Food Fabulous Food

The Women's Board
to Cooper Hospital/University Medical Center
Camden, New Jersey

Food Fabulous Food

Copyright © 1997
by
The Women's Board to Cooper
Hospital/University Medical Center

All rights reserved

The Women's Board to the Cooper Hospital
/University Medical Center is an organization
founded in 1921 dedicated to promoting
volunteerism and fundraising within the Cooper
Hospital/University Medical Center. Proceeds
from the sale of this cookbook will benefit The
Children's Regional Hospital.

Additional copies may be obtained by addressing:

Food Fabulous Food
The Women's Board to Cooper Hospital
/University Medical Center
One Cooper Plaza
Camden, New Jersey 08103

For your convenience, order forms
are included in the back of the book.

ISBN: 0-9655229-0-3
LCCN: 96-061667

First Edition - June 1997

Printed in the USA by

WIMMER
The Wimmer Companies, Inc.
Memphis

Table of Contents

Introduction

Food Fabulous Food is a book for those who love to eat, for those who love to cook, and for those who are inspired to experiment with healthier cooking. *Food Fabulous Food* is their safety net!

Healthful cooking is not about giving up our favorite foods. The Department of Food and Nutrition at The Cooper Health System has shown us how to modify some of our favorite recipes by substituting healthier ingredients and changing cooking techniques. These "Healthy Alternative" recipes (designated by the symbol **HA**) are printed on the facing or following pages of the original fabulous recipe. Some recipes did not lend themselves to a "Healthy Alternative" because fat played such an integral role in the final product. Those recipes were too good to change. The "Healthy Alternative" recipes featured in this cookbook are only those that taste as good or better in their lower fat version.

"The greatest gift a cook can receive — sincere and utter culinary appreciation. Ah, to the cook a plate licked clean is as a diadem!"

Anonymous

Appetizers

Appetizers

It was the Scandinavians who originated the custom of serving pre-dinner drinks with their "smorgasbord," a formal assortment of savories served in tiny portions. The Russians adapted the custom and served "zakuski" (little bits) to absorb their native vodka. The French renamed them "hors d'oeuvres a la russe," meaning outside the chef's main work.

Virtually every national cuisine features appetizers—the German "vorspiesen;" the Italian "antipasto;" the Middle Eastern "mesi;" the Spanish "tapas;" the South American "entremeses;" and the Japanese "zatsuki."

In America, appetizers and hors d'oeuvres are traditionally served to whet the appetite before a meal or as finger food at a cocktail party. But our tasty delicacies are far more versatile than tradition suggests. Many of the recipes in this chapter can be transformed into side dishes or even used to spark up the main dish of a meal.

Try the "Heavenly Horseradish Mousse" as a side dish with a rib roast of beef or use the "Micro Caponata" as a filling for omelets or crêpes.

"The hostess must be like a duck—calm and unruffled on the surface, and paddling like hell underneath."

Anonymous

Blue Cheese-Pecan Grapes

4 ounces blue cheese, crumbled
3 ounces cream cheese, softened
¼ pound seedless grapes
4 ounces pecans, finely chopped (1 cup),
   toasted

- Combine blue cheese and cream cheese in a bowl. Beat with an electric mixer at medium speed until smooth. Chill at least 1 hour.

- Wash, dry and remove stems from grapes. Cover each grape with cheese mixture. Roll in pecans. Chill at least 1 hour.

- Yield: 2 dozen

Island Crab Spread

1 pound backfin or lump crabmeat
1 cup sour cream (may use light)
½ cup mayonnaise (may use light)
¼ cup small onion, finely chopped
   (red onions look pretty)
¼ cup sweet relish
2 tablespoon dark rum

- Pick over crabmeat to remove any cartilage being careful not to break up lumps.

- Mix sour cream, mayonnaise, onion, relish, and rum. Add to crabmeat. Mix well but gently with fork.

- Chill at least 2 hours. Serve with crackers.

Bruschetta with Chopped Tomato Salsa

2 **medium tomatoes, chopped**
1 **medium red pepper, chopped**
1 **medium yellow pepper, chopped**
1 **medium onion, chopped**
2 **teaspoons capers**
3 **tablespoons chopped fresh basil**
1 **tablespoon balsamic vinegar**
2 **teaspoons lemon juice**
1 **clove garlic, peeled and minced**
1 **teaspoon dried oregano**
  black pepper
1 **loaf Italian bread, sliced**
3 **cloves garlic, halved**

- Combine tomatoes, peppers, onions, capers, basil, vinegar, lemon juice, minced garlic, oregano, and black pepper to taste in a large mixing bowl. Toss thoroughly.

- Cover and refrigerate for 1 hour.

- Preheat the broiler. Arrange bread on the broiler rack and broil for 2 minutes on each side, until browned. Remove the bread slices and rub them with the cut side of the garlic halves. Discard the garlic. Mound a tablespoon of salsa on each slice of bruschetta.

To speed the ripening of tomatoes, even green tomatoes, enclose them in a brown paper bag at room temperature.

The word Bruschetta comes from the Italian "bruscare", "to toast." This is an annual tradition that began in celebration of the newly pressed olive oil. Ancient Romans were the first to brush crusty grilled bread with olive oil, a custom that spread throughout central Italy, gathering other ingredients — tomatoes, garlic, herbs — as it traveled.

California Heaven

    2 large avocados, peeled and mashed
    2 teaspoons lemon juice
    1 tablespoon chopped onion
    2 cups sour cream
    1 (10-ounce) jar hamburger relish
    1 large tomato, chopped
    2 bunches green onions, tops only, chopped
    1 pound sharp cheddar cheese, grated
  1-2 bags taco chips

- Blend avocados, lemon juice, and onion. Spread on the bottom of a large flat dish with sides.

- Over the avocado, place a layer of sour cream then relish, tomatoes, and green onions. Sprinkle cheese on top. Make sure you spread the ingredients to all sides of the dish. Each ingredient should cover the previous ingredient.

- Cover with plastic wrap and refrigerate until served.

- Serve with taco chips.

The avocado or Alligator Pear was first cultivated by the Aztecs and references to it have been found in records kept by Spanish explorers as far back as 1519. The word is said to have come from the Indian word "ahuacatl," which was modified by the Spanish explorers into "aguacate." In Mexico, avocados are often called "the poor man's butter."

Heavenly Horseradish Mousse

This is a fabulous condiment with roast beef.

    nonstick cooking spray
  1 envelope unflavored gelatin
 ¼ cup cold water
  1 (3-ounce) package lemon flavored gelatin
 ½ cup boiling water
  1 cup sour cream
  1 (5-ounce) jar prepared horseradish
 ¾ cup mayonnaise

- Spray a 4-quart mold with nonstick cooking spray.

- Sprinkle unflavored gelatin over ¼ cup cold water. Let stand 1 minute.

- In a medium sized bowl, dissolve lemon flavored gelatin in ½ cup boiling water. Add unflavored gelatin mixture. Stir until dissolved.

- Add sour cream, horseradish, and mayonnaise. Stir until blended.

- Pour into mold, cover, and chill until firm. Unmold onto a plate garnished with curly endive or kale. Serve with party pumpernickel slices.

"In cooking, as in all the arts, simplicity is the sign of perfection."

— *Curnonsky*

Micro Caponato

*Serve with crisp crackers for an appetizer
or use as a filling for omelets or crêpes.
Dusted with freshly grated Parmesan cheese,
it makes a great luncheon dish.*

¼ **cup olive oil**
1 **large onion, chopped (1½ cups)**
1 **large celery stalk, cut in ¼-inch cubes**
¾ **pound eggplant, cut in ¼-inch cubes**
½ **pint cherry tomatoes, quartered**
½ **cup pitted black olives, quartered**
½ **cup stuffed green olives**
1 **(8-ounce) can tomato sauce**
¼ **cup sugar**
¼ **cup tomato paste**
¼ **cup red wine vinegar**
1½ **tablespoons capers, drained**
1½ **teaspoons salt**
1 **teaspoon dried basil**
¾ **teaspoon black pepper**
¼ **teaspoon cayenne pepper**

• Combine oil and onion in large microwavable bowl. Cover with plastic. Turn back one corner of plastic to vent. Microwave on high for 6 minutes, stirring every 2 minutes.

• Add celery. Cover and vent. Microwave on high for 6 minutes, stirring every 2 minutes.

• Add eggplant, tomatoes, black olives, green olives, tomato sauce, sugar, tomato paste, vinegar, capers, salt, basil, black pepper, and red pepper. Cover and vent. Microwave on high for 10 minutes, stirring every 3 minutes.

• Remove from microwave and let stand covered until cool, stirring occasionally.

• Serve with assorted crackers. Caponata may be frozen or it can be kept in the refrigerator for one month.

Italian Pesto Cheese Torta

A whole new way to say delicious!

      1 **cup pine nuts, toasted, divided**
  10-12 **fresh basil leaves**
      2 **(8-ounce) packages cream cheese,**
        softened
      1 **(16-ounce) container ricotta cheese,**
        drained
     ½ **pound fresh mozzarella cheese, drained**
     ¾ **cup pesto**
Pesto
      1 **cup fresh basil leaves, packed**
     ½ **cup walnuts**
     ½ **cup extra virgin olive oil**
      3 **ounces Parmesan or Romano cheese,**
        grated (⅔ cup)

- To toast pine nuts: preheat oven to 400°.
  Spread pine nuts in a single layer on a
  baking sheet and bake for 5 to 7 minutes.
  Stir once or twice during baking. When
  well browned, remove immediately and
  transfer to a cool plate.

- Line a standard bread pan with a double
  thickness of fine-weave cheesecloth.
  Allow enough cheesecloth to fold over top
  of mold after layering ingredients.

- Arrange fresh basil leaves in a decorative
  pattern on the bottom of the cheesecloth-
  lined bread pan and sprinkle with 1 to 2
  tablespoons of pine nuts.

- To make pesto: combine basil and walnuts in
  a food processor. Pulse briefly. With motor
  running, add olive oil in a slow, steady
  stream. Add cheese, salt, and pepper to taste.
  Process briefly and remove from processor.

- Combine cream cheese, ricotta, and
  mozzarella in a food processor. Process until
  smooth.

*Fresh basil can be
frozen and used
year-round. Just
remove leaves from
stems, rinse and
dry with paper
towels, and freeze
in a plastic
container or
freezer bag.*

(recipe continued on next page)

(Italian Pesto Cheese Torta, continued)

- Spread one-third of the cheese mixture evenly in the pan over the basil and pine nuts. Spread half of the pesto over top and sprinkle with half of the remaining pine nuts. Repeat these layers, ending with a cheese layer.

- Fold the cheesecloth over top of the cheese and press lightly to even up the mold.

- Refrigerate one to three days.

- To unmold torta: press down on the cheesecloth to make sure that the cheese is firmly in place. Fold back the top of the cheesecloth and pull up on the sides a little to loosen the mold. Invert a serving plate over the pan, keeping the cheesecloth away from the top of the mold. Turn over the mold together with the plate. Lift the pan away from the cheese. Peel the cheesecloth carefully off the torta.

Kielbasa and Apricot Nibbles

1½ **cups water**
1 **ring smoked kielbasa or low-fat kielbasa**
1 **(10-ounce) jar apricot preserves**
6 **dried apricots, sliced lengthwise**
2 **tablespoons Dijon mustard**
¼ **teaspoon ginger**

- Simmer kielbasa in water for 15 minutes. Slice ring of kielbasa like silver dollars.

- In a saucepan, add apricot preserves, apricots, mustard, and ginger. Mix and heat thoroughly. Add kielbasa.

- Serve warm with sliced French bread or on toothpicks.

Mushroom Almond Pâté

Delicate texture with a burst of flavor.
Guests will go "ga-ga" over this one.

nonstick cooking spray
1 **cup slivered almonds**
1 **garlic clove**
1 **small onion, cut in chunks**
¾ **pound mushrooms**
¼ **cup butter**
¾ **teaspoon salt**
½ **teaspoon dried thyme**
⅛ **teaspoon white pepper**
2 **tablespoons salad oil**

- Spray a wide frying pan with nonstick cooking spray. Toast almonds in frying pan over medium-low heat, stirring frequently, until lightly browned. Turn off pan and cool.

- In a food processor, using metal blade, process garlic until chopped. Add onions and process with on-off bursts until onion is chopped. Remove from processor and set aside.

- Cut mushrooms in half (if large), and put in processor bowl. Process with on-off bursts until coarsely chopped.

- Melt butter in frying pan over medium heat. Add garlic, onions, mushroom, salt, thyme, and pepper. Cook, stirring occasionally, until most liquid has evaporated. Remove and set aside.

- Process almonds until coarsely chopped. Remove 2 tablespoons of almonds and set aside.

- Process remaining nuts to form a paste. With motor running, slowly add oil and process until creamy. Add mushroom mixture and process until pâté is smooth.

- Add reserved nuts and blend with two on-off bursts.

- Cover and chill.

Oriental Peanut Popcorn

3 tablespoons butter
3 tablespoons smooth peanut butter
2 teaspoons soy sauce
1 small garlic clove
2½ quarts unsalted popped popcorn
salt (optional)

- Preheat oven to 300°.

- In a small saucepan, melt the butter with the peanut butter, soy sauce, and the garlic over moderately low heat. Stir until the mixture is smooth.

- Drizzle the mixture over the popcorn in a large baking pan, tossing it well.

- Sprinkle the popcorn with salt (if desired). Bake, stirring once or twice, for 10 to 15 minutes or until crisp.

- Yield: 2½ quarts

Repartee

4 avocados, peeled and mashed
1 (0.7-ounce) package of dry garlic salad dressing mix (the small dehydrated package)
1 tablespoon vinegar
1 teaspoon chopped chives
3 slices bacon, cooked crisp and crumbled
1-2 packages corn chips

- Blend avocados, salad dressing mix, vinegar, and chives.

- Cover and chill at least 2 hours.

- Stir in crumbled bacon.

- Serve with corn chips.

Red Pepper Dip with Walnuts

¼ **cup olive oil**
1 **small onion, chopped**
2 **large cloves of garlic, sliced**
1 **(12-ounce) jar roasted red peppers, drained and rinsed**
½ **cup walnuts, toasted**
⅓ **cup fresh basil, packed**
1 **slice firm white bread, chopped**
2 **tablespoons lemon juice**
  salt
  pita bread wedges, toasted

- Heat oil in a skillet and sauté onion and garlic until softened.

- Process roasted red pepper, walnuts, basil, white bread, and lemon juice in a food processor until walnuts are finely chopped.

- With the motor on, gradually add onion mixture and blend. Season with salt to taste.

- Serve with lightly toasted pita bread wedges.

Don't store fresh garlic in the refrigerator. Not only will it sprout, it will also both give off and absorb odors. Garlic keeps best in a dry, cool, dark spot that is also well ventilated.

"Garlic is the catsup of intellectuals."
— *Anonymous*

16

Cold Poached Salmon with Fresh Dill and Mustard Sauce

A seafood favorite.

nonstick cooking spray
½ side salmon filet
seasoned salt
pepper
margarine
lemon

Sauce
½ cup Dijon mustard
2 tablespoons dry mustard
6 tablespoons sugar
¼ cup white vinegar
⅔ cup oil
3 tablespoons chopped fresh dill

- Have fishmonger completely filet salmon and remove skin.

- Spray heavy duty aluminum foil with nonstick cooking spray. Place filet on foil and season with seasoned salt, pepper, and lemon. Wrap tightly and place on a cookie sheet.

- Bake at 400° for 20 to 30 minutes depending on thickness of filet.

- Refrigerate overnight.

- In a food processor, pulse Dijon mustard, dry mustard, sugar, and vinegar until smooth. While motor is running, slowly add oil. Add fresh dill. Refrigerate.

- When ready to serve, pour sauce over salmon.

Dill is an herb of ancient reputation. It is recorded in the medicinal rolls of ancient Egypt, and in the Middle Ages was accounted an excellent deterrent to witches, a reliable aid to flagging lovers.

Layered Shrimp Spread

- 1 **pound medium shrimp, cooked, peeled, and deveined**
- 1 **(8-ounce) package cream cheese, softened**
- ¼ **cup lemon juice**
- 1 **tablespoon mayonnaise**
- ½ **teaspoon seasoned salt**
- ¼ **teaspoon lemon-pepper seasoning**
- ¼ **teaspoon Worcestershire sauce**
- 1 **(12-ounce) jar cocktail sauce**
- 8 **ounces Monterey Jack cheese, shredded (2 cups)**
- 3 **green onions, chopped**
- ½ **large green pepper, chopped (½ cup)**
- ½ **cup black olives, sliced**

- Set aside 6 shrimp for garnish. Chop remaining shrimp. Chill chopped and whole shrimp.

- Beat cream cheese with an electric mixer at medium speed until light and fluffy. Add lemon juice, mayonnaise, seasoned salt, lemon-pepper seasoning, and Worcestershire sauce. Beat until smooth.

- Spread mixture in a circle on large serving platter (a pizza pan works well). Cover and chill 4 hours.

- Spread cocktail sauce evenly over cream cheese mixture. Layer chopped shrimp, Monterey jack cheese, green onions, green pepper, and olives over cocktail sauce. Top with whole shrimp.

- Cover and refrigerate 2 hours.

When boiling shrimp, try adding 1 teaspoon of caraway seed to the water; it will absorb much of the cooking odor.

Upstream Salmon Party Loaf

1 (1-pound) can salmon
1 (8-ounce) package cream cheese, softened
1 tablespoon lemon juice
2 teaspoons grated onion
1 teaspoon horseradish
¼ teaspoon liquid smoke
2 ounces pecans, chopped (½ cup)
3 teaspoons snipped parsley

• Mix salmon, cream cheese, lemon juice, onion, horseradish, and liquid smoke. Form into a loaf.

• Roll and coat loaf in chopped pecans and parsley.

• Refrigerate until serving.

Tapenade (or Olive Pâté)

1 (7-ounce) can pitted black olives, drained
3 garlic cloves, chopped
1 tin anchovies, drained and patted dry
1 tablespoon capers
1 tablespoon lemon juice
1 tablespoon brandy
¼ cup virgin olive oil
   black pepper

• Put olives, garlic, anchovies, capers, lemon juice, and brandy into a blender or a food processor and process until chopped rather than puréed.

• Stir in olive oil and add black pepper to taste.

• Store in a 16-ounce jar in the refrigerator. For best flavor, make 24 hours ahead. Serve at room temperature with crackers or vegetables.

Basil and Tomato Tart

1 refrigerated pie crust, unbaked
6 ounces mozzarella cheese, shredded
  (1½ cups)
8 plum or 4 medium tomatoes
1 cup fresh basil, loosely packed
4 garlic cloves
½ cup mayonnaise
¼ cup grated Parmesan cheese
⅛ teaspoon white pepper

- Prebake pie crust according to directions. Remove from oven. Sprinkle with ½ cup of the mozzarella cheese.

- Preheat oven to 375°. Cut tomatoes into wedges, seed, and drain on paper towels. Arrange tomato wedges on top of melted cheese.

- In a food processor, combine basil and garlic. Process and sprinkle over tomato wedges.

- In a medium bowl, combine the remaining mozzarella cheese, mayonnaise, Parmesan cheese, and pepper. Spoon cheese mixture over basil and spread evenly to cover the top of pie. Bake 375° for 35 to 40 minutes, or until the top is golden and bubbly. Serve warm.

"If I had to choose just one plant for the whole herb garden, I should be content with basil."
— Elizabeth David

Baked Brie with Crudités

Easy Entertaining.

1 tablespoon butter
1 large onion, chopped
2 tablespoons minced garlic
1 (8-ounce) package cream cheese
1 (8-ounce) round Brie cheese, no rind
¾ cup sour cream
1 teaspoon Worcestershire sauce
2½ teaspoons lemon juice
2 teaspoons brown sugar
   salt
   pepper
1 round loaf sourdough bread, unsliced
Crudités
   carrots sticks
   celery sticks
   green pepper sticks
   cauliflower
   broccoli

• Melt butter in a pan. Sauté onions and garlic until golden brown. Set aside.

• Cut cream cheese and Brie into pieces and place into bowl. Cover with plastic wrap. Microwave on medium until melted (around 2 minutes).

• Stir or whisk in onions and garlic, sour cream, Worcestershire, lemon juice, brown sugar, salt, and pepper.

• Cut off top of sourdough bread and tear out center, leaving a ¾ to 1-inch shell. Pour cheese mixture into bread and place bread lid on top. Wrap in foil.

• Refrigerate if making a day ahead. Take bread out of refrigerator 2 hours before baking. Let sit at room temperature for 1 hour.

• Preheat oven to 400°. Bake 1 hour. Unwrap foil and place bread on platter. Remove bread lid and sprinkle with paprika. Serve with crudités.

Chicken Almond Puffs

1 cup chicken broth
½ cup butter
1 cup flour
¼ teaspoon salt
4 large eggs
¾ cup cooked chicken, chopped
2 tablespoons chopped almonds, toasted
⅛ teaspoon paprika

- Preheat oven to 450°.

- Combine chicken broth and butter in a medium saucepan. Bring to a boil.

- Combine flour and salt. Add flour mixture to broth mixture all at once, stirring constantly over low heat until mixture forms a smooth ball. Remove from heat and cool slightly.

- Add eggs, one at a time, beating with a wooden spoon after each egg until batter is smooth. Stir in chicken, almonds, and paprika.

- Drop batter in heaping teaspoonfuls 2 inches apart onto an ungreased baking sheet. Bake for 10 minutes. Turn oven temperature to 350°. Bake an additional 5 to 10 minutes more or until puffs are golden brown.

To make sure your puffs bake thoroughly and are dry in the center, puncture the puffs with a skewer after baking, then replace in oven to dry out.

Chipped Beef Temptation

1 (8-ounce) package cream cheese, softened
2 tablespoons milk
1 (2½-ounce) jar dried beef, rinsed to remove salt, patted dry and chopped
2 tablespoons minced onion
2 tablespoons finely chopped green pepper
⅛ teaspoon pepper
½ cup sour cream
1 ounce walnuts, chopped (¼ cup)

- Preheat oven to 350°.

- Blend cream cheese and milk. Stir in dried beef, onion, green pepper, and pepper. Stir in sour cream. Mix well.

- Spoon into an 8-inch pie plate or shallow baking dish. Sprinkle with walnuts. Bake 20 minutes.

- Serve with assorted crackers.

Garlic Pretzels

16 ounces thick sourdough pretzels
1 cup oil
1 teaspoon garlic powder
1 teaspoon lemon-pepper seasoning
1 teaspoon dried dill weed

- Break pretzels into bite size pieces and place in a large plastic bowl with a lid.

- Mix the oil with garlic powder, lemon-pepper, and dill weed. Mix well and immediately pour over pretzels. Cover with tight fitting lid and shake so that the pretzels become saturated with oil mixture.

- Let pretzels sit for a few hours shaking every so often.

- Preheat oven to 350°. Pour pretzels in a 13 x 9-inch baking dish. Bake 25 minutes. Serve warm.

Buster Crab Rolls

½ **pound crabmeat, fresh (or 6½-ounces, canned)**
1 **(8-ounce) package whipped cream cheese, chive flavored**
1 **tablespoon minced onion**
Worcestershire sauce
18 **slices soft white bread**
26 **slices bacon**

- Combine crabmeat, cream cheese, onion, and two splashes of Worcestershire sauce.

- Trim off crusts from bread. Flatten slices with a rolling pin. Spread each slice of bread with about a tablespoon of the crab mixture and roll the bread in a jelly roll fashion. Cut into thirds.

- Cut bacon in half. Roll each piece of bacon around each bread roll. Secure with a toothpick. (Can be frozen at this time and cooked later.)

- Preheat oven to 375°.

- Place on a baking sheet and cook for 10 to 15 minutes.

Super Bowl Supper

Buster Crab Rolls

French Peasant Soup

Mom's Chicken Chili

Hearty Breads

Dos Equis Beer

Maple Walnut Crème Brûlée

Greek Spinach Pie

Cooking can be fun.

3 (10-ounce) packages frozen chopped
 spinach
1 medium onion, chopped
6 large eggs
1 pound feta cheese, crumbled
1 pound large curd cottage cheese
1 cup olive oil
1 pound phyllo dough
1 cup (2 sticks) butter, melted

- Preheat oven to 350°.

- Thaw spinach and squeeze out all of the moisture in a tea towel.

- Mix spinach, onion, eggs, feta cheese, cottage cheese, and olive oil in a bowl.

- Brush ten sheets of phyllo dough with butter and place in a jelly roll pan. Spread out filling evenly on top. Brush the remaining phyllo sheets with melted butter. Place the remaining sheets over filling and crimp edges with fork. Score top in diamond shapes.

- Bake 60 minutes or until brown.

"Cheese: Milk's leap toward immortality."
— Clifton Fadiman

Onion Pizza (Pissaladière)

2 tablespoon extra virgin olive oil
4 medium onions, thinly sliced
2 large garlic cloves, thinly sliced
1 large sprig fresh thyme or ½ teaspoon
   dried thyme
2 large tomatoes, peeled, seeded, and
   chopped
½ pound bread dough, if frozen, defrosted
8 flat anchovy fillets, rinsed and drained.
12 oil cured black olives, pitted and halved

- In a large skillet heat oil on medium-low heat. Add onions, garlic, and thyme and toss to coat. Cover and cook about 20 minutes, stirring occasionally.

- Stir in tomatoes and cook until liquid has evaporated and mixture is thick, about 5 minutes. Discard thyme sprig.

- On a lightly floured surface, roll out dough into an 11 x 14-inch rectangular pan.

- Transfer dough to a baking sheet. Cover and let rest 15 minutes.

- Preheat oven to 450°.

- Spread onion-tomato sauce evenly over dough. Arrange anchovies in spoke-like pattern on top and sprinkle with olives. Let stand 15 minutes.

- Bake until crust is crisp, about 15 to 20 minutes. Slice and serve warm or at room temperature.

"The taste of an olive is older than meat, older than wine."
— *Laurence Durell*

Sausage Stars

Watch for looks of surprised delight on guests' faces.

nonstick cooking spray
1½ pounds Italian sweet sausage, crumbled (3 cups)
6 ounces Cheddar cheese, grated (1½ cups)
6 ounces Monterey Jack cheese, grated (1½ cups)
1 cup ranch dressing
1 small can black olives
½ medium red pepper, chopped
1 package wonton wrappers
olive oil

- Preheat oven to 350°.

- Spray muffin tins with nonstick cooking spray.

- Sauté sausage until no longer pink. Drain well.

- Combine Cheddar cheese, Monterey Jack cheese, ranch dressing, black olives, and red pepper. Stir in sausage.

- Press 1 wonton wrapper in each muffin tin. Brush with oil. Bake 5 to 8 minutes until bubbly.

- Remove wontons from muffin tins and put on baking sheets. Fill with cheese mixture. Bake about 5 to 8 minutes until bubbly.

- Yield: about 35 to 40

Nearly every country boasts its own special kind of sausage. For instance, there's chorizo from Spain and Mexico, kielbasa from Poland, and wursts from Germany.

Sicilian Ground Beef Roll

½ **pound top round beef, ground twice**
½ **pound spicy ground sausage**
1 **teaspoon onion, minced**
   dash hot sauce
1 **large egg**
   dash pepper
1 **pie crust, from mix**

- Mix beef and sausage.

- Add onion, hot sauce, egg, and pepper.

- Blend and shape into a long 1-inch diameter roll. Wrap in thinly rolled pie crust. Keep in refrigerator until ready to cut into thin slices.

- Preheat oven to 450°. Bake 10 to 15 minutes or until crisp. Serve immediately.

Skordalia

1 **small potato**
3 **garlic cloves, minced**
⅓ **cup vinegar**
1 **teaspoon salt**
1 **cup olive oil**

- Peel potato and boil until tender.

- Put through a ricer or a food mill.

- In a blender, mix ½ cup of the potato, garlic, and salt. With motor running, gradually add olive oil, alternating with vinegar.

- Chill. Serve as a dip or over fish.

To peel garlic easily, place unpeeled garlic cloves in the microwave and cook on high for 10 seconds. Trim the root end of the clove with a sharp knife and the garlic will pop right out of its skin.

Soups
and
Salads

Soups

Soup has been a staple of the European diet since the Dark Ages. A slice of bread placed at the bottom of a bowl was covered with broth to create a hearty meal. The word "suppa" was used in Low Latin and has kept its original meaning in the Dutch "sopen," to soak, and with the English word "sop."

The secret to soup is in knowing your ingredients and knowing which herbs and spices to use to bring out their flavors. Great soup is the ultimate comfort food.

Soups, both hot and cold, are more fun when they are a bit unusual. Surprise your friends by starting your next dinner party with the deliciously different cold soup such as "Chilled Carrot-Orange Soup" or serve "Biltmore Peach Soup" as dessert.

"I live on a good soup, not on fine words."

Molière

Salads

The ancient Greeks had a taste for lettuce, what they considered the best of all the salad plants. The plant was popularized by the Romans and equally enjoyed by the English as "lettuce"; the Spanish as "lechuga"; and the Italians as "lattuca."

The popularity of salads is well deserved. The variety of flavors and the ease of preparation make a salad the perfect dish for today's lifestyle. The high nutritional value of a salad also has wide appeal for our health-conscious eaters.

Everyday our markets are filled with new kinds of lettuces, fresh herbs and greens. Choose the plumpest vegetables and the crispest, brightest greens. A mixture of different colors and shapes looks wonderful in a large wooden salad bowl. The "Florida Caesar" and the "Knock 'Em Dead Dinner Party Salad" are fabulous to view and to eat.

"It takes four men to dress a salad: a wise man for the salt, a madman for the pepper, a miser for the vinegar, and a spendthrift for the oil."

Anonymous

Autumn Soup

2 pounds ground beef or turkey
2 large onions, chopped (2 cups)
6 carrots, chopped (2 cups)
2 white potatoes, cut-up (2 cups)
4 celery stalks, chopped (2 cups)
2 (28-ounce) cans crushed tomatoes
1 bay leaf
4 tablespoons barley
2 quarts water
salt
pepper

- Lightly brown beef or turkey and onion in a nonstick skillet. Drain fat.

- Add onions, carrots, potatoes, celery, tomatoes, bay leaf, barley, and water. Simmer for 1 hour. Remove bay leaf. Salt and pepper to taste.

- Serve with bread and a green salad for a complete meal.

- Yield: 8 servings

Soups are the answer to any busy cook's prayers—not just because they are quickly prepared, but also because most soups taste better the next day.

"To make a good soup, the pot must only simmer or 'smile'."

— French proverb

Avgolemono Soup (Egg and Lemon Soup)

4 large egg yolks
4 tablespoons lemon juice
2 (2-pint 14-ounce) cans chicken broth
1 pound of noodles *or* 1 pound of orzo
   ***or* 2 cups rice**

- Beat eggs until light and fluffy, then slowly add the lemon juice, beating constantly. Put on low heat.

- Gradually add the chicken broth, and bring to a bare simmer. Keep the pan covered.

- In another pot, boil noodles or orzo or rice as directed on package. When cooked, add to the egg lemon broth.

- Yield: 10 servings

Summer Solstice Supper

Avgolemono Soup

Basil and Tomato Tart

*Mixed Greens
with California Dressing*

Crusty Bread

Cranberry Crunch

Black Kettle Soup

A hearty and robust soup for a blustery,
winter day. In fact for two blustery, winter days
because this soup is better reheated.

1 pound ground chuck
1 large egg
½ cup soft bread crumbs
6 tablespoons chopped parsley, divided
1 teaspoon salt
3 slices bacon
1 large onion, diced (1 cup)
2 garlic cloves, crushed
2 leeks, washed and sliced (2 cups)
3 carrots, sliced (1 cup)
2 potatoes, pared and diced (2 cups)
1 pound cabbage, shredded (4 cups)
4 (13¾-ounce) cans beef broth
1 bay leaf
½ teaspoon crushed thyme

- Combine ground chuck, egg, bread crumbs, 2 tablespoons of the parsley, and salt in a medium-sized bowl. Mix lightly with a fork.

- Shape into 32 balls about the size of a rounded teaspoon.

- Cook bacon until crisp in a large Dutch oven. Remove bacon and set aside.

- Brown meatballs in bacon drippings, single layer at a time. Remove when browned. Drain fat.

- Add onion, garlic, and leeks to Dutch oven. Sauté until soft, about 5 minutes. Stir in carrots, potatoes, cabbage, broth, bay leaf, and thyme. Bring to a boil. Lower heat and simmer covered for 20 minutes.

- Yield: 8 servings

French Peasant Soup

1 large onion, chopped (1 cup)
1 garlic clove, minced
2 tablespoons olive oil
1 pound mushrooms, sliced (4 cups)
2 tablespoons tomato paste
1 (2-pint, 14-ounce) can chicken broth
5 large egg yolks
¼ cup grated Parmesan cheese
2 tablespoons minced parsley
¼ cup Ruby Port
6 slices French bread, buttered and toasted

- In a large saucepan, cook the onion and garlic in olive oil over moderate heat for 6 minutes until lightly browned.

- Add the mushrooms and cook, stirring for 10 minutes.

- Add the tomato paste and chicken broth. Bring the liquid to a boil and simmer for 15 minutes.

- In a small bowl, combine the egg yolks, Parmesan and parsley. Add 1 cup of the hot broth in a stream, whisking constantly.

- Whisk this mixture into the broth. Add the Port and simmer for 5 minutes.

- To serve: place toasted bread in each bowl, ladle soup on top.

- Yield: 6 servings

"Only the pure in heart can make good soup."
— Ludwig van Beethoven

Habitant Split Pea Soup

1 (1-pound) package dried green split peas
6 cups water
1 tablespoon olive oil
1 large onion, chopped (1 cup)
2 garlic cloves, minced
3 carrots, chopped (1 cup)
2 large celery ribs, chopped (1 cup)
4 cups low sodium chicken broth
2 teaspoons reduced sodium soy sauce
¼ teaspoon freshly ground black pepper
½ cup snipped fresh dill
2 ounces smoked ham, diced (optional)
1 cup chicken broth or skim milk

- Place the peas in the water in a large, heavy saucepan. Bring the water to a boil. Boil the peas for 2 minutes. Turn off the heat and let the peas stand for 1 hour.

- Heat oil in a nonstick skillet. Add onions, garlic, carrots, and celery. Sauté and stir the vegetables for about 5 minutes. Add to the peas. Add the chicken broth, soy sauce, pepper, dill, and ham to the peas, stirring frequently.

- Bring the soup to a boil. Reduce the heat to low, and simmer the soup, partially covered for 1½ hours. (Check now and again to be sure the soup is not scorching and add more water if needed.)

- In a blender or food processor, purée the soup with the meat. Thin the soup to the desired consistency with broth or milk.

- Heat the soup before serving.

- Yield: 8 servings

Homestyle Fish Chowder

6 tablespoons butter
2 large onions, sliced
6 carrots, chopped (2 cups)
4 large celery stalks and leaves, chopped (2 cups)
7 medium potatoes, diced
1¾ teaspoons salt
water
2 pounds fresh or frozen cod or haddock
4 cups milk
pepper

- Melt butter in skillet. Sauté onions and celery, until soft.

- Add potatoes, carrots, and salt. Add water to cover vegetables and simmer for 10 minutes.

- Lay fish on top and cook, covered, until fish is flaky and potatoes are done (approximately 20 minutes).

- Add milk and pepper to taste.

- Yield: 8-10 servings

"Soup and fish explain half the emotions of human life."

— Sydney Smith

The Judge's Peanut Soup

4½ (13¾-ounce) cans chicken broth
½ cup (1 stick) butter
1 small onion, diced (½ cup)
2 large celery stalks, diced (1 cup)
3 tablespoons flour
1 (16-ounce) jar peanut butter
⅓ teaspoon celery salt
1 teaspoon salt
1 tablespoon lemon juice

- Heat chicken broth.

- Melt butter in large saucepan. Sauté onions and celery for 5 minutes. Do not brown.

- Sprinkle flour over vegetables. Add hot chicken broth stirring frequently. Simmer 30 minutes. Remove from stove and strain.

- Add peanut butter, celery salt, salt, and lemon juice.

- To serve: garnish with a sprinkling of the ground peanuts.

- Yield: 8 servings

The judge swore that his peanut soup had more healing properties than your mother's chicken soup. Lest you fall ill, he would appear on your doorstep with a big pot of peanut soup. You did feel better; but was it the soup or was it the judge?

Mulligatawny Soup

1 tablespoon oil
2 tablespoons butter
1 medium onion, chopped (¾ cup)
2 carrots, chopped (¾ cup)
1½ large ribs of celery, chopped (¾ cup)
1 medium bell pepper, chopped (¾ cup)
¼ pound turnip, chopped (½ cup)
1 apple, pared, cored and chopped (¾ cup)
2 teaspoons salt
½ teaspoon crushed red pepper
1½ teaspoons curry powder
4 (13¾-ounce) cans chicken broth
1 tablespoon cornstarch
¼ cup cold water
¼ cup tomato paste
2 cups cooked, diced chicken
1 (16-ounce) can garbanzo beans, puréed

- Heat oil and butter in a saucepan.

- Add onion, carrots, celery, bell pepper, turnips, apples, salt, red pepper, and curry powder. Sauté, stirring frequently, until onions are tender.

- Heat broth in a large pot until boiling.

- Make a smooth paste of cornstarch and water. Add to broth, stirring constantly, until broth returns to a boil.

- Add sautéed vegetables, tomato paste, chicken breast, and puréed beans. Heat to serving temperature.

- Serve garnished with chopped parsley.

- Yield: 8 servings

Pennsylvania Dutch Chicken Corn Chowder

1 pound Italian sausage
2 tablespoons butter
4 celery ribs, sliced (2 cups)
1 large onion, chopped (1 cup)
3 tablespoons flour
2 (13¾-ounce) cans chicken broth
1 (10-ounce) package frozen corn, thawed
1 cup cooked, diced chicken
1 cup heavy cream
1 large garlic clove, minced

- Brown sausage in a skillet and drain.

- In a large pot, melt butter and sauté celery and onion.

- Sprinkle flour over vegetables. Add chicken broth and boil, stirring frequently.

- Add corn, sausage, and chicken. Simmer 10 minutes. Add cream and return to simmer.

- To serve: garnish with parsley.

- Yield: 6 servings

"Chowder breathes reassurance. It steams consolation."
— *Clementine Paddleford*

Portuguese Bean Soup

Everyone loves this, especially men.
Use your imagination with ingredients,
additions or changes. You can't miss.

1 (1-pound) package dried kidney beans
3 tablespoons oil
2 green bell peppers, chopped (2 cups)
4 celery stalks and leaves, chopped (2 cups)
4 scallions, chopped
1 pound sweet Italian sausage
½ pound hot Italian sausage
3 (1-pound) cans chopped tomatoes
¼ cup red wine
1 bay leaf
1 (6-ounce) can tomato paste
1 cup chopped spinach or kale or escarole
2-3 potatoes, peeled and chopped
   salt
   pepper
   chicken broth or water

- Cover beans with water in excess of one-inch and bring to a boil for 3 minutes. Turn off heat and let soak for 2 hours, then drain and rinse.

- Heat oil in skillet and sauté peppers, celery, and scallions until tender. Remove with slotted spoon, set aside.

- Add sausage to same skillet, brown and break apart. Drain fat.

- Add sautéed vegetables, tomatoes, red wine, bay leaf, tomato paste, beans, chopped spinach, and potatoes to skillet. Add chicken broth or water to cover and simmer for 1½ to 2 hours (or until beans are tender).

- Season with salt and pepper.

- Yield: 8-10 servings

Potato, Ham, Corn and Spinach Chowder

This is one of those simple treats that gets praise out of proportion to the effort that went into it.

- **1 large onion, chopped (1 cup)**
- **1 tablespoon oil**
- **4 medium potatoes, peeled and diced**
- **3 cups water**
- **1 (10-ounce) package frozen corn**
- **½ (10-ounce) package frozen, chopped spinach**
- **2 cups diced ham**
- **3 cups milk**
- **3 tablespoons butter**
- **salt**
- **pepper**

- In a large saucepan, sauté onions in oil until slightly brown.

- Add potatoes and water. Cover and cook until potatoes are tender.

- Add corn, spinach, and ham. Cook 5 more minutes until frozen foods have separated.

- Add milk and butter. Simmer to heat thoroughly. Salt and pepper to taste.

- Yield: 8 servings

Chowder is a thick hearty soup that probably originated in New England, but takes its name from a large French kettle, the "chaudiere."

Pumpkin Shrimp Curry Bisque

A must for Thanksgiving dinner;
open the meal on a note of quiet elegance.

nonstick cooking spray
1 medium yellow onion, finely chopped
1 (2-pint 14-ounce) can chicken broth
1 (1-pound 13-ounce) can pumpkin
1 cup heavy cream
1 cup half & half
1 tablespoon curry powder
dash hot sauce and/or ½ teaspoon
cayenne pepper
salt
1 pound shrimp (medium to large) peeled,
deveined, briefly steamed or boiled, halved
lengthwise. If very large, cut cross-wise as
well as into bite sized pieces (keep whole
the number equal to the number of servings)
sour cream
chives

- Heat an 8-quart stock pan over high heat, then spray bottom with nonstick cooking spray and lower heat to medium high.

- Add onion and sauté until translucent.

- Add chicken broth and pumpkin. Bring to a simmer. Cook for about 20 minutes.

- Add curry powder and salt to taste. Simmer for another 10 minutes.

- Add cream and half & half, and bring to a bare simmer. Taste and adjust for seasonings. Add hot sauce and cayenne pepper if desired. If too thick add additional cream or half & half.

- A few minutes before serving, add halved (or cut up) shrimp and heat thoroughly. Ladle into

(recipe continued on next page)

(Pumpkin Shrimp Curry Bisque, continued)

warm soup plates or bowls. On each serving add a spoonful of sour cream, a sprinkling of chives and curl one whole shrimp on the edge of the cup or bowl.

- Yield: 12 servings

Pumpkin Soup

Smooth as velvet and delicious.

2 tablespoons peanut oil
1 onion, sliced
2 large celery ribs, sliced (1 cup)
1 large garlic clove, sliced
1½ teaspoons hot paprika
1 teaspoon ground cumin
1 teaspoon cinnamon
1 teaspoon ground coriander
1 bay leaf
few peppercorns, crushed
½ teaspoon sugar
1 (1-pound 13-ounce) can pumpkin
2½ (13¾-ounce) cans low sodium beef broth
2 tablespoons butter
2 tablespoons flour

- Heat oil in a large saucepan. Sauté onion and celery until soft.

- Add garlic, paprika, cumin, cinnamon, coriander, bay leaf, peppercorns, sugar, pumpkin, and beef broth. Simmer gently, partly covered.

- Purée and return to saucepan.

- Melt butter and stir in flour. Cook about 10 minutes or until brown. Whisk into soup and simmer another 10 minutes.

- Serve with a dollop of sour cream.

- Yield: 10 servings

Senate Black Bean Soup

This black bean soup is memorable.
Thick and dark and as satisfying as any meat dish.

1 **ham hock**
1 **(1-pound) package black beans**
6 **cups water**
½ **cup olive oil**
1 **large onion, chopped (1 cup)**
1 **green bell pepper, chopped (1 cup)**
2 **large garlic cloves, minced**
   salt
1 **tablespoon Dijon mustard** *or* ¼ **cup red**
   wine vinegar
1 **teaspoon cumin**
1 **teaspoon curry powder**
1 **tablespoon lemon juice**
1 **teaspoon Worcestershire sauce**

- In advance: simmer ham hock in 8 cups of water for 2 hours. Remove ham hock and refrigerate overnight. Place beans in a bowl, and cover with water. Soak overnight.

- The next day, skim off congealed fat from surface of the soup. Drain and rinse the soaked black beans. Place the beans in the ham hock broth. Bring to a boil. Reduce heat and simmer for 2 hours or until the beans are tender.

- Take out one cup of beans and purée. Return puréed beans to simmering beans.

- Add mustard or vinegar, cumin, curry powder, lemon juice, and Worcestershire sauce.

- Serve with condiments: chopped red onions, ripe olives, chopped hard cooked egg. Make a complete meal with a green salad and bread.

- Yield: 12 servings

Spring Pea Soup

A perfect fare for fair weather.

½ **cup (1 stick) butter**
1 **large onion, chopped (1 cup)**
2 **(1-pound) packages frozen petite pois**
1 **head Boston lettuce, chopped**
4 **tablespoons flour**
 pinch sugar
1 **(2-pint 14-ounce) can chicken broth**
2 **cups half & half**
 salt
 pepper

- Melt butter in a skillet. Sauté onions.

- Stir in frozen peas and lettuce. Sprinkle flour over vegetables and stir.

- Stir in sugar, chicken broth, cream or half & half, salt, and pepper. Simmer 10 minutes.

- Purée in a food processor or blender. Reheat and serve.

- Yield: 10 servings

"Beautiful soup! Who cares for fish, game, or any other dish? Who would not give all else for two pennyworth only of beautiful soup?"
 — "Alice in Wonderland", Lewis Carroll

Tomato Shrimp Bisque

1 (11-ounce) can tomato bisque soup,
   undiluted
1 (10¾-ounce) can cream of shrimp soup,
   undiluted
¾ cup water
½ cup milk
2 tablespoons chopped parsley
1 tablespoon minced onion
   freshly ground pepper to taste
⅓ cup dry sherry

- Combine soups in a medium saucepan, stirring well.

- Gradually add water and milk, stirring until smooth. Add chopped parsley, onion, and pepper.

- Cook over medium-high heat, stirring constantly, until bisque comes to a boil. Reduce heat, and simmer 5 minutes.

- Stir in sherry and cook an additional minute.

- Yield: 4 servings

A Ladies' Luncheon

Tomato Shrimp Bisque

Chicken Ham Pinwheels

*Lemon Rice Salad
with Cucumber*

*Tiny French Rolls
with Herb Butter*

Chocolate Indulgence

Winter Potage with Bacon

Soup - the ultimate comfort food.

8 strips bacon
8 medium leeks, (white parts only) washed and sliced
4 tablespoons butter
2 medium sweet potatoes, peeled and thinly sliced
1 (2-pint 14-ounce) can chicken broth
salt
pepper
3 tablespoons snipped fresh chives

- Fry bacon in stock pot over medium heat. Remove bacon and place on paper towel to drain. Drain fat from pot, reserving 2 tablespoons bacon drippings.

- Wipe stock pot clean. Add reserved bacon drippings and butter. Over low heat, sweat the leeks, stirring occasionally until very soft, about 25 minutes. Add sweet potatoes and broth. Cover and bring to a boil. Reduce heat and simmer uncovered until potatoes are very soft, about 35 minutes.

- Purée soup in a blender or processor. Reheat and add salt, pepper, and chives.

- To serve; crumble bacon and sprinkle on each bowl of soup.

- Yield: 6 servings

"Of all the items on the menu, soup is that which exacts the most delicate perfection and the strictest attention."
— Auguste Escoffier

Chilled Carrot-Orange Soup

       2 tablespoons butter
     ½ teaspoon grated fresh ginger
       9 carrots, thinly sliced
       1 leek, (white part only), cleaned and sliced
       2 (13¾-ounce) cans chicken broth
    1½ cups orange juice, freshly squeezed
         salt
         pepper

- Melt butter in a large saucepan. Add ginger, carrots, and leeks. Sauté until leeks are tender. Add 2 cups of the chicken broth and simmer until carrots are cooked, about 30 minutes.

- Purée in a blender or processor.

- Return to saucepan and stir in remaining broth and enough orange juice to produce the desired consistency—the thickness of heavy cream.

- Season with salt and pepper to taste. Cover and chill.

- To serve: garnish each serving with an orange slice, *or* grated carrot *or* chopped mint.

- Yield: 6 servings

Carrots have an honored place in history. The Greeks and Romans ate them in stews or as a vegetable. Elizabethan England adored them, and not only as food. They were prized for their delicate green foliage, worn like feathers in elegant ladies' hats.

Biltmore Cold Peach Soup

Serve this as a first course or as a surprise dessert.

1½ **pounds peaches, peeled, pitted, sliced**
2 **cups sour cream**
1 **cup orange juice**
1 **cup pineapple juice**
½ **cup dry sherry**
2 **tablespoons fresh lemon juice**
 sugar to taste

- Purée peaches in a food processor until smooth. Add sour cream, orange juice, pineapple juice, dry sherry, and lemon juice.

- Blend well and pass through a strainer. Add sugar to taste.

- Garnish with mint leaves. Serve chilled.

- Yield: 8-10 servings

Cold Tomato Cream

1 **cucumber, chopped**
1 **scallion, chopped**
1 **garlic clove, crushed**
1 **teaspoon honey**
4 **cups tomato juice**
1 **cup yogurt or sour cream**
1 **green bell pepper, chopped**

- Combine cucumber, scallion, clove, honey, tomato juice, yogurt or sour cream, and bell pepper.

- Chill.

- To serve: garnish with thinly sliced mushrooms.

- Yield: 4 servings

Chilled Red Pepper Soup

Soup of the season...beautiful soup!

4 red peppers
2 tablespoons butter
3 medium shallots or 1 medium onion,
finely chopped
1 (28-ounce) can Italian plum tomatoes,
undrained
1 cup dry red wine
1 teaspoon sugar
salt
pepper
1 cup tomato juice

- To roast peppers: cut peppers in half and discard ribs and seeds. Place cut side down on a nonstick baking sheet. Roast at 450° for about 20 minutes or until skin becomes blackened. Remove skin while pepper is hot (skin should slip right off).

- Purée three peppers. Slice remaining pepper for garnish and set aside.

- Melt butter in a saucepan. Add shallots and cook until softened and lightly browned about 3 to 5 minutes.

- Purée tomatoes (with liquid) and add to shallots.

- Stir in puréed peppers, wine, sugar, salt, and pepper. Bring to a boil and simmer for 20 minutes, stirring occasionally.

- Remove from heat. Stir in tomato juice. Cool and refrigerate overnight.

- Serve cool, garnished with the reserved roasted pepper slices.

- Yield: 4 servings

Apple Bavarian Slaw

4 medium McIntosh apples (about 1⅓
   pounds), peeled, cored and diced (3 cups)
2 tablespoons lemon juice
3 cups shredded white cabbage
¼ pound Swiss cheese, diced (1 cup)
4 ounces walnuts (¾ cup)
1 teaspoon salt
¼ teaspoon pepper
⅔ cup light mayonnaise
½ cup light sour cream
2 teaspoons sugar

- In a large bowl toss the apples and lemon juice. Add cabbage, cheese, walnuts, salt, and pepper.

- Mix together mayonnaise, sour cream, and sugar. Pour over slaw, toss well, and season to taste.

- Chill for at least four hours.

- Yield: 12 servings

Italian Style Cabbage Salad

½ head red cabbage, thinly sliced
½ head iceberg lettuce, thinly sliced
1 medium onion, thinly sliced into rings
12 pimento stuffed green olives, quartered
1 (3-ounce) can tuna (oil packed preferred),
   flaked
1 garlic clove
3 tablespoons Parmesan cheese
¼ cup extra virgin olive oil
2 tablespoons balsamic vinegar
1½ teaspoons dried oregano
   salt and pepper to taste

- Place all ingredients in a large bowl and toss.

- Refrigerate several hours prior to serving.

- Yield: 4 servings

Florida Caesar Salad

A light and lemony dressing.

4 medium garlic cloves
½ cup olive oil, divided
2 medium heads romaine lettuce
1 cup Italian salad croutons
3 anchovies, diced into small pieces
   (optional)
1 large egg
   juice of 1 lemon
⅛ teaspoon pepper
½ cup grated Romano or Parmesan cheese
   salt to taste

- Advance preparation: crush garlic and place in the oil. Cover and let stand for half a day.

- Wash lettuce thoroughly and pat dry. Break up into bite size pieces and refrigerate until ready to prepare salad.

- Sauté croutons in half of the oil and garlic mixture and lightly brown. Set aside.

- Before serving: place anchovies and lettuce in very large bowl and toss. Beat egg, lemon juice, and pepper together. Add to salad and toss. Add remaining oil and garlic and toss. Add croutons, sprinkle with cheese and toss. Salt to taste. One final toss and serve.

- Yield: 6 servings

Oriental Chicken Salad

2 pounds boneless, skinless chicken
6 ounces fresh bean sprouts (1½ cups)
2 cups bok choy, sliced in ¼-inch slices
2 bunches scallions (⅔ cup), cut in ¼-inch slices
1½ cups snow peas
⅓ cup bamboo shoots
½ (8-ounce) can sliced water chestnuts (½ cup), drained
romaine leaves
2 cups red cabbage, shredded
3 ounces whole, blanched almonds

Dressing

1 large egg
¼ cup sesame oil
¾ cup corn oil
1 teaspoon sugar
½ teaspoon pepper
3 tablespoons rice vinegar
2 teaspoons minced garlic
3 tablespoons Dijon mustard
2 tablespoons soy sauce
1 teaspoon lemon juice

- Put chicken onto baking pan and cook in oven for 20 minutes at 350°. Cut into bite size pieces and place in a large bowl.

- Add bean sprouts, bok choy, scallions, snow peas, bamboo shoots, and water chestnuts.

- To make dressing: whisk egg until light colored. Add sesame oil and corn oil. Add sugar, pepper, vinegar, garlic, mustard, soy sauce, and lemon juice.

- Toss salad with dressing.

- To serve: arrange on romaine leaves and red cabbage. Garnish with almonds.

- Yield: 6 servings

Knock 'em Dead Dinner Party Salad

The spiced pecans in this recipe will also make a fabulous nibble at your next cocktail party.

Spiced pecans
- ½ pound pecan halves (2 cups)
- 2½ tablespoons vegetable oil
- ¼ cup sugar
- 1 teaspoon salt
- 1 teaspoon ground cinnamon
- ¼ teaspoon nutmeg
- ¼ teaspoon ground cloves
- ½ teaspoon ginger
- ½ teaspoon dry mustard

Hot Cider Dressing
- 2 cups apple cider
- 8 bacon slices, cut into 1-inch pieces
- 3 shallots, minced
- 1 teaspoon cinnamon
- 1 tablespoon honey mustard
- ½ cup olive oil
- salt
- freshly ground black pepper

Salad
- 12 cups torn salad greens such as leaf lettuce, radicchio, endive, and watercress
- 1 cup thinly sliced fennel bulb (anise)
- 1½ large McIntosh apples, cored and thinly sliced
- 4 ounces crumbled chèvre, such as Montrachet

- To prepare the spiced pecans: place the nuts in a bowl, cover with boiling water, and let soak 15 minutes. Drain and pat dry on paper towels.

- Preheat the oven to 300°.

- Spread the nuts on an ungreased baking sheet and toast, stirring occasionally, for 45 minutes.

(recipe continued on next page)

(Knock 'em Dead Dinner Party Salad, continued)

Remove the nuts and increase the oven temperature to 350°.

- Whisk together the vegetable oil, sugar, salt, cinnamon, nutmeg, cloves, ginger, and mustard in a medium-sized bowl. Add the hot nuts and toss to coat thoroughly. Spread the nuts in a single layer on a baking sheet and roast for 15 minutes. Cool and store in a airtight container for up to 2 weeks.

- When ready to prepare the salad, place the cider in a small saucepan and boil until reduced to one-half cup, about 20 to 25 minutes.

- Sauté the bacon in a medium sized skillet over medium high heat until crisp. Drain on paper towels and discard all but three tablespoons of the bacon fat remaining in the skillet.

- Add the shallots to the skillet and sauté over medium heat until softened, about 3 minutes. Whisk in the cinnamon and the mustard and cook 1 minute more. Add the reduced cider and olive oil; season to taste with salt and pepper. Keep the dressing hot over low heat.

- Toss the salad greens, 1 cup of spiced pecans, bacon, fennel, apples, and chèvre in a large salad bowl. Toss with about two-thirds of the hot cider dressing and serve at once.

- Yield: 12 servings

"If you accept a dinner party invitation — you have a moral obligation to be amusing."
— The Duchess of Windsor

Green and Gold Salad

2 cucumbers, sliced
1 honeydew melon, seeded and cubed
2 (8-ounce) cans mandarin oranges, drained
3-4 bananas, sliced
3 kiwi fruit, peeled and sliced
1 head lettuce

Dressing

1 cup mayonnaise
1 cup sour cream
¼ cup olive oil
2 tablespoons vinegar
1 teaspoon curry powder
½ cup Major Grey's chutney
salt
hot sauce to taste

- Mix fruits in a large bowl.

- Blend mayonnaise, sour cream, oil, vinegar, curry, chutney, salt and hot sauce in blender. Pour over fruits and chill for 1 to 2 hours.

- To serve: line platter with lettuce leaves and cover with fruit salad.

- Yield: 6 servings

"Chutney is marvelous. I'm mad about it. To me, it's very imperial."

— *Diana Vreeland*

Spinach-Strawberry Salad

A faultless salad.

⅛ **cup cider vinegar**
¼ **cup sugar**
¼ **cup oil**
2 **tablespoons sesame seeds**
1½ **tablespoons minced onions**
1 **tablespoon poppy seed**
¼ **teaspoon Worcestershire sauce**
¼ **teaspoon paprika**
1 **(10-ounce) package fresh spinach, cleaned, stems removed**
1 **pint fresh strawberries, sliced**

- The day before serving: blend vinegar, sugar, oil, sesame seeds, onions, poppy seeds, Worcestershire sauce, and paprika in a blender.

- Serve over spinach mixed with sliced strawberries.

- Yield: 8 servings

For best results, always rinse strawberries before removing hulls so that the berries do not absorb moisture.

Avocado Salad Suzette

1 **pound potatoes, cooked, cubed and kept warm (2½ cups)**
2 **hard-cooked eggs, chopped**
6 **slices of bacon, cooked, drained and crumbled**
1 **small onion, minced (¼ cup)**
1 **tablespoon scallion tops, thinly sliced**
1 **tablespoon pimento, julienned**
   salt
   pepper
½ **cup mayonnaise**
2 **tablespoons lime juice**
2 **avocados, peeled, seeded and cubed**

- Mix warm potatoes, eggs, bacon, onion, scallions, pimento, and salt and pepper.

- Toss the mixture and chill covered for one hour.

- In a small bowl, mix the mayonnaise and lime juice. Fold into the potato mixture and add the avocados.

- Yield: 10 servings

Buy an avocado two to three days before you plan to use it since it will usually need some time to ripen. You can speed the process by placing the avocado in a closed paper bag with air holes.

Dublin Potato Salad

2 tablespoons vinegar
1 teaspoon celery seed
1 teaspoon mustard seed
3 medium-large potatoes
2 teaspoons sugar
1 teaspoon salt, divided
2 cups finely shredded cabbage
1 (12-ounce) can corned beef, chilled and
  cubed
¼ cup sliced green onion
¼ cup dill pickle, finely chopped
1 cup mayonnaise
1 cup milk

• Combine vinegar, celery seed, and mustard
  seed. Set aside.

• Pare and boil potatoes until fork tender. Drain
  and cube. While potatoes are still warm, drizzle
  with vinegar mixture. Sprinkle with sugar and
  ½ teaspoon of the salt, chill.

• Before serving, add cabbage, corned beef,
  onion, and pickle to potatoes.

• Combine mayonnaise, milk, and the remaining
  ½ teaspoon of salt. Pour over corned beef
  mixture and toss lightly.

• Yield: 8 servings

"Laughter is brightest where food is best."
— Irish Proverb

Dressy Green Bean Salad

1½ **pounds small red-skinned potatoes**
¾ **pound slenderest green beans available, stems trimmed**
1 **small red onion, coarsely chopped**
¼ **cup chopped fresh basil**

Dressing

¼ **cup balsamic vinegar**
2 **tablespoons Dijon mustard juice from small lemon (2 tablespoons)**
1 **garlic clove, minced dash Worcestershire sauce**
½ **cup extra virgin olive oil**

- Steam potatoes until tender. Cool; cut into quarters.

- Cook green beans in large pot of boiling salted water until crisp-tender, about 5 minutes. Drain and cut beans in half.

- Combine green beans, potatoes, onion, and basil in large bowl.

- Whisk balsamic vinegar, mustard, lemon juice, garlic, and Worcestershire sauce. Gradually whisk in oil.

- Pour dressing over vegetables. Toss to coat. Season to taste with salt and pepper. Can be prepared 4 hours ahead, just cover and keep at room temperature.

- Yield: 8 servings

"Extra virgin" olive oil means the olive oil will be more flavorful and aromatic.
If you prefer less olive oil taste, look for an olive oil that is lighter in color (it will also be lighter in taste).

Potato Salad for Fireworks

1½ **pounds small red potatoes**
1 **medium onion, chopped**
2 **tablespoons olive oil**
1 **large garlic clove, minced**
2 **large tomatoes, diced**
5 **tablespoons balsamic vinegar (or red wine vinegar)**
1 **tablespoon minced fresh basil or 1 teaspoon dried basil**
¼ **teaspoon dried oregano**

- Cook potatoes until fork tender, quarter and place in a large bowl.

- Sauté onion in oil until soft.

- Combine onion, garlic, tomatoes, vinegar, basil, and oregano with the potatoes.

- Serve warm or cold.

- Yield: 8 servings

Fourth of July Picnic

Sausage Stars

Chilled Red Pepper Soup

Grilled London Broil

Potato Salad for Fireworks

Summer Tomato Salad

Brag about Brownies

Scattered Confetti Rice Salad

2 cups uncooked rice
2 teaspoons mirin (Japanese sake)
2½ cups water
2 tablespoons rice or cider vinegar
½ cup sugar
1¼ teaspoons salt
6 tablespoons vegetable oil, divided
1 large egg
1 medium carrot, minced
1 small cucumber, peeled , seeded and minced
2 scallions, white and green, minced
handful of snow peas, cut into ½-inch lengths
2 cups frozen peas, lightly steamed
1 cup green beans, cut into ½-inch lengths, lightly steamed
1 small summer squash, minced
4 teaspoons minced fresh ginger
4 teaspoons sesame seeds

- Combine rice, water, and mirin. Bring to a boil and cook over low heat for 10 to 12 minutes.

- Remove rice from heat. Uncover and let stand for another 10 minutes.

- Combine vinegar, sugar, and salt in a small pan. Heat vinegar to dissolve sugar.

- Spread rice in a 9 x 13-inch pan. Sprinkle rice with half of the vinegar mixture. Mix gently with fork.

- Heat a medium size skillet, add 1 teaspoon of oil.

- Beat egg well. Pour on heated skillet. Make a thin omelet by tilting the pan in all directions, allowing the egg to run to its limits.

(recipe continued on next page)

(Scattered Confetti Rice Salad, continued)

- Remove the omelet from the skillet. Allow to cool thoroughly. Slice the cooled omelet into thin strips, then into ½-inch pieces.
- Gently mix the remaining oil, the vegetables, the omelet pieces, minced ginger, sesame seeds, and the remaining vinegar mixture with the rice.
- Serve cold or at room temperature.
- Yield: 8 servings

Lemon Rice Salad with Cucumber

This can be made up to 24 hours ahead of time.

- 1 tablespoon grated lemon peel
  juice from 1 large lemon (¼ cup)
- ¼ cup olive oil
- 1 teaspoon salt
- 1 teaspoon fresh ground pepper
- 2 medium size cucumbers, peeled, halved lengthwise and seeded
- 4 scallions, minced
- 1½ cups long-grain rice, cooked according to package directions

- Combine the lemon peel and lemon juice in a large salad bowl. Slowly whisk in the olive oil and add the salt and pepper. Set aside.
- Cut cucumbers into half-moon slices. Add the cucumber slices and scallions to the lemon vinaigrette. Toss.
- Place cooked rice in a colander and chill briefly under cold water until the rice is at room temperature. Drain well.
- Add the rice to cucumbers and toss. Cover and refrigerate for at least one hour before serving.
- Yield: 8 servings

Indonesian Rice Salad

Stir up your creativity.

2 cups cooked brown rice, cooled
½ cup raisins
2 scallions, chopped
¼ cup sesame seeds, toasted
4 ounces sliced water chestnuts (½ cup), drained
¼ pound fresh bean sprouts (1 cup)
1½ ounces toasted cashews (¼ cup)
1 large green pepper, chopped (1 cup)
1 celery stalk, sliced diagonally (½ cup)

Dressing

⅓ cup orange juice
¼ cup safflower oil
½ tablespoon sesame oil
2 tablespoons soy sauce
1 tablespoon dry sherry
juice of ½ lemon
¼ teaspoon grated fresh ginger root
1 garlic clove, minced
salt
pepper

Variations

½ cup thinly sliced bamboo shoots
fresh, raw snow peas
fresh pineapple
unsweetened toasted coconut

- In a large bowl, combine rice, raisins, scallions, sesame seeds, water chestnuts, bean sprouts, cashews, green pepper, and celery.

- To make dressing: combine orange juice, safflower oil, sesame oil, soy sauce, sherry, lemon juice, ginger, garlic, salt, and pepper in a wide mouth jar. Cover, shake to mix well.

- Pour dressing on rice mixture. Chill and serve on greens.

- Yield: 8 servings

Sunday Night Supper Salad

2 medium cucumbers, sliced
2 teaspoons salt, divided
⅔ cup olive oil
⅓ wine vinegar
2 large garlic cloves, minced
1 tablespoon chopped fresh basil
½ teaspoon pepper
10 medium mushrooms, sliced
4 scallions including tops, thinly sliced
½ cup parsley, minced
3 large tomatoes, peeled and chopped
1 medium green pepper, thinly sliced
½ pound Swiss cheese, cut into thin strips
6 bacon slices, cooked crisp, drained, and crumbled
4 hard cooked eggs, sliced

- Place cucumber slices in a bowl and sprinkle with 1 teaspoon of the salt. Let stand 30 minutes.

- In a large salad bowl, combine olive oil, vinegar, garlic, basil, remaining 1 teaspoon of salt, and the pepper. Add mushrooms and scallions.

- Drain cucumber slices and pat dry with a paper towel. Add to salad and chill 4 hours.

- Just before serving, add Swiss cheese and bacon. Toss gently and garnish with sliced, hard cooked eggs.

- Yield: 8 servings

"Parsley — the jewel of herbs, both in the pot and on the plate."

— Albert Stockli

Summer Tomato Salad

A beautiful dish for the summer buffet table.

  4 large, ripe, New Jersey beefsteak tomatoes, sliced
  1 bunch sweet basil leaves (same number as tomato slices)
1-2 large sweet onions: Spanish, Bermuda, Vidalia, or red; sliced very thin
1-2 brightly colored sweet peppers: red, green, yellow, orange, or purple, sliced in rounds (half the number of tomato slices)
  1 pound smoked mozzarella cheese, sliced thin
12-18 black or purple small Kalamata olives

Dressing
  ¼ cup balsamic vinegar
  1 teaspoon dry mustard
  ½ teaspoon minced garlic
  1 teaspoon dried herbes de Provence (or mix thyme, rosemary, marjoram)
  ¼ teaspoon salt
    freshly ground black pepper
  ¾ cup extra virgin olive oil

- On large platter, alternate tomato slices, basil leaves, onion slices, pepper rounds, and mozzarella slices, in a decorative pattern. Decorate further with strategically placed olives.

- Cover with plastic wrap and leave in a cool room, up to 2 hours. Do not refrigerate.

- In a wide-mouth jar, place balsamic vinegar, mustard, garlic, herbs, salt, and pepper. Cover tightly and shake vigorously.

- Uncover, add oil, recover tightly and shake even harder. Dressing should emulsify due to mustard. Cover and shake again before pouring the desired amount of dressing over salad. Dressing keeps for up to one week in refrigerator, but must be brought to room temperature before use.

- Yield: 20 servings

California Dressing

2 tablespoons balsamic vinegar
1 garlic clove, minced
¼ cup extra virgin olive oil
   splash of sherry vinegar
2 teaspoons pinenuts, toasted
4 sun-dried tomatoes, drained, thinly sliced
2 ounces creamy goat cheese, such as
   chèvre or Montrachet, crumbled
   ground pepper

- Combine balsamic vinegar, garlic, oil, sherry vinegar, pine nuts, sun-dried tomatoes and goat cheese in a wide mouth jar. Cover and shake.

- Yield: 6 servings

Luscious Lemon Dressing

1 garlic clove
   juice from 1 large lemon (makes about
   ¼ cup)
2 tablespoons sour cream
1 tablespoon sugar
½ cup safflower oil

- Chop garlic in a blender. Add lemon juice, sour cream and sugar. With the motor running, slowly add oil. (Can be prepared a day ahead.)

- Yield: 8 servings

Poppy Seed Dressing

1 cup sugar
½ teaspoon salt
1 teaspoon dry mustard
1½ teaspoons paprika
½ cup cider vinegar
1½ cups oil
1 teaspoon grated onion
2 tablespoons poppy seeds

- Combine sugar, salt, mustard, and vinegar in a blender. Add oil slowly and continue to blend until thick. Add poppy seeds and blend for a few minutes. Store in the refrigerator. (Can be prepared a day ahead.)

- Yield: 2½ cups

Ripply Raspberry Dressing

½ cup olive oil
¼ cup raspberry vinegar
½ teaspoon salt
¼ teaspoon ground pepper
¼ teaspoon ground ginger
¼ teaspoon Dijon mustard
1 egg yolk

- Combine oil, vinegar, salt, pepper, ginger, mustard, and egg yolk in a jar. Shake well. Refrigerate and shake to blend.

- Yield: 4 servings

Fresh Tomato Dressing

2 garlic cloves, minced
1-2 teaspoons salt
2 teaspoons sugar
½ teaspoon pepper
¼ cup mustard
½ cup oil
4 tablespoons tarragon vinegar
3-4 large tomatoes

- In a blender, mix garlic, salt, sugar, pepper, mustard, oil, and vinegar. Pour over sliced tomatoes.

- Yield: 8 servings

Strawberry Salad

Perfect for a ladies' luncheon.

1 (20-ounce) can crushed pineapple, drained
1 cup water
1 (6-ounce) package strawberry gelatin
2 (10-ounce) packages frozen strawberries, partially thawed
1 cup sour cream
4 ounces pecans, broken (1 cup)

- Combine drained juice from crushed pineapple and water.

- Boil liquid and dissolve gelatin. Add strawberries and pineapple.

- Put one-half of gelatin into a 9 x 13-inch pan and chill until firm (about 1 to 1½ hours).

- Spread sour cream over mixture. Pour other half of gelatin over sour cream and chill. Cut into squares and serve on decorative lettuce.

- Yield: 12 servings

Chicken Cranberry Layers

An easy and elegant luncheon entrée.

Cranberry layer
  1 **envelope unflavored gelatin**
  ¼ **cup water**
  1 **(16-ounce) can whole cranberry sauce**
  1 **(8-ounce) can crushed pineapple**
  2½ **ounces walnuts, chopped (½ cup)**
  1 **tablespoon lemon juice**
Chicken Layer
  1 **envelope unflavored gelatin**
  1 **cup light mayonnaise-type salad dressing**
  ¾ **cup water, divided**
  3 **tablespoons lemon juice**
  ¾ **teaspoon salt**
  2 **cups diced, cooked chicken**
  1 **large celery rib, diced (½ cup)**
  2 **tablespoons chopped parsley**

- To prepare cranberry layer: soften 1 envelope of gelatin in ¼ cup cold water. Dissolve over hot water.

- Add cranberry sauce, pineapple, walnuts, and lemon juice.

- Rinse a 9-inch square pan with cold water. Pour cranberry layer into the pan. Chill until firm.

- To make chicken layer: soften 1 envelope of gelatin in ¼ cup cold water. Dissolve over hot water.

- Whisk in light mayonnaise-type salad dressing, remaining ½ cup of the water, lemon juice, and salt.

- Add chicken, celery, and parsley.

- Pour over first layer; chill until firm.

- To unmold: dip pan in hot water, loosen edges with a knife and invert over serving platter decorated with greens.

- Yield: 8 servings

Christmas Ribbon Ring

1 (1-pound 4-ounce) can crushed pineapple
1 envelope unflavored gelatin
2 (3-ounce) packages raspberry gelatin
1 cup boiling water
1 (16-ounce) can whole cranberry sauce
1 cup port wine
5 ounces walnuts, chopped (1¼ cups)
Topping
1 (8-ounce) package cream cheese, softened
1 cup sour cream

- Drain ½ cup syrup from pineapple into saucepan and sprinkle with unflavored gelatin. Stir over low heat until dissolved.

- In a separate bowl, dissolve 2 packages raspberry gelatin in boiling water. Add syrup mixture. Stir in remaining undrained pineapple, cranberry sauce, and wine.

- Rinse a large ring mold with cold water. Pour pineapple gelatin mixture into mold and refrigerate

- When thick, stir in walnuts. Return to refrigerator and chill until firm.

- Blend cream cheese and sour cream together.

- Unmold on a bed of bright green lettuce and put cream cheese mixture in the center of the ring.

- Yield: 10 servings

"What is it?" Jelled Salad

1 tablespoon mayonnaise
3 (3-ounce) packages raspberry gelatin
1½ cups water
3 (16-ounce) cans stewed tomatoes, puréed
   and strained
3-4 dashes hot sauce
1 cup sour cream
1 tablespoon prepared horseradish

- Grease a 2½-quart mold with mayonnaise.

- Dissolve gelatin in 1½ cups water.

- Add tomato purée and hot sauce. Pour into mold. Chill until firm.

- To serve: mix sour cream with horseradish. Unmold jellied salad on a serving platter and pass sour cream mixture as a garnish.

- Yield: 14 servings

Midsummer's Night Supper

Baked Brie with Crudités

*Herb and Garlic
Marinated Leg of Lamb*

"What is it?" Jelled Salad

Garlicky Green Beans

French Bread

Fetzer's Fumé Blanc

Peaches Almondine

Apple Coffee Cake

Prepare the batter the night before and refrigerate.
Bake it in the morning.

nonstick cooking spray
1 **cup sugar**
½ **cup (1 stick) butter**
1 **large egg**
1½ **cups plus 2 tablespoons flour**
1 **teaspoon baking soda**
1 **teaspoon salt**
3 **apples, peeled, cored and finely chopped**
(preferably Granny Smith)
2 **tablespoons flour**
⅓ **cup brown sugar, firmly packed**
1 **teaspoon cinnamon**
1½ **ounces pecans, chopped (⅓ cup)**

- Preheat oven to 350°.

- Spray a 10 x 6 x 2-inch baking pan with nonstick cooking spray.

- Cream sugar and butter until light and fluffy. Add egg and beat well.

- Combine 1½ cups flour, baking soda, and salt. Add to butter mixture, mixing well.

- Combine apple with 2 tablespoons flour and stir into batter. Pour batter into baking pan.

- To make topping: combine brown sugar, cinnamon, and pecans. Sprinkle over batter.

- Bake for 40 to 45 minutes.

Our Favorite Banana Tea Loaf

1¾ **cups sifted flour**
¾ **teaspoon baking soda**
1¼ **teaspoons cream of tartar**
½ **teaspoon salt**
2 **large eggs**
⅓ **cup unsalted butter, softened**
2 **medium-sized ripe bananas, sliced**
⅔ **cup sugar**

- Preheat oven to 350°.

- Sift flour, baking soda, cream of tartar, and salt.

- Place eggs, butter, bananas, and sugar in blender and mix until smooth (about 30 seconds). Pour blended mixture over sifted dry ingredients; mix gently until barely combined.

- Pour into greased 8 x 4-inch loaf pan.

- Bake until lightly browned, about 45 minutes.

"Love and scandal are the best sweeteners of tea."

— Henry Fielding

Broccoli Bread

nonstick cooking spray
4 large eggs, beaten
½ cup (1 stick) butter, melted
6 ounces cottage cheese
1 large onion, finely chopped
1 teaspoon salt
1 package chopped frozen broccoli, thawed and drained
1 package corn bread mix

- Preheat oven to 400°.

- Spray a 9-inch square pan with nonstick cooking spray.

- Mix eggs, butter, cottage cheese, onion, salt, and broccoli. Fold in corn bread mix.

- Pour into baking pan. Bake 25 minutes.

- Serve with soup or salad.

- Yield: 6 servings

Broccoli is a member of the "Brassica" family and is closely related to cauliflower. In Greece and Italy, broccoli has been a favorite vegetable for some 2,000 years. Thomas Jefferson, it is said, grew broccoli at Monticello in the early 19th century.

Herbed Corn Bread

1½ cups flour, sifted
2 tablespoons sugar
4 teaspoons baking powder
½ teaspoon salt
1½ cups cornmeal
3 large celery ribs, chopped (1½ cups)
1 envelope onion soup mix
2 teaspoons rubbed sage
1 teaspoon dried thyme
3 large eggs, beaten
1½ cups milk
⅓ cup vegetable oil

- Preheat oven to 400°.

- Grease a 13 x 9 x 2-inch pan.

- Sift flour, sugar, baking powder, and salt into bowl. Add cornmeal, celery, soup mix, sage, and thyme. Mix thoroughly.

- Combine eggs, milk, and oil. Stir into dry ingredients and mix well.

- Pour batter into pan. Bake 35 to 40 minutes. Cut into squares and serve hot.

- Yield: 12 squares

Herbed Seasoned Bread Crumbs

3 cups herb seasoned stuffing
1 teaspoon dried oregano
¼ cup grated Parmesan cheese
½ teaspoon pepper
1 teaspoon salt

- Pulse in a food processor until ground to the right consistency for bread crumbs. Refrigerates well.

- Yield: 1 cup

Irish Soda Bread

*Irish Soda Bread freezes perfectly. To reheat;
preheat oven to 350°. Place bread in a moistened
brown paper bag. When the bag feels hot
(about 5 minutes), it's done.*

nonstick cooking spray
1½ **cups buttermilk**
2 **tablespoons butter, melted**
1 **large egg, slightly beaten**
1½ **cups raisins**
3 **cups flour**
⅔ **cup sugar**
1 **tablespoon baking powder**
1 **teaspoon baking soda**
1 **teaspoon salt**

• Preheat oven to 350°.

• Spray a 9 x 5 x 3-inch loaf pan with nonstick
  cooking spray.

• Combine buttermilk, butter, egg, and raisins.

• In a large bowl, combine dry ingredients. Add
  liquid ingredients. Mix with two forks for
  about one minute. Spoon into pan.

• Bake 50 to 55 minutes. Remove from oven and
  let sit in pan for a few minutes. Remove bread
  from pan and place on a wire rack to cool.

*The making of this traditional Gaelic bread
may date from the Middle Ages. Owing to the
shortage of wood fuel in the land, it is often
baked in a shallow-hearth oven over a
smoldering peat fire.*

Lemon Tea Bread

If you cannot find the lemon herbs, increase grated lemon peel to 2 tablespoons. By the way, lemon thyme and lemon balm are very easy to grow in a garden. In fact so easy to grow, that they can take over your entire backyard.

    nonstick cooking spray
¾ cup milk
1 tablespoon chopped lemon thyme
1 tablespoon chopped lemon balm
2 cups flour
1½ teaspoons baking powder
¼ teaspoon salt
6 tablespoons butter
1 cup sugar
2 large eggs, beaten
1 tablespoon grated lemon peel
    juice from 2 lemons
    confectioners' sugar

- Preheat oven to 325°.

- Spray a 9 x 5 x 3-inch loaf pan with nonstick cooking spray.

- Heat milk with lemon thyme and lemon balm.

- Mix flour, baking powder, and salt in a bowl.

- In another bowl, cream butter and gradually beat in sugar until light and fluffy. Beat in eggs, one at a time. Beat in grated lemon peel.

- Add flour mixture alternating with herbed milk. Mix until batter is just blended. Pour into prepared pan.

- Bake 50 minutes or until toothpick inserted in the center comes out clean.

- To make glaze: put the juice of 2 lemons in a bowl and add confectioners' sugar until a thick pourable paste forms.

- Remove bread from pan onto wire rack set over a sheet of wax paper. Pour lemon glaze over hot bread. Serve with Pennsylvania Lemon Butter.

Pennsylvania Lemon Butter

3 large eggs
2 cups sugar
juice and grated peel from 3 lemons
½ cup (1 stick) butter

- Combine eggs, sugar, juice, peel, and butter in a saucepan over low heat. Stir only until thickened. Serve on your favorite sweet bread.

Orange Nut Bread

nonstick cooking spray
1½ cups flour
½ cup sugar
2 teaspoons baking powder
½ teaspoon salt
1½ ounces walnuts, chopped (⅓ cup)
¼ cup raisins, chopped
2 tablespoons grated orange peel
1 large egg, beaten
½ cup orange juice
2 teaspoons vegetable oil

- Spray an 8 x 4-inch loaf pan with nonstick cooking spray.

- Preheat oven to 350°.

- Combine flour, sugar, baking powder, and salt in a mixing bowl. Stir in nuts, raisins, and orange peel.

- Combine beaten egg, orange juice, and oil. Pour into flour mixture. Mix only until flour is dampened and fruit and nuts are well distributed.

- Turn into loaf pan and bake for 40 minutes.

- Let cool in pan for 10 minutes, remove and cool completely. Wrap in wax paper and store overnight before serving.

Toast your nutmeats and while hot, add a little butter; your nutbread will take on a new aristocracy.

Pumpkin Apple Streusel Muffins

nonstick cooking spray
2½ cups flour
2 cups sugar
1 tablespoon pumpkin pie spice
1 teaspoon baking soda
½ teaspoon salt
2 large eggs, lightly beaten
1 cup canned pumpkin, packed
½ cup vegetable oil
3 medium apples, peeled, cored and finely chopped (2 cups)
2 tablespoons flour
¼ cup sugar
½ teaspoon cinnamon
4 teaspoons butter

- Preheat oven to 350°.

- Spray muffin cups with nonstick cooking spray.

- In large bowl, combine flour, sugar, pumpkin pie spice, baking soda, and salt. Set aside.

- Combine eggs, pumpkin, and oil. Add liquid ingredients to dry ingredients; stir just until moistened. Fold in apples.

- To make streusel topping: in a small bowl, combine flour, sugar, and cinnamon. Cut in butter until mixture is crumbly.

- Spoon batter into muffin cups, fill three-fourths full. Sprinkle streusel topping over batter. Bake for 35 to 40 minutes or until a toothpick inserted in the center comes out clean.

- Yield: 18 muffins

Pumpkin Bread

*Make this bread in two 1-pound coffee
tins as a great gift for the holidays.
Spray the coffee tins with nonstick cooking
spray. The bread easily slides out of the coffee
tin and is a perfect size for gift giving. Add a
festive touch by wrapping in bright colored
plastic wrap.*

nonstick cooking spray
1⅔ cups flour
1½ cups sugar
¼ teaspoon salt
1 teaspoon baking soda
1 teaspoon baking powder
½ teaspoon ground cloves
½ teaspoon cinnamon
½ teaspoon nutmeg
2 large eggs, beaten
½ cup vegetable oil
1 cup canned pumpkin
2 ounces nuts, chopped (½ cup)
½ cup raisins

*Dust raisins and
nuts with flour
before adding them
to cake batter to
prevent them
sinking to the
bottom of the pan.*

- Preheat oven to 325°.

- Spray a 9 x 5 x 3-inch loaf pan with
  nonstick cooking spray.

- Sift flour, sugar, salt, baking soda, baking
  powder, cloves, cinnamon, and nutmeg in
  a bowl.

- Add eggs, oil, and canned pumpkin. Add
  nuts and raisins.

- Bake 60 minutes or until a toothpick
  inserted in the center comes out clean.

Sweet Lime Bread

nonstick cooking spray
4 large eggs
1 cup milk
3 cups flour
2 teaspoons baking powder
1 teaspoon salt
1 cup (2 sticks) butter
2 cups sugar
2 tablespoons grated lime peel
Glaze
½ cup sugar
3 teaspoons lime juice
finely shredded lime peel

- Spray 2 loaf pans with nonstick cooking spray.

- In a medium bowl, mix together eggs and milk.

- Combine flour, baking powder, and salt. Add to the egg mixture.

- Cream butter, sugar, and grated lime peel. Add flour mixture, a little at a time to the butter mixture.

- Divide batter into loaf pans. Bake for 55 minutes.

- To make glaze: cook sugar, lime juice, and finely shredded lime peel until sugar dissolves.

- As soon as bread comes out of the oven, prick several times with a two-prong fork. Drizzle the glaze over breads. Allow loaves to cool in pan. The loaves freeze well.

Tea Time Scones

Scones need butter to be a scone.
A scone doesn't turn out when margarine
is substituted for butter.

½ **cup golden raisins**
   minced peel of 1 orange
¼ **cup plus 1 tablespoon water**
2 **cups flour**
1¼ **teaspoons baking powder**
1 **tablespoon sugar**
¼ **teaspoon salt**
½ **cup (1 stick) butter**
¾ **cup half & half**
1 **large egg yolk**
2 **tablespoons sugar**

- Preheat oven to 400°.

- Combine flour, baking powder, sugar, and salt. Blend in butter with a pastry cutter until the mixture is the size of small peas. Incorporate the half & half, raisins and orange peel; handling the dough as little as possible.

- Gather the dough together and roll it out on a lightly floured board until it is ½ to ¼-inch thick. Cut in heart shapes with a cookie cutter.

- Combine egg yolk and 1 tablespoon water; brush on scone as a glaze. Sprinkle with sugar.

- Bake for about 15 minutes until golden.

- Yield: 15 large or 30 small scones

To store extra egg yolks or whites: cover yolks with cold water and store in the refrigerator; leftover whites can be frozen or stored in a jar in the refrigerator.

June Fête Zucchini Bread

nonstick cooking spray
3 large eggs
1 cup oil
1½ cups sugar
2 teaspoons vanilla
1½ pounds zucchini, grated (3 cups)
3 cups flour
1 teaspoon baking powder
1 teaspoon baking soda
1 teaspoon salt
2½ teaspoons cinnamon
½ cup raisins

- Preheat oven to 325°.

- Spray 2 loaf pans or 4 small loaf pans with nonstick cooking spray.

- Beat eggs until light and fluffy. Add oil and continue beating until combined. Add sugar and vanilla and beat well.

- Combine the grated zucchini with the egg mixture.

- Combine flour, baking powder, baking soda, salt, and cinnamon in a separate bowl. Add the raisins.

- Combine the wet and dry ingredients; mix well.

- Pour into loaf pans. Bake 50 to 60 minutes, depending on size of pan.

Although zucchini is considered a summer squash, it is available year-round in many areas. For lowest cost and greatest freshness and flavor, late spring through summer is the peak season.

**Healthy
Alternative
Broccoli
Breakfast
Quesadilla**

*Sauté vegetables
with nonstick
cooking spray, use
1½ cups of egg
substitute for the
eggs and use 2
ounces of sharp
Cheddar cheese.
Per serving: 284
Calories • 22% Fat*

*Microwave
vegetables for a
more beautiful
color. It's quick
and easy. For
smaller amounts of
vegetables, cooking
time is as little as
15 seconds. For
larger amounts of
vegetables, cooking
time is 2 to 3
minutes.*

Broccoli Breakfast Quesadillas

*These are delicious frozen and reheated
in the oven or microwave.*

½ **medium onion, chopped**
¼ **green pepper, chopped**
¼ **red pepper, chopped**
2 **teaspoons olive oil**
6 **large eggs**
¼ **cup broccoli, steamed or
   microwaved
   until tender/crisp**
6 **slices of bacon, cooked crisp,
   drained and crumbled**
4 **ounces sharp Cheddar cheese,
   grated (1 cup)**
4 **soft flour tortillas**
   salsa
   sour cream

- Preheat oven to 350°.

- Sauté onions and peppers in oil. Remove vegetables, scramble eggs in same pan. When eggs are almost done, add onion, peppers, broccoli, and bacon.

- Put 1 ounce of the cheese and one-quarter of the egg mixture in the center of each tortilla. Leave enough room to tuck down the top and bottom flaps and then the sides, creating a totally enclosed tortilla.

- Place on a cookie sheet, bake for 25 minutes, or until lightly browned on top.

- Garnish with salsa and sour cream.

- Yield: 4 servings

- Per serving: 487 Calories • 50% Fat

Pan Fried Apple Rum Pancake

For a simply delicious breakfast, try this family pancake—a single pancake serves four.

> 2 **large eggs, beaten**
> ⅓ **cup sugar**
> ½ **cup milk**
> ¾ **cup flour**
> 2 **tablespoons dark rum (optional)**
> 2 **Golden Delicious apples (¾ pound), peeled, quartered and thinly sliced (2 cups)**
> 2 **tablespoons oil**
> 1 **tablespoon confectioners' sugar**

- In a small mixing bowl, blend eggs, sugar, and milk.

- Place flour in a large bowl. Whisk the egg mixture into the flour. Add rum, one tablespoon at time.

- Stir the apples and oil into the batter.

- Heat a large (12-inch) nonstick skillet. Pour batter into skillet and cook over gentle heat for about 5 to 7 minutes or until the pancake is almost set.

- Place a serving dish on the top of the pancake and flip the skillet so the pancake is on the dish. Slide pancake back into skillet, brown side up, and continue cooking for about another 10 minutes or until set.

- Turn out pancake onto a plate. With a sieve, sprinkle with confectioners' sugar. To serve, cut into wedges.

- Yield: 4 servings

- Per serving: 301 Calories • 33% Fat

HA

Healthy Alternative Pan Fried Apple Rum Pancake

Use ½ cup of skim milk, ½ cup egg substitute and 1 tablespoon of oil in this recipe.
Per serving: 255 Calories • 23% Fat

Bacon 'n Egg Sophisticate

*When opening a package of bacon,
roll it into a long tube. This loosens the slices
and keeps them from sticking.*

> 2 teaspoons butter
> ¼ cup bread crumbs
> 8 slices of bacon, cooked crisp, drained
>   and broken in halves
> 6 large eggs, separated
> ¾ teaspoon salt
> ⅛ teaspoon pepper
> 1½ cups milk
> 3 ounces Swiss cheese, grated (¾ cup)

- Preheat oven to 350°.

- Coat a 1½-quart round casserole with butter. Sprinkle with bread crumbs. Place bacon in casserole dish.

- In a medium bowl, whisk egg yolks with milk, salt, and pepper. Add cheese.

- In a separate bowl, with an electric mixer, beat egg whites until they stand in stiff peaks. Fold into egg yolk mixture.

- Pour egg mixture into casserole dish. Bake 25 minutes, let stand 5 minutes.

- Yield: 6 servings

- Per serving: 244 Calories • 63% Fat

"Omelets are not made without breaking eggs."
— *Robespierre*

ᴴᴬ
Healthy Alternative
Ham 'n Egg Sophisticate

*Ham is a fabulous lower fat
replacement for bacon.*

nonstick cooking spray
¼ cup bread crumbs
4 ounces ham, diced
1½ cups egg substitute
2 large egg whites
½ teaspoon salt
⅛ teaspoon pepper
1½ cups skim milk
3 ounces Swiss cheese, grated (¾ cup)

- Preheat oven to 350°.

- Spray a 1½-quart round casserole with nonstick cooking spray. Sprinkle with bread crumbs. Place diced ham in casserole.

- In a medium bowl, whisk egg substitute with skim milk, salt, and pepper. Add cheese.

- In a separate bowl, beat egg whites until they stand in stiff peaks. Fold into egg substitute mixture.

- Pour egg mixture into casserole. Bake 25 minutes, let stand 5 minutes.

- Yield: 6 servings

- Per serving: 145 Calories • 32% Fat

Question of the century is: should I use low-fat or non-fat cheese? The tastiest answer is neither. We suggest less of the real thing in a recipe. The best way for a little of a great cheese to go a long way is to grate the cheese: 1 ounce of cheese is ¼ cup of grated cheese.

Sunday French Toast

8 slices French bread, ¾-inch thick
4 eggs, or 1 cup egg substitute
1 cup milk
2 tablespoons Grand Marnier or
orange juice
1 tablespoon sugar
½ teaspoon vanilla extract
¼ teaspoon salt
2 tablespoons butter
confectioners' sugar

To keep French toast from getting soggy, freeze the bread overnight.

- Arrange bread in a single layer in a 12 x 8-inch baking dish.

- In a medium bowl, combine eggs, milk, Grand Marnier, sugar, vanilla, and salt until well blended. Pour over bread. Turn slices to coat evenly.

- Refrigerate, covered, overnight.

- In hot butter in a skillet, sauté bread until golden, about 4 minutes on each side. Sprinkle with confectioners' sugar.

"Start every day with a smile and get it over with."

— *W. C. Fields*

Ham Roulades

1 (11-ounce) can mandarin oranges, drained
1½ cups cooked long grain rice
⅓ cup mayonnaise
1 tablespoon grated onion
3 tablespoons chopped pecans
2 tablespoons chopped parsley
  salt
  pepper
8 thin slices of ham (2 ounces)
½ cup orange marmalade
2 tablespoons lemon juice
½ teaspoon ginger

- Preheat oven to 350°.

- Chop mandarin orange sections, reserving eight for garnish.

- In a medium bowl, combine chopped mandarin oranges, rice, mayonnaise, onion, pecans, and parsley. Salt and pepper to taste.

- Spoon about two tablespoons of mixture onto each ham slice. Roll up to enclose filling.

- In a small bowl, combine marmalade, lemon juice, and ginger. Brush over ham roulades.

- Bake for 15 minutes, basting occasionally with orange sauce. Garnish each roulade with a mandarin slice.

- Yield: 8 servings

- Per serving: 192 Calories • 47% Fat

⊣⊢A
Healthy Alternative
Ham Roulades

*For a creamy, delicious, substitute for mayonnaise;
try yomayo...mix a tiny bit of mayonnaise with
nonfat plain yogurt. Yomayo also works in tuna
or chicken salad.*

1 **(11-ounce) can mandarin oranges, drained**
1½ **cups cooked long grain rice**
⅓ **cup nonfat yogurt**
1 **tablespoon mayonnaise**
1 **tablespoon grated onion**
3 **tablespoons chopped pecans**
2 **tablespoons chopped parsley**
  salt
  pepper
8 **thin slices of ham (2 ounces)**
½ **cup orange marmalade**
2 **tablespoons lemon juice**
½ **teaspoon ginger**

- Preheat oven to 350°.

- Chop mandarin orange sections, reserving eight for garnish.

- In a medium bowl, combine chopped mandarin oranges, rice, nonfat yogurt, mayonnaise, onion, pecans, and parsley. Salt and pepper to taste.

- Spoon about two tablespoons of mixture onto each ham slice. Roll up to enclose filling.

- In a small bowl, combine marmalade, lemon juice and ginger. Brush over ham roulades.

- Bake for 15 minutes, basting occasionally with orange sauce. Garnish each roulade with a mandarin slice.

- Yield: 8 servings

- Per serving: 149 Calories • 24% Fat

Belgian Onion Pie

½ **cup (1 stick) butter**
3 **large Spanish onions, cut into half**
   moons and sliced thin
3 **tablespoons flour**
¼ **cup hot milk**
¼ **cup hot light cream**
2 **large eggs, beaten**
⅛ **teaspoon nutmeg**
2 **tablespoons grated Parmesan and**
   Romano mix
¼ **teaspoon salt**
⅛ **teaspoon pepper**
1 **baked 9-inch pie shell**

- Preheat oven to 400°.

- Heat butter until foamy in a large frying pan. Add onions and sauté until limp.

- Cover and cook for 5 minutes. Mix in flour, then add cream and milk. Remove from heat and cool slightly.

- Add eggs, nutmeg, Parmesan and Romano cheese mix, salt, and pepper.

- Pour into a baked pie shell. Bake for 30 to 40 minutes, until brown and center is set.

- Yield: 10 servings

To help avoid tears when chopping onions, peel under cold running water, close your mouth and breathe through your nose, hold a bread crust or celery stalk in your mouth or chop near an open flame.

Blueberry Pouffe Sunday Morning

Serve with maple syrup and sausage links.

nonstick cooking spray
3 large eggs, separated
½ cup sour cream
⅓ cup milk
1 teaspoon grated orange peel
½ teaspoon nutmeg
¼ teaspoon salt, divided
1 cup flour, sifted
⅔ cup fresh blueberries

- Preheat oven to 375°.

- Spray a 1½-quart soufflé dish with nonstick cooking spray.

- In a large bowl, combine egg yolks, sour cream, milk, orange peel, nutmeg, and ⅛ teaspoon of salt. Stir in flour.

- In a separate bowl, with an electric mixer, beat egg whites and remaining salt until they stand in stiff peaks. Fold egg whites into egg yolk mixture.

- Gently fold in blueberries.

- Pour mixture into soufflé dish. Bake 45 minutes or until puffed and browned and knife inserted in the center comes out clean.

- Yield: 6 servings

- Per serving: 167 Calories • 37% Fat

HA
Healthy Alternative Blueberry Pouffe Sunday Morning

Serve with blueberry topping and Canadian bacon.

nonstick cooking spray
½ **cup egg substitute**
½ **cup yogurt cheese**
⅓ **cup skim milk**
1 **teaspoon grated orange peel**
½ **teaspoon nutmeg**
¼ **teaspoon salt, divided**
3 **large egg whites**
1 **cup flour, sifted**
⅔ **cup fresh blueberries or frozen blueberries that have been thawed and patted dry with paper towels**

- Advance preparation: make yogurt cheese.

- Preheat oven to 375°.

- Spray 1½-quart soufflé dish with nonstick cooking spray.

- In a large bowl, combine egg substitute, yogurt cheese, milk, orange peel, nutmeg, and ⅛ teaspoon of the salt. Stir in flour.

- In a separate bowl, beat egg whites with remaining salt until they stand in stiff peaks. Fold egg whites into egg mixture.

- Gently fold in blueberries.

- Pour mixture into soufflé dish. Bake 45 minutes or until puffed and browned and knife inserted in the center comes out clean.

- Yield: 6 servings

- Per serving: 124 Calories • 12% Fat

A fabulous, calcium-enriched, tasty tip: use yogurt cheese in place of sour cream. To make yogurt cheese: line a strainer with a coffee filter and place the strainer in a shallow bowl. Fill the strainer with plain nonfat yogurt. Refrigerate the whole thing for 2 to 4 hours. Discard the clear liquid that separates into the bowl. A 32-ounce container of nonfat plain yogurt will make about 1½ cups of yogurt cheese. What do you do with leftover yogurt cheese after you have made Healthy Alternative Blueberry Pouffe Sunday Morning? Add your favorite spices and use it as a tasty vegetable dip.

Crab Quiche to Die For

Rich and savory fare.

nonstick cooking spray
8-9 slices bread, crust removed and toasted
1 cup light cream
1 oup mayonnaise
5 large eggs
16 ounces Swiss cheese, grated (4 cups)
1 pound crabmeat (the best available, large pieces preferred)

- One hour in advance: spray an 8-inch square pan with nonstick cooking spray. Line bottom and sides with toast. Refrigerate for 1 hour.

- Preheat oven to 350°.

- Whisk cream, mayonnaise, and eggs thoroughly. Add cheese. Fold in crabmeat. Pour into the refrigerated crust.

- Bake for 45 minutes or until top is set.

- Yield: 9-12 servings

"Tell me what you eat and I will tell you what you are."
— *Anthelme Brillat-Savarin*

Gratin of Eggs with Fine Herbs

2 pounds asparagus
10 large eggs, hard cooked and peeled
½ teaspoon Worcestershire sauce
1 teaspoon grated onion
1 teaspoon dry mustard, divided
1 tablespoon cream
2 teaspoons salt, divided
⅛ teaspoon pepper, divided
2 (4½-ounce) cans deviled ham
½ cup (1 stick) butter, divided
6 tablespoons flour
3 cups half & half
8 ounces Cheddar cheese, grated (2 cups)
1 cup cornflakes, crushed

For eggs that are difficult to peel, refrigerate in a pan of cold water for an hour or longer.

- Preheat oven to 400°.

- Cook asparagus in microwave, until fork tender.

- Slice hard cooked eggs in half and remove yolks. Mash yolks and blend with Worcestershire sauce, onion, ¾ teaspoon of the mustard, cream, ½ teaspoon of the salt, dash of the pepper, and deviled ham.

- Fill egg whites.

- Melt 6 tablespoons of the butter. Stir in flour. Add half & half, stirring until thick (takes about 5 minutes). Remove from heat. Add cheese, the remaining mustard, salt, and pepper.

- Line a 9 x 11-inch baking dish with asparagus, arrange eggs on top. Pour cheese sauce overall. Mix cornflakes with remaining 2 tablespoons of the butter and sprinkle over casserole.

- Bake for 20 minutes.

- Yield: 8 servings

Leek & Cheddar Tart

1 unbaked 9-inch pie shell
4 tablespoons butter
2½ pounds leeks (about 6 medium), trimmed
   and sliced thin (use white and light green
   parts only).
6 ounces mild white Cheddar cheese
   (1½ cups), grated, divided
3 large egg yolks
1 cup heavy cream
1 teaspoon salt
½ teaspoon pepper
½ teaspoon mace

- Preheat oven to 350°.

- Bake pie shell until light brown, about 20 minutes. Cool.

- Melt butter in heavy skillet over low heat. Add leeks and sauté until tender but not soft, about 15 minutes. Spread leeks onto pie crust. Sprinkle with 1 cup of the cheese.

- In a medium bowl, whisk egg yolks, cream, salt, pepper, and mace. Pour over leeks in pie crust. Sprinkle with remaining cheese.

- Bake about 40 minutes, until filling is set and golden. Cool at least 40 minutes before serving.

- Yield: 8 servings

Leeks became the national emblem of Wales, for, as legend has it, Saint David told Welshmen to wear a leek in their cap when they went to war against the invading Saxons lest they mistake friends for enemies.

Noodle Kugel

*Kugel recipes are traditionally handed down
from generation to generation and have a
starring role in the holiday menu.*

  1 **(8-ounce) package cream cheese, softened**
  1 **cup (2 sticks) butter, melted and divided**
  1 **(16-ounce) container creamed cottage
     cheese**
1½ **cups sugar**
  2 **tablespoons vanilla**
  2 **cups sour cream**
 10 **large eggs**
  1 **pound wide egg noodles, cooked and
     drained**
 ¼ **cup graham cracker crumbs**

- Preheat oven to 350°.

- Using an electric mixer, blend cream cheese,
  cottage cheese, sugar, vanilla, sour cream, and
  eggs. Mix into noodles.

- Pour ½ cup melted butter in a 9 x 13-inch
  baking dish. Add the noodle mixture and then
  the remaining melted butter. Sprinkle with
  graham cracker crumbs. Bake for 1 hour.

- Yield: 15 servings

*"To invite a person into your house is to take
charge of his happiness for as long as he is under
your roof."*
                                    — Brillat-Savarin

Sausage Apple Ring

A centerpiece for your next holiday brunch.

nonstick cooking spray
12 **large eggs, divided**
2 **pounds sausage**
1½ **cups cracker crumbs**
½ **cup milk**
1 **small onion, finely chopped (¼ cup)**
2 **medium apples, finely chopped (1 cup)**
½ **cup grated Parmesan cheese**

- Preheat oven to 350°.

- Spray a ring mold with nonstick cooking spray.

- Lightly beat 2 eggs.

- Combine sausage, cracker crumbs, the 2 beaten eggs, milk, onion, and apples.

- Press lightly into the ring mold. Place on a cookie sheet.

- Bake 1½ to 2 hours. Pour off grease as it accumulates.

- Just before serving, scramble the remaining eggs with grated cheese. Unmold sausage ring and fill center with scrambled eggs.

- Yield: 10 servings

Smoking or salting meat to preserve it probably goes back to the time of the ancient Egyptians. Although sausage is usually made of pork, there is virtually no meat that cannot be used. Sausage-eating customs differ as much from one country to another as the spices used in making them. In Germany every type of sausage has its hour — or meal — when it is traditionally eaten. The French prefer sausage as an appetizer.

Sour Cream Brunch Bake

nonstick cooking spray
2 tablespoons flour
1 (15 to 16-ounce) container of ricotta cheese
⅔ cup confectioners' sugar, divided
1 large egg, separated
9 large eggs
1½ cups sour cream
⅛ teaspoon salt
sour cream
raspberry preserves

- Preheat oven to 350°.

- Spray an 8 x 12-inch baking dish with nonstick cooking spray and lightly flour.

- Combine ricotta, ⅓ cup of confectioners' sugar, and 1 egg yolk. Spread evenly in bottom of baking dish.

- In medium mixing bowl, combine eggs, the egg white, sour cream, the remaining ⅓ cup of confectioners' sugar, and salt. Beat with an electric mixer on medium speed for 2 minutes.

- Pour egg mixture over ricotta. Bake for an hour or until puffy and set.

- Cut into squares and serve topped with a spoonful of sour cream and raspberry preserves.

- Yield: 9 servings

"I always like to have the morning well-aired before I get up."
— *Beau Brummell*

Angel Hair Pasta with Lemon and Garlic

This is a fabulous low-fat recipe.

1 teaspoon olive oil
2 garlic cloves, minced
½ cup dry white wine
 juice of a medium lemon (¼ cup)
1 medium tomato, chopped (1 cup)
8 ounces angel hair pasta
¼ cup fresh basil, chopped
2 tablespoons grated Parmesan cheese
 freshly ground black pepper to taste

- Bring a large pot of water to boil and maintain at a boil.

- Heat olive oil in skillet and sauté garlic over medium heat, just until garlic begins to brown. Remove pan from the heat and add wine.

- Return to heat and reduce by half, about 1 to 2 minutes. Stir in lemon juice and tomato.

- Place the pasta in the boiling water and cook to desired doneness; 30 seconds to 1 minute. Drain and put in a warm serving bowl.

- To serve: toss hot drained pasta with tomato mixture, basil, Parmesan cheese, and black pepper.

- Yield: 4 servings

Fettucine with Shrimp and Spinach

¼ **cup olive oil**
2 **small dried hot red peppers (optional)**
4 **garlic cloves, minced**
1 **pound medium shrimp, peeled and deveined**
1 **(10-ounce) bag spinach, washed and stems removed**
1 **(28-ounce) can plum tomatoes, drained and chopped**
1½ **cups grated Parmesan cheese**
1 **pound fresh fettucine, cooked**

- Heat olive oil in a skillet. Sauté hot peppers until black. Remove from pan.

- Add garlic to pan and sauté (do not brown). Add shrimp and sauté just until pink.

- Lower heat, add tomatoes and spinach. Sauté until wilted (use full package, it really cooks down). Simmer over low heat.

- In a large bowl, toss shrimp mixture over cooked pasta. Sprinkle with cheese.

- Yield: 8 servings

Raw spinach has just 28 calories per cup and it's loaded with vitamins, namely A, B, and C.

Fettucine Soufflé

*Okra, corn and tomatoes served on the side will make
a colorful, delicious and inviting accompaniment*

nonstick cooking spray
¼ pound fresh fettucine, cooked al dente
¼ cup grated Parmesan cheese, divided
1⅓ cups milk
1 garlic clove, minced
4 ounces fontina cheese, grated (1 cup)
8 tablespoons (1 stick) butter, cut into small pieces
pepper
1-2 tablespoons chopped parsley
6 large eggs, separated

- Preheat oven to 350°.

- Spray a 2-quart soufflé dish with nonstick cooking spray and dust with 3 tablespoons of the Parmesan.

- Bring milk to a simmer.

- In a large bowl, mix cooked, drained fettucine with hot milk, garlic, remaining Parmesan cheese, fontina cheese, and butter. Season with pepper. Add parsley. Cool about 30 minutes.

- Add lightly beaten egg yolks to cooled fettucine mixture.

- Beat egg whites until they stand in stiff peaks. Fold carefully into fettucine mixture. Pour into soufflé dish.

- Bake approximately 40 minutes.

- Increase heat to 425°. Bake another 5 minutes to form a crusty top.

- Yield: 6 servings

Orzo with Mustard Balsamic Vinaigrette

5 tablespoons balsamic vinegar
1 teaspoon salt
freshly ground pepper
2 tablespoons Dijon mustard
¼ cup minced shallots
1 teaspoon sugar
1 cup olive oil
4 quarts water
1 pound orzo (rice shaped pasta)

- To make dressing: combine balsamic vinegar, salt, pepper, mustard, shallots, sugar, and olive oil in a blender or food processor. Blend until smooth.

- Bring water to a rapid boil in a large saucepan. Add orzo and cook until tender, approximately 8 minutes. Drain, but do not rinse.

- Pour dressing over warm orzo.

- Yield: 8 servings

A Spring Celebration

Italian Pesto Cheese Torta

Boneless Turkey Breast with Peanut Sauce

Orzo with Mustard Balsamic Vinaigrette

Mixed Green Salad with Poppy Seed Dressing

Tott's California Champagne

Strawberries Bourbonaisse

Out of the Ordinary Orzo

nonstick cooking spray
2 quarts water
1 pound orzo (rice shaped pasta)
6 garlic cloves, unpooled
1 cup heavy cream
1 cup chicken broth
1 cup grated Parmesan cheese, divided
1¼ cups minced parsley, divided
¼ teaspoon salt
pepper
4 tablespoons dry bread crumbs
3 tablespoons butter

- Spray 2-quart baking dish with nonstick cooking spray.

- Bring the water to a rapid boil in a large saucepan. Add orzo and garlic and boil for 10 minutes. Drain in a colander. Rinse under cold water and drain again. Place in prepared baking dish.

- Remove garlic and peel. Place in large bowl and mash with a fork.

- Whisk cream into the mashed garlic. Add broth, ¾ cup of the Parmesan cheese, 1 cup of the parsley, salt, and pepper. Mix well.

- Pour mixture over orzo.

- To make the topping: in a small bowl, mix the bread crumbs with the remaining Parmesan and parsley. Sprinkle mixture evenly over orzo. Dot the top with butter.

- Bake at 325° for one hour, or until it is bubbly around the edges and the top is golden.

- Yield: 10 servings

Pasta with Caramelized Onions and Spinach

1 **tablespoon olive oil**
2 **tablespoons unsalted butter, divided**
4 **medium onions, peeled and cut into
   ¼-inch rings**
1 **teaspoon sugar**
3 **(13¾-ounce) cans chicken broth
   salt
   pepper**
1 **pound fettucine**
1 **(10-ounce) bag fresh spinach, washed,
   stems removed, leaves torn into pieces**

- Heat oil and 1 tablespoon of the butter in a large heavy skillet over medium high heat (do not use nonstick pan).

- Add onions and sugar. Cook, stirring once or twice until well browned, about 10 minutes (watch carefully).

- Remove half the onions and set aside.

- Add broth to the pan and bring to a boil. Cook over high heat for 10 minutes, scraping bottom of pan to deglaze. Season to taste with salt and pepper.

- Cook pasta in boiling salted water until a little underdone. Drain and add to broth. Simmer for 2 to 3 minutes.

- Add spinach. Cover and cook until spinach is wilted (about 1 minute). Stir in remaining tablespoon of butter and top with reserved onions.

- Yield: 6 servings

Pasta and Shrimp

A breeze to prepare.

4 tablespoons butter
1 medium onion, diced
1 garlic clove, minced
½ green pepper, diced
¼ pound mushrooms, sliced
1 teaspoon ground ginger
1 (8-ounce) can minced clams, undrained
½ pound cooked shrimp, diced to ¾-inch
1 tablespoon chopped fresh cilantro
1 pound angel hair pasta
Parmesan cheese to taste

- Boil water and cook pasta al dente. Drain well.

- While water is heating, melt butter in skillet and sauté onions and garlic.

- Add peppers and mushrooms, cook until soft. Add ginger, clams, and shrimp. Stir and cook for 5 minutes. Add the cilantro.

- Spoon shrimp and vegetable mixture over hot, cooked pasta.

- Sprinkle with Parmesan cheese to taste.

- Yield: 6 servings

- Per serving: 397 Calories • 23% Fat

HA

Healthy Alternative Pasta and Shrimp

Our healthier version of Pasta and Shrimp is made with olive oil instead of butter. Cooper-tested and rated, "as good as the original". You will love it.
Per serving: 397 Calories • 23% Fat

"Too much of a good thing can be wonderful."
— *Mae West*

Penne for your Thoughts

This is a "keep life simple" recipe. Prepare a day ahead, cover and refrigerate. Just bring to room temperature before baking the day of serving.

    ½ **pound penne pasta**
        nonstick cooking spray
    3 **medium zucchini, trimmed, halved**
        lengthwise
    1 **tablespoon olive oil**
    ½ **pound HOT Italian sausage, casings**
        removed
    1 **onion, chopped**
        salt
        freshly ground pepper
    1 **cup heavy cream**
    1 **teaspoon dried oregano**
    8 **ounces fontina cheese, grated (2 cups)**

- Boil water for pasta. Cook al dente. Drain well.

- Preheat oven to 375°.

- Spray a 2½ to 3-quart deep casserole with nonstick cooking spray.

- Transfer cooked pasta into casserole dish.

- Cut each zucchini half into thirds lengthwise, then crosswise into 1½-inch long pieces. Set aside.

- Heat oil in heavy skillet over medium heat. Add sausage and cook until no longer pink, breaking up with a fork. Drain all but 2 tablespoons of fat from pan. Using a slotted spoon, transfer to a bowl.

- Add onion to skillet and cook until beginning to soften, stirring occasionally. Add zucchini. Season with salt and pepper, and sauté to almost tender, about 4 minutes.

(recipe continued on next page)

(Penne for your Thoughts, continued)

- Return sausage to skillet. Add heavy cream and oregano. Bring to a boil. Add half of fontina cheese to sauce and stir just until melted. Stir cheese mixture into pasta. Top with remaining cheese.

- Bake until heated through, about 15 minutes.

- Yield: 4 servings

A Bistro Dinner

Tapenade (or Olive Pâté)

Homestyle Fish Chowder

Green Salad with
Luscious Lemon Dressing

Penne for your Thoughts

Beaujolais Nouveau

Brandy Alexander Cream Pie

Lip-Smacking Tomato Sauce with Meatballs

This is so great...and worth the effort.
While you are at it, double the recipe and freeze half.
Memories are made of this.

    4 garlic cloves, minced
    1 medium onion, chopped
    1 (12-ounce) can tomato paste
    1 (16-ounce) can tomato sauce
    1 (28-ounce) can tomato purée
    1 (28-ounce) can crushed tomatoes
Sauce Seasonings
    1 large bay leaf
    1 tablespoon sugar
    ½ teaspoon black pepper
    1 tablespoon dried oregano
    1 tablespoon dried thyme
    1 teaspoon dried coriander
  1-2 teaspoons cilantro (optional)
    2 teaspoons dried sage
    2 tablespoons dried parsley
    2 teaspoons dried basil
    ½ teaspoon crushed red pepper flakes
    ⅓ cup olive oil
    1 tablespoon sesame oil
Meatballs
    1 pound lean ground beef or ground turkey
    ¼ cup Worcestershire sauce
    2 teaspoons sesame oil
    2 tablespoons olive oil
    ⅓ cup bread crumbs
    1 teaspoon dried sage
    2 teaspoons dried rosemary
    1 teaspoon dried thyme
    1 teaspoon dried basil
    ½ cup dry sherry

• Combine garlic, onion, tomato products, and sauce seasonings. Bring to a simmer in a large pot.

(recipe continued on next page)

(Lip-smacking Tomato Sauce with Meatballs, continued)

- In a bowl, combine meatball ingredients except for the sherry. Shape the mixture into small balls or break into bits as preferred

- Heat a skillet and sauté the meat until cooked to rare. Do not overcook or singe the meat.

- Remove the grease from the meat mixture by straining in a colander, then return meat to the skillet and reheat. Add sherry and reduce.

- Add meat to the sauce. Simmer the mixture at the lowest possible heat for 6 to 7 hours. Stir occasionally.

- Yield: 10 servings

Kitchen Table Family Dinner

Florida Caesar Salad

Lip-Smacking Tomato Sauce with Meatballs and Pasta

Garlic Bread

Deep Dish Rhubarb Pie

Roasted Vegetable Rigatoni

3 tablespoons olive oil, divided
1 small onion, chopped
1 large eggplant, cut into 1-inch cubes
1¼ pounds medium mushrooms, cleaned and quartered
2 large red peppers, cut into 1-inch pieces
1¼ teaspoons salt, divided
½ teaspoon pepper
1 pound rigatoni
4 cups tomato sauce
2 tablespoons finely chopped fresh basil
½ pound provolone cheese, cut into ½-inch pieces
¾ cup grated Parmesan cheese
nonstick cooking spray

- Preheat oven to 425°.

- In a large roasting pan, combine 2 tablespoons of the olive oil, onions, eggplant, mushrooms, and red peppers. Mix to coat all ingredients.

- Roast vegetables 40 to 45 minutes, or until soft. Turn occasionally to keep them from sticking. Remove from oven, cool, and season with ¼ teaspoon of the salt and the pepper.

- Boil water in a large pot. Add the remaining olive oil and salt. Add the pasta. Cook over high heat until al dente, about 12 minutes and drain well.

- Place the pasta in a large mixing bowl. Pour 3½ cups tomato sauce over the pasta, mix well. Add basil, provolone,

Instead of roasting vegetables in olive oil, spray the vegetables with nonstick cooking spray. Roasted Vegetable Rigatoni will go from 34% fat to 25% fat.

(recipe continued on next page)

(Roasted Vegetable Rigatoni, continued)

¼ cup of the Parmesan cheese and roasted vegetables. Season to taste.

- Spray a 9 x 13-inch baking dish with nonstick cooking spray. Spoon the pasta mixture into the dish. Dot the top with the remaining ½ cup of tomato sauce. Sprinkle the remaining Parmesan on the top.

- When ready to bake, decrease oven to 400°. Bake pasta for 20 minutes or until piping hot. Serve immediately.

- Yield: 10 servings

- Per serving: 376 Calories • 34% Fat

Vermicelli with Napoli Salsa

4 medium size, ripe tomatoes, chopped
¼ cup extra virgin olive oil
2 garlic cloves, minced
4 tablespoons chopped fresh basil
   salt and pepper to taste
½ teaspoon dried oregano
1 pound vermicelli

- In a large bowl, combine tomatoes, oil, garlic, basil, salt, pepper, and oregano. Marinate at least 30 minutes at room temperature.

- When ready to serve, cook pasta according to directions on box.

- Drain well and combine with tomato mixture. Mix well and adjust seasoning. Add more oil if desired. Serve warm or at room temperature.

- Yield: 6 servings

Shrimp with Oriental Vegetables and Pasta

*This recipe makes a quick dinner,
suitable even for company.*

1½ **pounds medium shrimp shelled, and
  deveined**
  2 **tablespoons hot sesame oil, divided**
  2 **tablespoons corn oil**
 10 **asparagus stalks, cut in 1-inch pieces**
  1 **small red onion, coarsely chopped**
 ½ **red pepper, julienned**
 ½ **green pepper, julienned**
  3 **garlic cloves, minced**
 ½ **pound snow peas, ends trimmed**
  2 **tablespoons cornstarch, dissolved
  in 2 tablespoons of chicken broth**
  1 **cup chicken broth
  soy sauce to taste**
 10 **ounces angel hair pasta**

- Boil water for pasta.

- Heat 1 tablespoon sesame oil in a skillet. Sauté shrimp until pink. Set aside.

- In a separate large frying pan or wok, heat 2 tablespoons of corn oil. Stir-fry asparagus briefly; then onion, peppers, garlic, then snow peas.

- Add cornstarch mixture, chicken broth, and soy sauce.

- Cook pasta briefly in boiling water, drain and toss with the remaining tablespoon of sesame oil.

- Mix vegetables with pasta and serve.

- Yield: 6 servings

It Hasta be Pasta

nonstick cooking spray
6 ounces spaghetti (⅓ package)
2 teaspoons butter
½ cup grated Parmesan cheese
2 large eggs, well beaten
1 medium onion, chopped (½ cup)
¼ green bell pepper, chopped (¼ cup)
1 pound lean ground beef
1 (16-ounce) can chopped tomatoes
1 (6-ounce) can Italian tomato paste
1 teaspoon sugar
1 teaspoon oregano
½ teaspoon garlic salt
1 cup cottage cheese
2 ounces mozzarella cheese, shredded
(½ cup)

- Spray 10-inch pie pan with nonstick cooking spray.

- Boil water and cook pasta al dente according to directions on package. Drain well. Stir butter into hot spaghetti. Add Parmesan cheese and eggs. Pour into the pie pan.

- Preheat oven to 350°.

- Spray a skillet with nonstick cooking-spray. Sauté onions and green pepper until tender.

- Add ground beef and cook until browned. Drain off excess fat. Stir in tomatoes, tomato paste, sugar, oregano, and garlic salt. Heat through.

- Spread cottage cheese over top of spaghetti in pie pan. Top with ground beef mixture.

- Bake uncovered for 20 minutes. Sprinkle mozzarella cheese on top of pie and bake for an additional 5 minutes until cheese melts.

- Yield: 8 servings

- Per serving: 341 Calories • 44% Fat

HA

Healthy Alternative It Hasta be Pasta

Our "It Hasta be Pasta" healthier version drew rave reviews. A couple of very simple changes: use 1 teaspoon olive oil for the butter, use ½ cup egg substitute instead of eggs and use low-fat dairy products; low-fat cottage cheese and part skim mozzarella. Per serving: 282 Calories • 29% Fat

Rags to Riches Pasta

*This is a fabulous low-fat recipe with
an amazing amount of flavorful sauce
from a little bit of roasted garlic.*

8 **medium garlic cloves, peeled**
½ **teaspoon dried thyme**
½ **teaspoon dried rosemary**
2 **tablespoons olive oil**
   salt
   pepper
1 **pound rotini, twists or spirals**
3 **medium zucchini, coarsely grated**
   (5 to 6 cups)

- Preheat oven to 450°.

- Place garlic on a 12-inch square of foil. Sprinkle thyme and rosemary over garlic. Drizzle oil over herbs and garlic. Draw up edges and seal. Bake for 20 minutes.

- Placed cooked garlic in large bowl. Mash and season with salt and pepper.

- Cook pasta. In the final 2 minutes of cooking, add zucchini to water. Drain and mix into mashed garlic.

- Yield: 6 servings

"Seasoning is in Cookery what chords are in music."
             — Louis Eustache

Asparagus Bread Pudding

nonstick cooking spray
12-16 slices of bread
2½ cups milk, divided
1 pound asparagus, diagonally sliced into 2-inch pieces
1 teaspoon chopped fresh tarragon
1 teaspoon chopped fresh chives
1 teaspoon chopped fresh parsley
4 ounces fontina cheese, sliced
4 ounces Swiss cheese, sliced
5 large eggs
½ teaspoon pepper
1 teaspoon butter, cut into 4 pieces

- Spray a 3-quart baking dish with nonstick cooking spray.

- Place bread in a single layer on a baking sheet with sides. Pour 2 cups of the milk over bread and soak until milk is absorbed, about 30 minutes. Squeeze bread and place in the bottom of the baking dish.

- Steam asparagus for 3 minutes. Rinse in cold water and layer over bread (reserve a few pieces of asparagus). Sprinkle tarragon, chives, and parsley over asparagus. Cover with the sliced fontina and Swiss cheeses. Garnish with the reserved asparagus.

- Beat eggs, pepper, and the remaining ½ cup of milk. Pour over the asparagus and dot with butter bits.

- Bake 45 minutes.

- Yield: 6-8 servings

Outrageous Asparagus

nonstick cooking spray
5 tablespoons butter, divided
1 pound asparagus, diagonally sliced
1 large onion, sliced (1 cup)
1 tablespoon flour
¼ teaspoon salt
pepper
1 cup sour cream
4 ounces Swiss cheese, grated (1 cup)
¼ cup cracker crumbs

- Spray a shallow baking dish with nonstick cooking spray.

- Preheat oven to 400°.

- Melt 2 tablespoons of the butter in a large skillet. Sauté asparagus for 2 to 3 minutes or until barely tender. Remove and set aside.

- Add 2 more tablespoons of butter to skillet and sauté onion until tender. Stir in flour, salt, and pepper. Cook for 1 minute or until flour is well blended. Add sour cream and grated cheese. Cook, stirring constantly, over low heat, until cheese melts.

- Spoon asparagus into baking dish. Top with sour cream mixture. Sprinkle with crumbs. Dot with remaining butter.

- Bake for 20 minutes.

- Yield: 6 servings

"Do that in less time than it takes to cook asparagus."
                              — A Roman Saying

Spring Asparagus

2 pounds fresh asparagus
3 tablespoons minced parsley
2 tablespoons olive oil
2 tablespoons melted butter
salt
pepper

- Preheat oven to 400°.

- Arrange asparagus in large baking pan in single layer. Sprinkle parsley over asparagus.

- Combine oil and melted butter. Pour over asparagus and parsley. Season with salt and pepper.

- Cover with foil and bake for 15 minutes.

- Yield: 6 servings

Corn Pudding Delicious

Bake in a pretty ovenproof dish and serve it for company. The delicate custard is so delicious.

nonstick cooking spray
2 (10-ounce) packages frozen corn, thawed
1 tablespoon flour
2 tablespoons sugar
2 large eggs
¾ teaspoon salt
¾ cup milk
4 tablespoons butter, sliced

- Preheat oven to 375°.

- Spray a 1-quart casserole dish with nonstick cooking spray.

- Place corn, flour, sugar, eggs, salt, and milk in a blender. Blend for 10 seconds at high speed. Pour into the casserole dish.

- Top with butter slices.

- Bake 45 minutes. Let sit 5 minutes before serving.

Pennsylvania Dutch Cabbage Sauté

Wonderfully satisfying on a cold winter's night.

4 strips bacon
1 tablespoon butter
2 pounds cabbage, coarsely shredded (about 8 cups)
1 large apple, peeled, cored and sliced
1 small onion, chopped (½ cup)
1 tablespoon poppy seeds
1 teaspoon salt
1 teaspoon caraway seeds
¼ cup cider vinegar, divided
2 cups cooked medium egg noodles, drained
½ cup sour cream

- Sauté bacon in skillet until crisp. Drain bacon on paper towels, crumble and set aside.

- Add butter to bacon drippings. Add cabbage, apple, onion, poppy seeds, salt, caraway seeds, and 2 tablespoons of the vinegar. Toss to blend well. Cook 10 minutes.

- Add noodles. Cover and simmer 15 minutes. Stir in the remaining vinegar.

- To serve: sprinkle with reserved bacon and garnish with sour cream.

- Yield: 8 servings

Carrot Soufflé Supreme

Sweet and pungent carrot soufflé.

nonstick cooking spray
1 pound carrots, cooked
3 large eggs
½ cup sugar
3 tablespoons flour
1 teaspoon baking powder
1 teaspoon vanilla
½ cup (1 stick) butter, melted
dash nutmeg

Topping
1 cup cornflakes, crushed (⅓ cup)
3 tablespoons brown sugar
1 ounce walnuts, chopped (¼ cup)
dash cinnamon
dash nutmeg
1 tablespoon butter, melted

• Spray a 1½-quart soufflé dish with nonstick cooking spray.

• Blend carrots, eggs, sugar, flour, baking powder, vanilla, butter, and nutmeg in a blender. Pour into soufflé dish.

• To make topping: combine cornflake crumbs, brown sugar, walnuts, cinnamon, nutmeg, and melted butter. Sprinkle on top.

• Bake for 45 minutes at 350°.

• Yield: 10 servings

Roasted Carrots with Garlic

nonstick cooking spray
1½ pounds carrots, peeled
4 garlic cloves, sliced
2 tablespoons olive oil
½ teaspoon salt
½ teaspoon pepper
1 tablespoon chopped fresh coriander
1 tablespoon chopped fresh Italian (flat-leaf) parsley

- Preheat oven to 425°.

- Slice carrots on an angle about ¾-inch thick.

- Spray baking dish with nonstick cooking spray. (Select a baking dish that will hold the carrots snugly in a single layer.) Place carrots in the baking dish.

- Combine garlic, oil, salt, pepper, coriander, and parsley. Pour over carrot layer.

- Put in oven and roast until brown, about 40 minutes. Turn once during roasting.

- Serve hot or at room temperature.

- Yield: 4 servings

Out of fresh herbs? Substitute ½ teaspoon crushed dried herbs for each tablespoon chopped fresh herbs.

Zesty Carrots

1 **pound carrots (6 to 8), sliced and cooked**
¼ **cup carrot liquid**
2 **teaspoons grated onion**
1 **teaspoon prepared horseradish**
½ **cup mayonnaise**
½ **teaspoon salt**
¼ **teaspoon pepper**
2 **tablespoons bread crumbs**
1 **tablespoon butter, melted**
½ **tablespoon paprika**

- Preheat oven to 375°.

- Place cooked carrots in a baking dish.

- Mix carrot liquid, onion, horseradish, mayonnaise, salt, and pepper. Pour over cooked carrots.

- To make topping: combine bread crumbs, butter, and paprika. Sprinkle on carrots.

- Bake for 15 to 20 minutes. Can be prepared a day in advance. Before baking sprinkle on the topping.

- Yield: 6 servings

For dramatically improved color and flavor in cooked carrots do not cut, peel or boil as usual. Instead boil carrots whole and rinse under cold water and scrape off the skin using the back of a knife. Slice and add sweet butter, white pepper and a dash of sugar.

In the fourteenth century, carrots were among life's basic necessities. The vegetable was one of the few which could be stored throughout the winter; its vivid color enlivened otherwise drab Lenten fare; and it was considered a cure for a variety of ills.

Incredible Edible Eggplant

nonstick cooking spray
2 **medium eggplants, peeled and diced**
1 **onion, diced**
½ **cup water**
2 **(14½-ounce) cans tomatoes**
½ **cup cracker crumbs**
2 **ounces Cheddar cheese, grated**
  (½ cup)
¼ **teaspoon salt**
  pepper

- Spray 2-quart casserole dish with nonstick cooking spray.

- Boil eggplants and onion until tender. Drain well.

- Preheat oven to 350°.

- Place half of the eggplant in the casserole dish. Season with salt and pepper. Cover with half of the tomatoes and half of the cracker crumbs. Top with half of the cheese. Repeat the eggplant, tomato, and cracker crumb layers, reserving the cheese.

- Bake 40 minutes. Sprinkle the remaining cheese on the casserole and bake for another 5 minutes.

- Yield: 6 servings

Male eggplants have fewer seeds and are less likely to be bitter. To differentiate between male and female eggplant, inspect the flower end. The male has a small round and smooth end; the female is irregular and less smooth.

Hot tip; how to control the personality of your onions. If sautéed slowly, onions become mild and sweet. A quick sauté over high heat produces a more robust onion flavor.

Eggplants are low in calories, high in fiber and carbohydrates, and have little protein, almost no fat, and no cholesterol.

Eggplant and Onions

An excellent side dish or use as an omelet or quiche filling.

10 tablespoons butter, divided
3 onions, chopped
2 medium eggplants, peeled and diced
½ cup bread crumbs

• Melt 2 tablespoons butter in a large skillet and brown onions lightly.

• Preheat oven to 350°.

• Boil eggplant in water to cover just until tender. Drain well.

• Add eggplant to onions and mix thoroughly. Put into a 1-quart baking dish.

• Sprinkle bread crumbs over eggplant. Slice remaining butter into bits. Place over bread crumbs.

• Bake until hot and lightly browned on top (5 to 10 minutes).

• Yield: 6 servings

Green Beans with Bacon and Mushrooms

12 slices bacon
1 tablespoon bacon drippings
1 medium onion, chopped (¾ cup)
2 (4½-ounce) cans sliced mushrooms, drained
3 (9-ounce) packages frozen whole green beans, thawed
1 tablespoon sugar

- Cook bacon in large skillet until crisp. Remove bacon, reserving 1 tablespoon drippings. Crumble bacon and set aside.

- Sauté onion in bacon drippings over medium heat until tender.

- Add mushrooms and cook 2 minutes. Stir in green beans and sugar. Cover and cook 10 minutes or until desired degree of doneness, stirring occasionally.

- Transfer beans to a serving dish. Add bacon, stirring gently and serve immediately

- Yield: 12 servings

Garlicky Green Beans

This dish is delicious enough to set before a king.

1 **pound fresh green beans, tips removed**
2 **tablespoons butter**
? **tablespoons olive oil**
4 **garlic cloves, minced**
8 **sun dried tomatoes, finely chopped**
3 **tablespoons bread crumbs**
3 **tablespoons grated Parmesan cheese**
  salt
  pepper

- Rinse beans and microwave for 3 to 5 minutes on full power.

- Heat butter and olive oil in skillet. Add garlic and tomatoes and sauté for 3 minutes.

- Add beans, bread crumbs, and cheese. Mix and remove from heat. Season with salt and pepper.

- Yield: 6 servings

Vegetables were slow to gain a respectable place on the European menu. The first of many European vegetarian societies was begun in 1847, based on the notion that "meat-eating begets ferocious dispositions, a callousness...but a vegetarian diet develops the gentler affections."

Lima Bean Casserole

nonstick cooking spray
3 (10-ounce) packages frozen lima beans
6 bacon slices, diced
3 tablespoons flour
2 large onions, sliced
1¾ cups milk
1 (⅝-ounce) package dry Italian salad dressing mix
½ teaspoon oregano
8 ounces mozzarella cheese, sliced

- Preheat oven to 350°.

- Spray a 2-quart casserole dish with nonstick cooking spray.

- Cook lima beans as directed on package; drain. Set aside.

- In skillet, sauté bacon until crisp; drain and set aside. Reserve 3 tablespoons of bacon fat.

- In bacon fat, sauté onion until tender. Remove onions and add to bacon.

- In the fat remaining in skillet, stir in flour to make a smooth paste. Blend in milk. Cook, stirring, over medium heat until thickened and smooth. Remove from heat.

- Add lima beans, dry Italian salad dressing mix, and oregano.

- Pour one-third of the lima bean mixture into a casserole dish; top with one-third of the reserved bacon and onion slices, then one-third of the cheese. Repeat twice.

- Bake covered for 30 minutes.

- Yield: 10 servings

Parrillo's Roasted Peppers

1 (4-ounce) can pitted black olives, sliced into rings
2 (2-ounce) cans anchovies (in oil) undrained
1 (1¾-ounce) jar capers
1 cup oil
½ teaspoon garlic powder
¼ teaspoon pepper
12 peppers (red, green, and yellow), sliced lengthwise
1 cup bread crumbs

- Preheat oven to 350°.

- Combine black olives, anchovies, capers, and oil. Season with garlic powder and pepper. Mix well and place in large baking dish.

- Add peppers and mix to coat well.

- Cover with foil and bake for 20 to 30 minutes until peppers soften. Take off foil, sprinkle top with bread crumbs. Continue baking about an hour or longer until top is crispy.

- Serve at room temperature.

- Yield: 15 servings

A must for the antipasti table. Make sure you have plenty of bruschetta on hand!

Custard Potatoes

4-5 tablespoons butter, divided
1 garlic clove, minced
6 medium potatoes, peeled and sliced paper thin
¼ teaspoon salt
pepper
4 large eggs
1 cup milk
¼ cup heavy cream
1 cup sour cream

- Preheat oven to 350°.

- Butter a 1-quart casserole dish using 2 to 3 tablespoons of butter. Sprinkle the garlic over the butter.

- Place the potatoes in the casserole dish and season with salt and pepper.

- In a separate bowl, whisk the eggs, milk, and cream. Pour over the potatoes and dot with remaining butter.

- Bake for one hour.

- Serve the sour cream in a separate dish to be used as a garnish.

- Yield: 8 servings

Keep peeled potatoes white by placing them in a bowl of water to which 1 teaspoon of lemon juice or vinegar has been added.

Roasted Mustard Potatoes

Served with a steak or a roast, green beans, and a hearty red wine, this potato dish will bring the house down.

nonstick cooking spray
4 tablespoons Dijon mustard
2 teaspoons paprika
1 teaspoon ground cumin
1 teaspoon chili powder
⅛ teaspoon cayenne pepper
2 pounds baby red potatoes (16)

- Preheat oven to 400°.

- Spray a roasting pan three times with nonstick cooking spray.

- Put the mustard, paprika, cumin, chili powder, and cayenne pepper in a large bowl. Whisk to blend.

- Prick the potatoes several times with a fork and add them to the bowl. Toss to coat the potatoes evenly.

- Pour the coated potatoes into the prepared roasted pan, leaving a little space between them. Bake for about 45 minutes to 1 hour until potatoes are fork tender.

- Yield: 4 servings

When boiling red potatoes, remove a thin strip of peel from around the centers. This prevents the skin from bursting and makes for a pretty presentation.

O-C Potatoes

Keep on low heat for late dinners. Serve in or out of foil, depending upon elegance of dinner.

4 large white potatoes, peeled and sliced
½ cup (1 stick) butter, softened
2 packages dry onion soup mix
1 (8-ounce) package Muenster or brick Swiss cheese, sliced into ¼-inch strips

• Divide potatoes into four portions. Place each portion on a large piece of aluminum foil. Dab butter between slices.

• Pour packaged onion soup into a small bowl and mix well. Sprinkle onion soup over each portion of potatoes. Place cheese on each portion.

• Seal and bake at 350° for one hour.

• Yield: 8 servings

September Song Feast

Mushroom Almond Pâté

Autumn Soup

Tangy Pork

O-C Potatoes

Pennsylvania Dutch Cabbage Sauté

Robert Mondavi Chardonnay Reserve

Shoo Fly Pie à la mode

Party Potatoes
Food for friends.

6 medium potatoes, boiled, cooled and peeled
¼ cup (1 stick) butter, melted
½ cup chopped green onions
2 cups sour cream
½ pound Cheddar cheese, shredded (2 cups)
¼ teaspoon salt
paprika

- Preheat oven to 350°.

- Spray 2-quart casserole dish with nonstick cooking spray.

- Coarsely grate potatoes into a large bowl.

- Mix melted butter, onions, sour cream, cheese, and salt. Fold into grated potatoes. Put into casserole dish. Sprinkle top with paprika.

- Bake, covered, for 1½ hours. Uncover and bake an additional 15 minutes.

- May be prepared ahead of time, frozen, and baked later.

- Yield: 12 servings

"Strange to see how a good dinner and feasting reconciles everybody."
— Samuel Pepys

Praise the Potatoes

nonstick cooking spray
3 large potatoes (2½ to 3 pounds),
peeled and cubed
1 (8-ounce) carton commercial green
onion dip
1 (3-ounce) package cream cheese,
softened
4 tablespoons butter, melted
2 tablespoons milk
½ teaspoon garlic salt
paprika

- Spray a 1½-quart baking dish with nonstick cooking spray.

- In a saucepan cover potatoes with water. Boil potatoes for 15 minutes or until tender. Drain and mash.

- Add green onion dip, cream cheese, butter, milk, and garlic salt. Beat at medium speed with an electric mixer until smooth.

- Spoon potato mixture into baking dish. Sprinkle with paprika.

- Bake at 350° for 30 minutes.

- Yield: 6 servings

Premature sprouting warning: store potatoes and onions separately. The high moisture content of the onions causes the potatoes to sprout prematurely.

"If beef's the King of Meat, Potato's the Queen of the Garden World."
— Old Irish Saying

Sweet Potato Mousse

4 pounds sweet potatoes, baked
½ cup (1 stick) butter, softened
1 cup milk
1 tablespoon honey
¼ teaspoon nutmeg
  salt
  pepper

- Remove skins from potatoes and mash in a heavy saucepan.

- Beat in the butter, milk, honey, nutmeg, salt, and pepper.

- Heat thoroughly, stirring frequently. Adjust seasoning and serve.

- Yield: 10 servings

Not-so-Plain Jane Rice

For gourmets on the run.

  nonstick cooking spray
3 cups cooked rice
¼ cup flour
1 teaspoon salt
⅔ cup sliced green onions
½ cup finely chopped parsley
2½ cups light cream

- Preheat oven to 350°.

- Spray a 1½-quart casserole dish with nonstick cooking spray.

- Mix rice, flour, salt, onions, and parsley. Spoon into casserole dish. Pour cream over rice mixture.

- Bake uncovered 30 minutes or until set.

- Yield: 6 servings

Wild Rice with Walnuts and Dates

Flavor and variety.

1 celery stalk, chopped (¼ cup)
½ small onion, chopped (¼ cup)
1 tablespoon butter
1 cup uncooked wild rice
1 cup chicken broth
1 cup water
⅓ cup pitted dates, chopped
1 ounce walnuts, chopped (¼ cup)

- Sauté celery and onion in butter for about 10 minutes.

- Add wild rice and stir for 3 minutes. Add chicken broth and water. Bring to a boil. Cover and simmer for one hour.

- Add dates and walnuts to mixture. Cook uncovered for 3 to 4 minutes.

- Yield: 6 servings

In China, where rice is almost a religion, even the imperial court were expected to do their share to ensure a bountiful crop. Each year at the beginning of the planting season, and with great ceremony, they plowed their appointed rows — three for the emperor, six for his sons, and so on down to the mandarin's fifteen.

Down Home Spoon Bread

5 tablespoons butter, divided
1⅔ cups milk
1 cup white cornmeal
1 cup water
1 tablespoon sugar
2 teaspoons salt
4 large eggs, separated
2 teaspoons baking powder
4 strips bacon, cooked, drained and
   crumbled

- Preheat oven to 375°.

- With 1 tablespoon of the butter, coat a baking dish.

- In a heavy saucepan combine the milk, cornmeal, water, 3 tablespoons of the butter, sugar, and salt. Bring the liquid to a simmer over low heat. And continue simmering, stirring vigorously, for 2 minutes. Scrape the mixture into a large bowl and cool slightly.

- With an electric mixture, beat the egg whites until they stand in stiff peaks. Set aside.

- In a separate bowl, beat the yolks with the baking powder until the mixture is light and lemon colored.

- Stir the yolks into the cornmeal mixture quickly. Stir in one-quarter of the whites. Fold in the remaining whites and pour into the buttered baking dish.

- Bake for 25 to 30 minutes. Top with the remaining butter and a sprinkling of crumbled bacon.

- Yield: 8 servings

Top Gun Tomatoes

3 **strips bacon**
½ **medium onion, chopped (¼ cup)**
1 **(10-ounce) package fresh spinach, stems removed, leaves chopped**
½ **cup sour cream**
   dash hot sauce
4 **medium tomatoes**
   salt
   pepper
2 **ounces mozzarella cheese, grated (½ cup)**

- Cook bacon until crisp, remove and crumble. Reserve 2 tablespoons of drippings.

- Cook onion in drippings until tender. Stir in spinach and cook, covered, 2 to 3 minutes. Stir in bacon, sour cream, and hot sauce. Set aside.

- Cut tops from tomatoes; remove centers, leaving shells. Drain on paper towels for 10 minutes. Season shells with salt and pepper. Fill with spinach mixture.

- Place in a 8-inch square pan. Bake in 375° oven 20 to 25 minutes.

- Top with cheese and bake an additional 2 to 3 minutes or until cheese melts.

- Yield: 4 servings

The plump, sanguine tomato, a gift conveyed by Spaniards from the New World to the Old, was thought to be a favorite of Venus and was credited with aphrodisiac powers.

Winter Vegetable Potpourri

4 cups water
6 small red potatoes, cubed, unskinned
1 red bell pepper, cubed
1 green bell pepper, cubed
½ pound mushrooms, stemmed and halved (if large)
10 garlic cloves, chopped
¼ cup olive oil
2 teaspoons chopped rosemary, fresh or dried
¼ teaspoon salt
pepper
2 tablespoons balsamic vinegar

• Bring the water to a rapid boil in a large saucepan. Boil the potato cubes for five minutes. Drain the potatoes.

• In a large bowl, toss the cooked potatoes, bell peppers, mushrooms, garlic, olive oil, and rosemary until the vegetables are well coated with rosemary and oil.

• Spread the vegetables on a broiler pan covered with foil, sprinkle generously with salt and pepper.

• Broil 10 to 12 minutes, until slightly browned at the edges. Stir once or twice to ensure even cooking.

• Return to the bowl and toss with vinegar. Serve hot or at room temperature.

• Yield: 6 servings

Puccini Zucchini Soufflés

1 **pound zucchini, grated (2 cups)**
½ **cup salt**
 nonstick cooking spray
4 **large eggs, separated**
3 **tablespoons butter**
¼ **cup flour**
¼ **teaspoon dry mustard**
1 **cup milk**
2 **ounces feta cheese, crumbled (½ cup)**
1 **tablespoon grated Parmesan cheese**

- Sprinkle zucchini with salt and let stand for 30 minutes. Rinse well. Drain and squeeze out liquid.

- Spray six 6-ounce ramekins with nonstick cooking spray.

- Beat egg yolks and set aside.

- Beat whites until they stand in stiff peaks. Set aside.

- Melt butter in a saucepan, stir in flour and dry mustard. Add milk and simmer until bubbly. Remove from heat. Stir in zucchini and cheeses. Gradually add beaten egg yolks.

- Fold one-half of the egg whites into zucchini mixture and slowly add the other half. Spoon into ramekins.

- Bake at 375° for 20 to 25 minutes or until a knife inserted in the center comes out clean.

- Yield: 6 servings

Posh Squash

nonstick cooking spray
2 pounds summer squash or zucchini, sliced
1 cup mayonnaise
1 cup grated Parmesan cheese
1 small onion, chopped (¼ cup)
2 large eggs, beaten
2 tablespoons butter, melted
½ cup bread crumbs

- Spray casserole dish with nonstick cooking spray.

- Cook squash in boiling water until tender. Drain and cool. Mash cooked squash.

- Combine mayonnaise, cheese, onion, and eggs. Mix into mashed squash. Pour into casserole dish.

- To make topping: combine butter and bread crumbs. Spoon on top.

- Bake at 350° for 30 minutes.

- Yield: 4 servings

Chinese Sauce for Vegetables

Good over broccoli, green beans, asparagus or sautéed zucchini.

½ cup butter
½ teaspoon salt
½ teaspoon pepper
1 teaspoon dried minced onions
1 can sliced water chestnuts
¼ cup lemon juice
2 tablespoons soy sauce

- In a microwave safe bowl, melt butter. Add remaining ingredients and heat in the microwave a few minutes to blend flavors. Pour over vegetables and serve.

Yellow Pepper Sauce

Best on green beans.

2 yellow bell peppers
1 head garlic, unpeeled
4 tablespoons extra virgin olive oil, divided
  salt
2¼ pounds green beans
1 tablespoon chopped parsley

- Cook peppers with unpeeled garlic for 20 minutes in a 400° oven.

- Peel peppers and discard seeds.

- Peel garlic. Blend in a food processor with 2 tablespoons of the oil. Add salt and reserve.

- Cook beans in a saucepan of salted water until crispy but barely tender (about 5 minutes). Drain and then sauté over low heat in a frying pan with the remaining oil for 5 minutes.

- Heat the pepper sauce.

- Arrange beans on a platter. Pour over pepper sauce. Sprinkle with chopped parsley and serve.

- Sauce is great on many things, use your imagination!

This dish will establish your reputation as a master chef!

Chaing Mai Chicken Curry

Béchamel Sauce
- ¼ **cup butter**
- ¼ **cup flour**
- ½ **teaspoon salt**
- **dash pepper**
- 2 **cups half & half**

Curry
- 3 **tablespoons corn oil**
- 1 **ounce green Thai curry paste**
- 4 **skinless, boneless chicken breast halves, cooked and cut into ½-inch strips**
- ¼ **teaspoon salt**
- ¼ **cup sugar**
- 1 **teaspoon minced garlic**
- ¼ **cup soy sauce**
- 3 **cups broccoli florets, cooked tender/crisp in a microwave**
- 2 **ounces roasted salted peanuts (½ cup)**
- 1 **red pepper, sliced**
- 3 **cups cooked rice**
- **peanuts**
- **coconut**
- **sliced bananas**

- To make béchamel sauce: melt butter in a medium saucepan. Stir in flour, salt, and pepper. Stir in half & half and cook over medium heat until sauce thickens. Set aside.

- To make curry: heat corn oil in a large skillet. Stir in curry paste and cook 1 minute. Turn heat to medium high. Add chicken, salt, sugar, and garlic. Stir-fry until it caramelizes. Keep pan hot. Add soy sauce.

- Blend in béchamel sauce, adding more half & half if necessary. Add broccoli, peanuts, and pepper. Heat thoroughly, add more curry paste as desired.

- Serve over rice with optional garnish of chopped peanuts, coconut, or sliced bananas.

- Yield: 5 servings

- Per serving: 678 Calories • 50% Fat

HA
Healthy Alternative
Chaing Mai Chicken Curry

*If you like chicken flavorful, spicy hot and you're
keeping an eye on fat, try this Healthy Alternative
Chaing Mai chicken. The secret is the versatile
velouté—a very special sauce; Cooper rated for
excellence.*

Low-fat Velouté Sauce:
- 2 tablespoons cornstarch
- dash pepper
- 1 cup evaporated skim milk
- 1 chicken bouillon cube

Curry
- 2 tablespoons corn oil
- 1 ounce green Thai curry paste
- 4 skinless, boneless chicken breast halves, cooked and cut into ½-inch strips
- ¼ teaspoon salt
- ¼ cup sugar
- 1 teaspoon minced garlic
- ¼ cup soy sauce
- 3 cups broccoli florets, cooked tender/crisp in the microwave
- 1 ounce roasted, salted peanuts (¼ cup)
- 1 red pepper, sliced
- 3 cups cooked rice
- peanuts
- coconut
- sliced bananas

- To make low-fat velouté sauce: dissolve cornstarch in evaporated skim milk. Cook over medium heat until thickened. Stir in salt and pepper. Set aside.

- To make curry: heat corn oil in a large skillet. Stir in curry paste and cook 1 minute. Turn heat to medium high. Add chicken, salt, sugar, and garlic. Stir-fry until it caramelizes. Keep pan hot. Add soy sauce.

(recipe continued on next page)

(Healthy Alternative Chaing Mai Chicken Curry, continued)

- Blend in velouté sauce, adding evaporated skim milk if too thin.
- Add broccoli, peanuts, and pepper.
- Heat thoroughly, add more curry paste as desired.
- Serve over rice with optional garnish of peanuts, coconut, or sliced bananas.
- Yield: 5 servings
- Per serving: 487 Calories • 20% Fat

The King and I
Dinner Party

Blue Cheese Pecan Grapes

Chaing Mai Chicken Curry

*Sliced Cucumber Salad
with Yogurt and Mint*

Fairy Sherbet

Beacon Hill Chocolate Cookies

Cheese Stuffed Chicken Breasts

6 large skinless, boneless chicken breast halves
1 tablespoon Dijon mustard, divided
2 (3-ounce) packages cream cheese, room temperature
1½ ounces blue cheese (⅓ cup), room temperature
3 ounces Swiss cheese, grated (¾ cup)
5 tablespoons butter, room temperature
⅛ teaspoon nutmeg
1 large egg, beaten
⅓ cup flour
¼ cup dry bread crumbs
4 tablespoons clarified butter

- Place chicken, skin side down, on a cutting board. Cover with plastic wrap and gently pound to about ½-inch thick with a wooden mallet.

- Spread each breast with ½ teaspoon of the Dijon mustard.

- In a bowl, cream together cream cheese, blue cheese, and butter. Add grated Swiss cheese and nutmeg.

- Place 2 tablespoons of cheese mixture onto the center of each breast and enclose the cheese completely with the chicken breast. Freeze for 1 hour.

- Preheat oven to 400°.

- Place the flour, egg, and bread crumbs in separate bowls. Roll each chicken breast in flour, coat with egg and then cover with bread crumbs. Chill.

- In a heavy ovenproof skillet, sear each chicken breast in the clarified butter over high heat for 3 to 4 minutes, or until lightly browned.

- Place in oven and bake for 40 minutes.

- Yield: 6 servings

- Per serving: 630 Calories • 69% Fat

HA
Healthy Alternative Cheese Stuffed Chicken Breasts

The "glorious golden baked crust" of
Healthy Alternative Cheese Stuffed Chicken Breasts
is a feast for the eyes as well the palate.

6 **large skinless, boneless chicken breast halves**
1 **tablespoon Dijon mustard, divided**
4 **ounces Neufchâtel cheese (½ cup), room temperature**
1 **ounce blue cheese (¼ cup), room temperature**
2 **ounces Swiss cheese, grated (½ cup)**
⅛ **teaspoon nutmeg**
½ **cup egg substitute**
⅓ **cup flour**
5 **cups cornflakes, crushed (1⅔ cups crushed)**

- Place chicken, skin side down, on a cutting board. Cover with plastic wrap and gently pound to about ½-inch thick with a wooden mallet.

- Spread each breast with ½ teaspoon of the Dijon mustard.

- In a bowl, cream together Neufchâtel and blue cheese. Add grated Swiss cheese and nutmeg.

- Place 1 heaping tablespoon of cheese mixture onto the center of each breast and enclose the cheese completely with the chicken breast. Freeze for 1 hour.

- Preheat oven to 400°.

- Put flour, egg, and cornflake crumbs in three separate bowls. Roll each chicken breast in flour, coat with egg substitute and cover in cornflakes. Chill.

- Bake for 40 minutes.

- Yield: 6 servings

- Per serving: 366 Calories • 27% Fat

Chicken with Basil Cream Sauce

*An enticing offering…all ingredients
go splendidly with the chicken.*

4 skinless, boneless chicken breast halves
¼ cup milk
½ cup Italian bread crumbs
3 tablespoons butter
1 cup chicken broth
2 cups dry white wine
1 cup heavy cream
½ cup sliced pimentos
½ cup fresh basil, chopped
¼ cup grated Parmesan cheese
⅛ teaspoon pepper

- Dip chicken in milk, then coat with bread crumbs.

- Sauté chicken in melted butter until golden brown on both sides (about 10 minutes). Set aside on a heat proof serving dish and keep warm.

- In the same pan, heat broth and wine to a boil. Loosen brown bits. Add cream and pimentos. Reduce heat. Add basil, Parmesan, and pepper. Pour sauce over chicken.

- Sauce is rich and a little goes a long way. Delicious served over pasta.

- Yield: 4 servings

- Per serving: 593 Calories • 56% Fat

HA
Healthy Alternative
Chicken with
Basil Cream Sauce

4 skinless, boneless chicken breast halves
¼ cup skim milk
½ cup Italian bread crumbs
   nonstick cooking spray
1 cup evaporated skim milk
1 tablespoon cornstarch
1 cup chicken broth
1½ cups dry white wine
½ cup sliced pimentos
½ cup fresh basil, chopped
¼ cup grated Parmesan cheese
⅛ teaspoon pepper

• Place chicken, skin side down on a cutting board. Cover with plastic wrap. Pound with a wooden mallet to about 1-inch thickness. Dip chicken in milk, then coat with bread crumbs.

• Sauté chicken in pan sprayed with nonstick cooking spray until golden brown on both sides (about 10 minutes). Set aside on a heat proof serving dish and keep warm.

• In separate pan, heat broth and wine to a boil. Reduce heat. Dissolve cornstarch in evaporated milk. Whisk into simmering broth. Add basil, pimentos, Parmesan, and pepper. Pour sauce over chicken.

• Yield: 4 servings

• Per serving: 318 Calories • 14% Fat

"Things are seldom what they seem, skim milk masquerades as cream."
             — Sir William Gilbert

Chicken Breasts in Cream with Sesame Seeds

Serve this on a bed of fresh, steamed spinach,
drizzled with the sauce from the chicken.
It is a quick, easy and delicious meal.

6 skinless, boneless chicken breast halves
1 teaspoon paprika
½ teaspoon salt, divided
3 tablespoons butter
1 cup dry white wine
¼ pound mushrooms, sliced (1 cup)
¾ cup half & half
2 tablespoons cornstarch
¼ cup grated Parmesan cheese, divided
2 tablespoons sesame seeds

- Preheat oven to 325°.

- Pat chicken dry and sprinkle with paprika and ¼ teaspoon of the salt.

- Sauté chicken over medium heat in butter until golden brown. Add wine, cover and bake for 25 to 30 minutes. Remove chicken from pan and place in an ovenproof dish.

- Add mushrooms to sauce, simmer 4 minutes. Add half & half and cornstarch, stirring until thick. Add remaining salt and 2 tablespoons of the Parmesan.

- Pour over chicken. Top with remaining Parmesan cheese and sesame seeds. Broil until golden.

- Yield: 6 servings

- Per serving: 378 Calories • 43% Fat

Healthy Alternative Chicken Breasts in Low-Fat Cream Sauce with Sesame Seeds

6 skinless, boneless chicken breast halves
1 teaspoon paprika
½ teaspoon salt, divided
1 tablespoon olive oil
¾ cup dry white wine
¼ pound mushrooms, sliced (1 cup)
¾ cup evaporated skim milk
2 tablespoons cornstarch
¼ cup grated Parmesan cheese, divided
2 tablespoons sesame seeds

- Preheat oven to 350°.

- Place chicken, skin side down, on a cutting board. Cover with plastic wrap. Pound with a wooden mallet to about ½-inch thick. Sprinkle with paprika and ¼ teaspoon of the salt.

- Sauté chicken over medium heat in oil until golden brown. Add wine, cover and bake for 25 minutes. Remove chicken from pan and place in an ovenproof dish.

- Add mushrooms to sauce, simmer 4 minutes. Add evaporated skim milk and cornstarch, stirring until thick. Add remaining salt and 2 tablespoons of the Parmesan.

- Pour over chicken. Top with remaining Parmesan cheese and sesame seeds. Broil until golden.

- Yield: 6 servings

- Per serving: 290 Calories • 28% Fat

Chicken Cacciatore

½ **cup olive oil**
2 **(2 to 3-pound) whole chickens, cut into serving pieces**
1 **garlic clove**
½ **teaspoon dried rosemary**
½ **teaspoon dried oregano**
1¼ **teaspoons salt**
¼ **teaspoon pepper**
6 **anchovy fillets, chopped**
⅔ **cup wine vinegar**
1 **cup Chianti**
3 **tablespoons tomato paste**
⅓ **cup chicken broth**

- Heat oil at high heat. Sauté chicken and garlic for about 5 minutes, turning constantly. Remove garlic.

- In a bowl, mix rosemary, oregano, salt, pepper, anchovies, vinegar, and Chianti. Add to chicken and simmer uncovered until liquid is reduced one third, about 10 minutes.

- In a separate bowl, dissolve tomato paste in chicken broth, and pour over chicken.

- Simmer covered for 20 minutes.

- Yield: 6 servings

- Per serving: 461 Calories • 55% Fat

An easy tip to reduce fat in a recipe…think 1 teaspoon of oil per serving.

Healthy Alternative Chicken Cacciatore
Reduce the ½ cup of olive oil to 2 tablespoons of olive oil.
Per serving: 342 Calories • 39% Fat

Chicken Ham Pinwheels

When your bridge club comes for lunch,
serve this fabulous low-fat entrée.
It's not only delicious, but it looks wonderful.

   2 **whole chicken breasts, skinned and boned**
 1/8 **teaspoon dried basil**
 1/8 **teaspoon salt**
 1/8 **teaspoon pepper**
 1/8 **teaspoon garlic salt**
   3 **very thin slices cooked ham**
   2 **teaspoons lemon juice**
 1/4 **teaspoon paprika**
     parsley

- Place chicken breasts, skin side down, on a cutting board. Cover with plastic wrap and gently pound with a wooden mallet to 1/4-inch thickness.

- Combine basil, salt, pepper, and garlic salt. Sprinkle on chicken.

- Place 1 1/2 slices of ham on each chicken breast. Roll up. Place seam side down on baking sheet. Drizzle with lemon juice. Sprinkle with paprika.

- Bake at 350° for 30 minutes.

- Cool and slice into 1/4-inch slices. Serve on a platter of parsley.

- Yield: 4 servings

"Poultry is for the cook what canvas is for the painter."
                                        — Brillat-Savarin

Chicken Magnifique

*One of our registered dietitian taste-testers
said this recipe inspired her to go home
and try more new recipes.*

10 pounds chicken parts, skin removed
1 head of garlic, peeled and puréed
¼ cup dried oregano
  salt and pepper
½ cup red wine vinegar
½ cup olive oil
1 cup pitted prunes
½ cup pitted Spanish green olives
½ cup capers with 1 teaspoon of juice
6 bay leaves
1 cup white wine
1 cup brown sugar, firmly packed
¼ cup finely chopped Italian parsley

• Advance preparation: combine garlic, oregano, salt, pepper, vinegar, oil, prunes, olives, capers, and bay leaves in a large bowl. Pour over chicken. Cover and refrigerate overnight.

• Preheat oven to 350°.

• Arrange chicken in a single layer in 1 or 2 shallow baking pans and spoon marinade evenly over chicken. Pour wine over chicken and sprinkle with brown sugar.

• Bake 50 minutes to 1 hour, basting frequently.

• Garnish with parsley. Serve marinade in a sauceboat. Delicious served at room temperature.

• Yield: 15 servings

Chicken Lasagne

1 (3 to 4-pound) whole chicken
¾ pound lasagna noodles
3¼ teaspoons salt, divided
½ cup olive oil, divided
    nonstick cooking spray
1 large onion, chopped
1 garlic clove, minced
1 (6-ounce) can tomato paste
1 (28-ounce) can of whole tomatoes, chopped
1 teaspoon sugar
¼ teaspoon pepper
    water
16 ounces mozzarella cheese, shredded
1 (15 to 16-ounce) container ricotta cheese
¾ cup grated Parmesan cheese

- Advance preparation: simmer chicken in a pot of water. Remove skin and bones from meat and dice.

- Cook noodles in a large pot of boiling water with 3 teaspoons of salt and 1 tablespoon of the olive oil as directed on package. Drain and separate noodles on a tray or cookie sheet sprayed with cooking spray.

- Heat the remaining olive oil in a skillet and sauté onions and garlic. Add tomato paste, chopped tomatoes, sugar, remaining salt, and pepper. Mix well and simmer for 15 minutes. Add water to sauce to make 4 cups of sauce.

- In a separate bowl, mix mozzarella and ricotta cheese.

- Preheat oven to 350°.

- In a 9 x 11-inch baking pan, layer sauce, chicken, noodles, and cheese. The final layer is noodles, sauce, and Parmesan cheese.

- Bake for 15 to 20 minutes, cheese on top will brown lightly.

- Yield: 8 servings

- Per serving: 698 Calories • 40% Fat

Healthy Alternative Chicken Lasagne

Take the challenge: use part-skim mozzarella and low-fat cottage cheese in this Chicken Lasagne. You won't be able to tell the difference.

- 1 (3 to 4-pound) whole chicken
- ¾ pound lasagna noodles
- 1 tablespoon olive oil, divided
  nonstick cooking spray
- 1 large onion, chopped
- 1 garlic clove, minced
- 1 (6-ounce) can Italian tomato paste
- 1 (28-ounce) can of whole tomatoes, chopped
- 1 teaspoon sugar
- ¼ teaspoon pepper
  water
- 16 ounces part skim mozzarella cheese, shredded
- 1 (15 to 16-ounce) container low-fat cottage cheese
- ¾ cup grated Parmesan cheese

- Advance preparation: simmer chicken in a pot of water. Remove skin and bones from meat and dice.

- Cook noodles in a large pot of boiling water with 1 teaspoon of olive oil as directed on package. Drain and separate noodles on a tray or cookie sheet sprayed with nonstick cooking spray.

- Sauté onions and garlic in the remaining olive oil. Add tomato paste, chopped tomatoes, sugar, and pepper. Mix well and simmer for 15 minutes. Add water to make 4 cups of sauce.

- Cream cottage cheese in a blender. Mix with mozzarella.

Flavor seal: to enhance the flavor and maintain a moist food when baking try the "Flavor Seal". Seal with plastic wrap and cover with aluminum foil. By the way, not all plastic wraps are alike. Look for a thicker plastic wrap…around 18.5 m2. (It will say it on the label underneath the square feet information.)

(recipe continued on next page)

(Healthy Alternative Chicken Lasagne, continued)

- Preheat oven to 350°.

- In a 9 x 11-inch baking pan, layer sauce, noodles, chicken and cheese. The final layer is noodles, sauce, and Parmesan cheese.

- "Flavor Seal": seal with plastic wrap and cover with aluminum foil.

- Bake for 20 to 30 minutes, uncover and bake for an additional 5 minutes.

- Yield: 8 servings

- Per serving: 574 Calories • 30% Fat

"Poulet Basquaise"

We don't know the author of this recipe,
we just know it's signed "from a friend in France".

> 4 **chicken legs or thighs or boneless breasts—as you like**
> 1 **teaspoon salt**
> **pepper**
> 2 **teaspoons butter**
> 1 **large onion, chopped (1 cup)**
> 1 **large tomato, diced**
> 1 **green pepper, cut in wide strips and then in half**
> ½-1 **cup water**
> 1 **teaspoon thyme**
> 3 **bay leaves**

- Sauté chicken in butter for about 2 minutes on each side. Salt and pepper chicken while sautéing.

- Add onion, tomatoes, green pepper, and water. Season with thyme, bay leaves, salt, and pepper.

- Cook over low to medium heat for about 45 minutes. The herbs make it smell divine.

- Yield: 4 servings

Hot Chicken Salad from Alabama

"An old family favorite."

3 **cups cooked, cubed chicken**
1 **cup mayonnaise**
½ **cup sour cream**
3 **tablespoons lemon juice**
1 **teaspoon salt**
1 **teaspoon pepper**
4 **celery ribs, chopped (2 cups)**
4 **ounces slivered almonds (⅔ cup)**
1 **(8-ounce) can sliced water chestnuts, drained**
1 **(4-ounce) jar pimentos, drained and diced**
¼ **pound mushrooms, sliced (1 cup)**
3 **ounces Cheddar cheese, grated (¾ cup)**
3 **ounces potato chips, crushed (1 cup)**

- Preheat oven to 350°.

- Place cut up chicken in a 9 x 13-inch baking dish.

- In a large bowl, blend mayonnaise, sour cream, lemon juice, salt, and pepper. Add celery, almonds, water chestnuts, pimentos, and mushrooms.

- Pour mixture over chicken and stir. Sprinkle Cheddar cheese and potato chips on the top.

- Bake for 30 minutes.

- Yield: 8 servings

- Per serving: 466 Calories • 75% Fat

HA
Healthy Alternative Hot Chicken Salad from Alabama

We are proud to introduce to you
a healthful updating of this family favorite!

3 cups cooked, cubed chicken
1 cup nonfat yogurt, drained
½ cup low-fat mayonnaise
½ cup skim milk
2 tablespoons flour
3 tablespoons lemon juice
1 teaspoon salt
1 teaspoon pepper
4 celery ribs, chopped (2 cups)
2 ounces dried apricots (20 whole), chopped
1 (8-ounce) can sliced water chestnuts, drained
1 (4-ounce) jar pimentos, drained and diced
¼ pound mushrooms, sliced (1 cup)
2 ounces Cheddar cheese, grated (¾ cup)
3 cups cornflakes, crushed (1 cup crushed)

- Preheat oven to 350°.

- Place cut up chicken in a 9 x 13-inch baking dish.

- To drain yogurt: set a sieve on top of a bowl. Line the sieve with a coffee filter. Pour yogurt in a paper-towel lined sieve. Let drain for about 30 minutes.

- Blend drained yogurt, low-fat mayonnaise, milk, flour, lemon juice, salt, and pepper. Add celery, apricots, water chestnuts, pimentos, and mushrooms.

- Pour mixture over chicken. Sprinkle Cheddar cheese and cornflakes on the top.

- Bake for 30 minutes.

- Yield: 8 servings

- Per serving: 202 Calories • 33% Fat

Chicken with Sun Dried Tomatoes

Serve with wild rice for a party dish.

4 **skinless, boneless chicken breast halves**
3 **tablespoons unsalted butter**
½ **teaspoon salt**
¼ **teaspoon pepper**
1 **large shallot, minced**
⅔ **cup heavy cream**
½ **cup dry white wine**
¼ **teaspoon marjoram**
1 **ounce (about 12) sundried tomatoes, coarsely chopped**

- Cut each breast into six diagonal pieces.

- Melt butter in a heavy skillet at moderate heat. Add chicken pieces and sprinkle with salt and pepper. Sauté until chicken is opaque (about 5 minutes). Remove chicken.

- Add shallots and sauté for about 1 minute until soft, stirring constantly. Add cream, wine, marjoram, sun dried tomatoes and bring to a boil. Cook uncovered, occasionally stirring until sauce thickens (about 5 minutes).

- Return chicken to skillet, simmer gently, spooning sauce over chicken until heated throughout (about 3 minutes).

- Yield: 4 servings

- Per serving: 411 Calories • 67% Fat

"The ornament of a house is the friends who frequent it."
— *Ralph Waldo Emerson*

HA
Healthy Alternative Chicken with Sun Dried Tomatoes

4 skinless, boneless chicken breast halves
nonstick cooking spray
½ teaspoon salt
¼ teaspoon pepper
¼ teaspoon marjoram
1 large shallot, minced
⅔ cup evaporated skim milk
1 tablespoon cornstarch
5 tablespoons dry white wine
1 ounce (about 12) sun-dried tomatoes,
coarsely chopped

- Cut each breast into six diagonal pieces.

- Spray heavy skillet with nonstick cooking spray and heat at moderate heat. Add chicken pieces and sprinkle with salt, pepper, and marjoram. Sauté until chicken is opaque (about 5 minutes). Remove chicken.

- Add shallot to skillet and sauté for about 1 minute until soft, stirring constantly. Add wine, simmer to reduce volume by one-half. Mix cornstarch with evaporated milk. Add milk mixture and sun dried tomatoes. Cook uncovered, occasionally stirring until sauce thickens (about 5 minutes).

- Return chicken to skillet, simmer gently, spooning sauce over chicken until heated throughout (about 3 minutes).

- Yield: 4 servings

- Per serving: 218 Calories • 13% Fat

Chicken with Spinach and Feta

1 (10-ounce) package frozen spinach
4 large skinless, boneless chicken
   breast halves
2 tablespoons olive oil
¼ pound mushrooms, sliced (1 cup)
1 medium onion, chopped (½ cup)
1 tablespoon minced garlic
½ cup white wine
2 teaspoons dried thyme
2 teaspoons dried basil
1 teaspoon salt
1 teaspoon pepper
8 ounces feta cheese

- Defrost spinach and squeeze out excess water.

- Place chicken, skin side down, on a cutting board. Cover with plastic wrap. Gently pound with a wooden mallet to about ¼-inch thick.

- Preheat oven to 350°.

- Heat olive oil in a skillet. Sauté spinach, mushrooms, onion, and garlic until liquid evaporates. Add wine, thyme, basil, salt, and pepper. Mix thoroughly.

- Place one-quarter of spinach mixture and 2 ounces of feta on half of each chicken breast. Fold over the other half of the chicken breast to cover the spinach and feta cheese.

- Place in a covered baking dish and bake for 1 hour.

- Yield: 4 servings

- Per serving: 444 Calories • 41% Fat

Healthy Alternative Chicken with Spinach and Feta

Sauté spinach, mushrooms, onion, and garlic in ½ cup of chicken broth until liquid evaporates. Use 1 ounce of feta cheese in each chicken breast.
Per serving: 310 Calories • 32% Fat

Company Chicken Casserole

This is even better when prepared a day in advance; chill uncooked ~~~ ~~ overnight in the refrigerator.

1 (20-ounce) bag frozen broccoli florets
  or mixed vegetables
2-3 cups cooked chicken (leftovers are great)
¼ teaspoon garlic powder
¼ teaspoon lemon pepper
2 (10¾-ounce) cans cream of chicken soup
1 tablespoon lemon juice
1 medium onion, chopped (½ cup)
1 cup mayonnaise
½ teaspoon curry powder (or more to taste)
2 ounces Cheddar cheese, grated (½ cup)
½ cup bread crumbs (plain or Italian)
¼ cup grated Parmesan cheese
4 tablespoons butter
3 cups rice, cooked according to package
  directions

- In a large casserole dish, put frozen vegetables in a single layer.

- Cover with a layer of chicken. Season with garlic powder and lemon pepper.

- Combine soups, lemon juice, onion, mayonnaise, curry powder, and Cheddar cheese and pour mixture over chicken layer.

- Mix bread crumbs and Parmesan and sprinkle on top. Drizzle butter over entire top.

- Chill for 3 hours or more, best if chilled overnight.

- Preheat oven to 350°. Cook for one hour or until middle of casserole is very hot. Serve over rice.

- Yield: 8 servings

- Per serving: 586 Calories • 56% Fat

HA
Healthy Alternative Company Chicken Casserole

A heart healthy company casserole sure to please everyone, kids to grandparents.

- 2 (11-ounce) cans evaporated skim milk
- 3 teaspoons chicken bouillon granules
- 3 tablespoons cornstarch
- 1 (20-ounce) bag frozen broccoli florets or mixed vegetables
- 2-3 cups cooked chicken
- ¼ teaspoon garlic powder
- ¼ teaspoon lemon pepper
- 1 tablespoon lemon juice
- 1 medium onion, chopped (½ cup)
- ½ cup low-fat mayonnaise
- ½ teaspoon curry powder (or more to taste)
- 2 ounces Cheddar cheese, grated (½ cup)
- 3 cups cornflakes, crushed (1 cup)
- ¼ cup grated Parmesan cheese
- 3 cups rice, cooked according to package directions

What about cream sauces in low-fat foods? Try velouté—a sauce made from evaporated skim milk, chicken bouillon, and cornstarch. Here's a Healthy Alternative Company Chicken that has received rave reviews… Thanks to velouté.

- Combine evaporated milk, chicken bouillon granules, and cornstarch in a saucepan. Heat, stirring frequently until thickened.

- In a large casserole dish, put frozen vegetables in a single layer. Cover with a layer of chicken. Season with garlic powder and lemon pepper.

- Combine evaporated milk mixture, lemon juice, onions, mayonnaise, curry powder, and Cheddar cheese. Pour mixture over chicken layer.

(recipe continued on next page)

(Healthy Alternative Company Chicken Casserole, continued)

- Sprinkle cornflakes and Parmesan on top.

- Chill for 3 hours or more, best if chilled overnight.

- Preheat oven to 350°. Cook for one hour or until middle of casserole is very hot. Serve over rice.

- Yield: 8 servings

- Per serving: 378 Calories • 15% Fat

Ginger Chicken

The interesting combination of soy sauce, ginger, and cinnamon is most unusual and gives this dish a Middle Eastern flair. Added bonus; it's low in fat and a breeze to prepare.

4 chicken breast halves (ribs in), skin removed
⅓ cup soy sauce
2 tablespoons water
1 small onion, thinly sliced
2 teaspoons ginger
2 teaspoons cinnamon

- Combine soy sauce, water, onions, ginger, and cinnamon in a frying pan. Add chicken breasts. Bring to a boil.

- Cover, reduce heat and simmer slowly for 30 to 40 minutes.

- Yield: 4 servings

Kung Pao Chicken

Cuisine from the orient has always known the secret of low-fat cooking—flavor, flavor and more flavor.

   5 **tablespoons soy sauce, divided**
   4 **teaspoons cornstarch, divided**
   6 **skinless, boneless chicken breast halves,
     cut into thin strips**
   2 **tablespoons dry white wine**
1½ **tablespoons sugar**
   1 **tablespoon cider vinegar**
1½ **teaspoons sesame oil**
   ½ **teaspoon salt**
   4 **tablespoons vegetable oil, divided**
1-2 **teaspoons dried red pepper, crushed**
   3 **ounces salted peanuts (¾ cup)**
   1 **teaspoon fresh ginger, minced**
   3 **cups cooked rice**

• Blend 2 tablespoons soy sauce and 2 teaspoons of the cornstarch until smooth. Stir in the chicken. Refrigerate 30 minutes.

• Combine remaining soy sauce, wine, sugar, cider vinegar, the remaining cornstarch, sesame oil, and salt together. Set aside.

• In a frying pan, heat 2 tablespoons of the vegetable oil and the crushed dried red pepper for 2 minutes. Add peanuts. Stir-fry until pepper is almost black. Remove from pan and set aside.

• Heat remaining 2 tablespoons oil about 1 minute. Add minced ginger. Add chicken mixture. Stir-fry about 3 minutes or until chicken is no longer pink. Add cooking sauce. Stir-fry until sauce thickens. Remove pan from heat. Stir in reserved peanuts and blackened pepper. Serve over rice.

• Yield: 8 servings

Labor Day Brunswick Stew

*The flavor of this low-fat stew is enhanced by
serving it the following day. This stew is a keeper—
it freezes beautifully.*

1 (6-pound) stewing chicken
2 large onions, sliced
½ pound okra, sliced (2 cups)
3 pounds tomatoes skinned, diced (4 cups)
2 pounds lima beans, shelled (2 cups)
1 pound potatoes, diced (3 medium)
8 ears of corn, kernels removed (4 cups)
3 teaspoons salt
1 teaspoon pepper
1 tablespoon sugar

• Cut chicken in pieces and simmer in 3 quarts of water until the meat can be easily removed from the bones (about 2½ hours).

• Remove chicken from the broth. In the refrigerator, chill the broth until fat congeals on the surface. Remove fat. Reheat chicken broth and add onions, okra, tomatoes, lima beans, and corn. Simmer uncovered until the beans and potatoes are tender.

• Remove skin and bones from chicken. Dice chicken and add to broth (after vegetables are tender). Add salt, pepper, and sugar to broth. Heat thoroughly.

• Yield: 10 servings

"You may stroll to the garden to cut the corn...but you had darn well better run back to the kitchen to make it."
— *New England Adage*

Spicy Noodle Salad with Chicken

½ **pound thin spaghetti**
¾ **cup water**
¼ **cup soy sauce**
1 **tablespoon sugar**
3 **tablespoons red wine vinegar**
2 **tablespoons peanut oil**
2 **tablespoons sesame oil**
1 **teaspoon red pepper flakes**
1 **teaspoon grated fresh ginger**
⅛ **teaspoon pepper**
2 **cups cooked and shredded chicken**
6-7 **scallions, sliced**

• Cook pasta to al dente. Drain, rinse under cold water; drain again. Refrigerate until chilled.

• In a blender or food processor, combine water, soy sauce, sugar, vinegar, oils, red pepper flakes, ginger, and pepper for ten seconds. Pour sauce over chicken.

• Cover and marinate for at least 30 minutes.

• Combine cold noodles with chicken and sauce. Garnish with sliced scallions.

• This is delicious also served over hot pasta.

• Yield: 4 servings

Sesame oil is to Chinese cuisine as butter is to the French. The pressed seeds of the sesame plant, introduced to China in about the fifth century A.D., provide a basic cooking fat. When toasted, they impart a delicate nutlike flavor to all types of recipes.

Mushroom Stuffed Chicken Breasts

4 whole chicken breasts, skinned, boned and halved

¾ cup (1½ sticks) butter, divided

½ pound mushrooms, chopped fine (3 cups)

½ teaspoon salt

¼ teaspoon pepper

6 slices of white bread, crust removed and made into fresh bread crumbs (1½ cups)

¼ teaspoon nutmeg

1 cup heavy cream

- Preheat oven to 350°.

- Place chicken, skin side down, on a cutting board. Cover with plastic wrap and gently pound with a wooden mallet to about ½-inch thick.

- Melt ½ cup of the butter in a skillet. Add mushrooms, salt, and pepper. Cook, stirring often, until mushrooms turn dark and absorb most of the butter. Remove from heat and stir in ¾ cup of the bread crumbs and the nutmeg.

- Divide mushroom stuffing into eight portions and place in the center of each piece of chicken. Fold chicken around stuffing, and place seam side down in a shallow casserole.

- Melt remaining butter and brush over chicken. Sprinkle with remaining bread crumbs. Pour cream over top.

- Bake 30 minutes until lightly browned.

- Yield: 8 servings

- Per serving: 473 Calories • 63% Fat

HA
Healthy Alternative
Mushroom Stuffed
Chicken Breasts

*Here's a delicious variation, replacing cream
with some "unlikely" ingredients—yogurt,
apricot preserves, and mustard.*

4 **whole chicken breasts, skinned, boned
and halved**
1 **tablespoon olive oil**
½ **cup chicken broth**
½ **pound of mushrooms, chopped fine
(3 cups)**
½ **teaspoon salt**
¼ **teaspoon pepper**
3 **slices of white bread, crust removed and
made into fresh bread crumbs (¾ cup)**
¼ **teaspoon nutmeg**
⅔ **cup nonfat plain yogurt**
⅔ **cup apricot all-fruit preserves**
2 **tablespoons mustard**

• Preheat oven to 350°.

• Place chicken, skin side down, on a cutting
board. Cover with plastic wrap and gently
pound with a wooden mallet to about ½-inch
thick.

• Place olive oil in a heated skillet and sauté
mushrooms, salt, and pepper. Add chicken
broth. Cook, stirring often, until mushrooms
turn dark and absorb most of the broth.
Remove from heat and stir in ¾ cup bread
crumbs and nutmeg.

• Divide mushroom stuffing into eight portions
and place in the center of each piece of chicken.
Fold chicken around stuffing, and place seam
side down in a shallow casserole.

(recipe continued on next page)

(Healthy Alternative Mushroom Stuffed Chicken Breasts, continued)

- Mix yogurt, preserves, and mustard. Spread yogurt mixture over top and sides of chicken breasts.

- Bake 30 minutes until lightly browned.

- Yield: 8 servings

- Per serving: 272 Calories • 16% Fat

Turkey Quick-as-a-Wink

Who says stir-fry has to be served over rice? Try it over bean sprouts.

1 cup jellied cranberry sauce
⅓ cup dry sherry
¼ cup soy sauce
¼ cup vinegar
¼ cup water
2 tablespoons cornstarch
2 tablespoons peanut oil
2 large garlic cloves, minced
1 pound carrots, thinly sliced (2 cups)
1 pound zucchini, julienned (2 cups)
2 cups cooked turkey breast, cubed
1 pound bean sprouts (4 cups), lightly steamed or microwaved

- Combine cranberry sauce, sherry, soy sauce, vinegar, water, and cornstarch. Mix until smooth.

- Preheat wok or large skillet over high heat; add oil. Stir-fry garlic for 30 seconds. Add carrots, stir-fry 3 minutes. Add zucchini and turkey, stir-fry 1 minute.

- Stir in cranberry mixture. Mix to coat vegetables and turkey. Cook and stir until bubbly. Cover and cook 1 minute more. Serve over sprouts.

- Yield: 6 servings

Spinach-Stuffed Turkey Meatloaf

1 tablespoon butter
1 (10-ounce) package frozen chopped spinach, thawed and drained
¼ pound mushrooms, coarsely chopped (1 cup)
½ medium onion, chopped (¼ cup)
2 ounces Swiss cheese, shredded (½ cup), divided
¼ cup grated Parmesan cheese
1 pound ground turkey
½ pound ground beef
¾ cup oats
½ cup milk
1 large egg, beaten
1 teaspoon Italian seasoning
½ teaspoon salt
¼ teaspoon pepper

- Preheat oven to 375°.

- Heat butter in a skillet. Sauté spinach, mushrooms, and onions over medium heat for 3 to 4 minutes. Stir in ¼ cup of the Swiss cheese and the Parmesan cheese.

- Combine turkey, beef, oats, milk, egg, Italian seasoning, salt, and pepper. Mix well.

- Spoon two-thirds of the meat mixture lengthwise down the center of an 11 x 7-inch glass baking dish. Make a deep indentation down center of meat. Fill with spinach mixture. Top with remaining meat mixture to encase spinach filling.

Keep an eye out for ground turkey made from turkey breast. It is hard to find. The label will read, in extremely small print: "made from breast". It's worth the search because it is considerably lower in fat. If you cannot find ground turkey breast, make your own. Buy a breast of turkey and cut into cubes. In a food processor with a steel blade, process until ground.

(recipe continued on next page)

(Spinach-Stuffed Turkey Meatloaf, continued)

- Bake 50 to 55 minutes. Take out of oven and sprinkle with remaining Swiss cheese. Bake another 1 to 2 minutes, until cheese melts. Let stand 5 minutes before slicing.

- Yield: 8 servings

- Per serving: 266 Calories • 55% Fat

Teen Night In

Onion Pizza (Pissaladière)

California Heaven

*Spinach-Stuffed
Turkey Meatloaf*

Zesty Carrots

Party Potatoes

Sparkling Cider

Back Yard Banana Boats

HA
Healthy Alternative Spinach-Stuffed Turkey Meatloaf

Try our Healthy Alternative Spinach-Stuffed Meatloaf with a surprise ingredient: raisins. If it's been Cooper tested you know it's delicious.

　　nonstick cooking spray
1 **(10-ounce) package frozen chopped spinach, thawed and drained**
¼ **pound mushrooms, coarsely chopped (1 cup)**
½ **medium onion, chopped (½ cup)**
2 **ounces Swiss cheese, shredded (½ cup), divided**
¼ **cup grated Parmesan cheese**
1½ **pounds ground turkey**
¾ **cup oats**
½ **cup applesauce**
¼ **cup raisins**
1 **apple, peeled and cubed**
1 **large egg white**
1 **teaspoon Italian seasoning**
½ **teaspoon salt**
¼ **teaspoon pepper**

- Preheat oven to 375°.

- Spray a skillet with nonstick cooking spray.

- Sauté spinach, mushrooms, and onions over medium heat for 3 to 4 minutes. Stir in ¼ cup of the Swiss cheese and the Parmesan cheese.

- Combine turkey, oats, applesauce, raisins, apples, egg white, Italian seasoning, salt, and pepper. Mix well.

- Spoon two-thirds of the meat mixture lengthwise down center of 11 x 7-inch glass baking dish. Make a deep indentation down

(recipe continued on next page)

(Healthy Alternative Spinach-Stuffed Turkey Meatloaf, continued)

center of meat. Fill with spinach mixture. Top with remaining meat mixture to encase spinach filling.

- Bake 50 to 55 minutes. Remove from oven and sprinkle with remaining Swiss cheese. Bake an additional 1 to 2 minutes, until cheese melts. Let stand 5 minutes before slicing.
- Yield: 8 servings
- Per serving: 173 Calories • 30% Fat

Gourmet Club Night

Island Crab Spread

Chilled Red Pepper Soup

Spinach-Stuffed Turkey Meatloaf

Roasted Carrots with Garlic

Praise the Potatoes

Geyser Peak Sauvignon Blanc

Lemondown Fancies

Boneless Turkey Breast with Peanut Sauce

1 (3-pound) skinless, boneless turkey
  breast
½ cup peanut butter
¼ cup soy sauce
¼ cup sesame oil
1 large garlic clove, minced
¼ cup cider vinegar
2 teaspoons sugar
1½ tablespoons hot pepper oil
1 cup sour cream
  milk

- Advance preparation: place turkey, skin side down, on a cutting board. Cover with plastic wrap. Pound with a wooden mallet to about 1-inch thick.

- Combine peanut butter, soy sauce, sesame oil, garlic, vinegar, sugar, hot pepper oil, and sour cream. Thin this with milk to make the consistency of softly whipped cream. Spread turkey with sauce and marinate several hours or overnight.

- Grill turkey over moderately hot fire, turning and basting with sauce for 15 to 20 minutes.

- If you do not have a grill, or it's covered with ice and snow, broil in an oven (six inches from heat) 15 to 20 minutes. Serve sliced either warm or cold.

- Yield: 6 servings

Nonfat plain yogurt can be used in place of sour cream in a marinade. It acts like a moisturizing cream and makes a flavorful juicy turkey breast.

Marinated Filet of Beef

Try a little tenderness.

1 cup soy sauce
2 cups red wine
4 garlic cloves, crushed
2 tablespoons Dijon mustard
2 tablespoons caraway seeds
1 (5-pound) beef filet
2 tablespoons olive oil
2 tablespoons butter

- Advance preparation: combine soy sauce, wine, garlic, mustard, and caraway seeds and pour into a doubled ziploc bag. Add filet and marinate overnight in the refrigerator, turning several times.

- Preheat oven to 425°.

- Heat oil and butter in a heavy skillet. Remove meat from marinade and pat dry. Sear the meat in the butter and oil until brown, then transfer to a roasting pan.

- Roast in oven for 30 to 40 minutes (depending on desired doneness).

- May serve hot, or cool to room temperature for 1 hour before slicing.

- Yield: 8 servings

" 'Roast Beef Medium' is not a food. It is a philosophy."
— Edna Ferber

Lobster Stuffed Tenderloin of Beef

Living well is the best revenge.

2 (4-ounce) frozen lobster tails
1 teaspoon salt
1 (3 to 4-pound) whole beef tenderloin
½ cup butter, melted and divided
  juice from ½ of a large lemon
  (1½ tablespoons)
6 slices bacon, partially cooked
½ cup green onions, sliced
½ cup dry white wine
⅛ teaspoon garlic salt

- Fill a large pot with water and add 1 teaspoon salt. Bring to a boil.

- Place frozen lobster tails in boiling water and cover. Simmer 5 minutes. Remove lobster tails from boiling water and shell. Cut lobster tails in half.

- Preheat oven to 425°.

- Cut tenderloin lengthwise to within ½-inch of bottom. Place lobster end to end inside of beef. Combine 1 tablespoon of the melted butter and lemon juice. Drizzle on lobster. Close meat around lobster and tie roast together with a string. Place in roasting pan on a rack.

- Roast for 30 minutes. Place bacon on top, roast 5 minutes longer.

- To make wine sauce: while tenderloin is roasting, sauté onion in remaining butter in a saucepan. Add wine, garlic salt and simmer.

- To serve: slice roast and spoon on wine sauce.

- Tenderloin can be stuffed ahead of time and then refrigerated until ready to cook.

- Yield: 8 servings

Grilled London Broil

Red meat has taken a lot of heat, not all of it deserved.
Take this low-fat London broil off the fire and enjoy.

1 **(2-pound) London broil, fat removed,**
pierced with a fork
3 **cups dry red wine**
1 **cup red wine vinegar**
2 **whole garlic heads, chopped**
3 **bay leaves, crushed**
6 **peppercorns**
4 **Vidalia onions, unskinned**

• Advance preparation: marinate (no less than 8 hours) London broil in wine, vinegar, garlic, bay leaves, peppercorns. Turn several times.

• To cook on a gas grill: heat to medium high. Place London broil on grill, sear both sides. Lower heat and slowly grill to desired doneness. For a 1-inch steak, grill about 10 minutes on each side.

• At the same time, place whole unskinned onions on grill, allow the onion skins to brown and burn.

• To serve: slice London broil (if you are using top round cut on a diagonal to increase tenderness. If you are using flank, slice vertically). Remove onion from skin and layer on top of sliced London broil.

• Yield: 4 servings

"The wonderful world of home appliances now makes it possible to cook indoors with charcoal and outdoors with gas."
— Bill Vaughan

Meeting Your Daughter's Future-in-laws Roast Filet of Beef

In cook's heaven.

- ½ **cup tomato purée**
- 2 **cups Médoc wine**
- 6 **beef bouillon cubes**
- 8 **cups water**
- 8 **tablespoons butter, divided**
- ½ **cup celery, minced**
- ½ **cup onions, minced**
- ½ **cup carrots, minced**
- ½ **pound mushrooms, divided**
- 6-10 **tablespoons flour**
- 1 **tablespoon fresh lemon juice**
- 1 **(6-pound) filet mignon, trimmed**
- ¼ **teaspoon salt**
- ¼ **teaspoon pepper**
- 1 **garlic clove, crushed**
  parsley

- Combine the tomato purée, wine, bouillon cubes, and water in a large pot.

- Reduce over medium heat to about five cups (takes about 2½ hours).

- Melt 1 tablespoon of the butter in a skillet. Sauté celery, carrots, and onions over low heat about 20 minutes or until tender.

- Put vegetables in a blender with ½ cup of tomato mixture and blend. Remove from blender, strain vegetables. Add strained liquid to the reduced tomato mixture. Discard pulp of vegetables.

- Finely chop ¼ pound of the mushrooms. Sauté in 1 tablespoon of the butter and set aside.

Bruised greens can be used to keep rare meat rare during reheating. Line a baking dish with greens, layer leftover meat slices on top, then blanket with additional greens. Warm about 10 minutes in a very slow oven.

(recipe continued on next page)

(Meeting Your Daughter's Future-in-Laws Roast Filet of Beef, continued)

- To make sauce: melt 6 tablespoons of butter in a saucepan. With a whisk, stir in flour, one tablespoon at a time. Slowly add the tomato mixture to the roux, stirring constantly to avoid lumps. Cook until thick enough to coat the back of a spoon. Add sautéed mushrooms, lemon juice, and parsley. If sauce is too thick, add more wine. Set aside to be warmed prior to serving roast. Sauce may be made days in advance and refrigerated.

- Preheat oven to 375°.

- Place the remaining whole mushrooms on a sheet of heavy duty aluminum foil. Seal and bake for 30 minutes. Remove from aluminum foil and use to garnish roast.

- To cook roast: rub surface of roast with salt, pepper, and garlic.

- Bake in a shallow baking pan until thermometer registers desired doneness (140° for rare, 165° for medium and 180° for well done). It takes about 35 to 45 minutes to cook to rare.

- Heat sauce.

- To serve: when roast is done, put on platter and carve. Pour some of the sauce on top and garnish with the whole mushrooms and fresh parsley.

- Yield: 12 servings

The leanest cuts of beef are top round, eye of the round, tip round, sirloin, top loin and tenderloin.

Sauerbraten

Sauerbraten, the second day, is better
(if that's possible) than the first.

  1 **(4-pound) rump or round roast (select meat**
    with layer of fat)
  2 **cups red wine vinegar**
    water
  4 **bay leaves**
 12 **cloves**
 12 **peppercorns**
 ¼ **cup flour**
  1 **teaspoon salt**
 ½ **teaspoon pepper**
 ¼ **teaspoon allspice**
  1 **pound carrots (6-7), pared and sliced**
 12 **small onions**
 12 **gingersnaps, crumbled**
  1 **tablespoon sugar**

- To make marinade: wipe meat with paper towels. Place meat in a deep bowl and add vinegar and enough water to cover meat completely. Add bay leaves, cloves and peppercorns and put in the refrigerator for three days.

- To prepare: remove meat and reserve the spicy vinegar marinade.

- Combine flour, salt, pepper, and allspice. Rub meat with seasoned flour.

- Heat a heavy kettle until smoking. Brown roast on all sides, fat side down first. Add sliced carrots, onions, and two cups of the reserved spiced vinegar marinade.

- Cover and cook over low heat about two hours until meat is tender.

- Add crumbled gingersnaps and sugar to liquid around meat. Cook 10 minutes more.

- Traditionally Sauerbraten is served with pancakes, applesauce, and red cabbage.

- Yield: 8 servings

Beef it up Stew

A very satisfying, delicious low-fat dish.

2 (16-ounce) cans tomatoes
1 (15-ounce) can tomato sauce
1 small onion, sliced
6 carrots, sliced
4 medium potatoes, diced
½-1 cup Burgundy wine
3 tablespoons minute tapioca
1 tablespoon sugar
¾ tablespoon salt
½ teaspoon pepper
2 pounds lean chuck, cubed
1 (4-ounce) can button mushrooms, drained
2 tablespoons cream sherry (optional)

- Preheat oven to 250°.

- Combine tomatoes, tomato sauce, onion, carrots, potatoes, wine, tapioca, sugar, salt, and pepper in a large oven casserole.

- Add chuck. Cover and bake for 5½ hours.

- Add mushrooms and cream sherry (if desired) and bake uncovered for an additional 30 minutes.

- Serve with salad and hot crusty bread.

- Yield: 8 servings

"There is no sight on earth more appealing than the sight of a woman making dinner for someone she loves."
— Thomas Wolfe

Peppered Chutney Roast Beef

1 (3 to 4-pound) beef tenderloin
¾ cup unsweetened pineapple juice
½ cup steak sauce
⅓ cup Worcestershire sauce
⅓ cup port wine
¼ cup lemon juice
2 teaspoons seasoned salt
1 teaspoon lemon pepper seasoning
1 teaspoon dry mustard
2 teaspoons cracked pepper
3 slices bacon
⅓ cup Major Grey's chutney

• Advance preparation: place tenderloin in a large ziploc bag. In a small bowl, combine pineapple juice, steak sauce, Worcestershire sauce, wine, lemon juice, seasoned salt, pepper, lemon pepper, and dry mustard. Pour over meat in plastic bag. Seal and refrigerate overnight, turning meat occasionally. (Don't lose any sleep over this. Just turn once before bed and once in the morning.)

• Preheat oven to 425°.

• Drain, reserving marinade. Rub beef with cracked pepper and place in shallow roasting pan. Arrange bacon slices over tenderloin.

• Roast uncovered for 30 to 40 minutes. Baste tenderloin twice during roasting with marinade.

• Spoon chutney over tenderloin. Bake 5 to 10 minutes more until meat thermometer registers 140°.

• Let stand 15 minutes before slicing.

• Yield: 12 servings

Glorified Meat Loaf

1 (4-ounce) can sliced mushrooms
water
1 pound lean ground beef
½ cup plus 2 tablespoons whole wheat bread
crumbs
1 large egg, beaten
½ teaspoon salt
¼ teaspoon garlic powder
4 slices bacon, cooked, drained, and
crumbled
1 small onion, chopped
4 ounces mozzarella cheese, shredded
(1 cup)
1 teaspoon parsley flakes
½ teaspoon dried oregano
½ teaspoon dried basil
½ teaspoon dried thyme
1 (15-ounce) can tomato sauce

- Drain mushrooms and reserve juice. Add enough water to juice to make ½ cup.

- Combine mushroom liquid, beef, ½ cup of the bread crumbs, egg, salt, and garlic powder. Mix well. Cover and chill 30 minutes.

- Shape mixture into a 12 x 8-inch rectangle on a sheet of wax paper. Sprinkle with mushrooms, bacon, onions, cheese, 2 tablespoons of the bread crumbs, and seasonings. Leave a one-inch margin around the edges.

- Beginning at the short end, roll meat up (jelly roll style), lifting wax paper to help in rolling. Press edges and ends together to seal. Place in a loaf pan.

- Place tomato sauce on top and cover with aluminum foil. Bake at 350° for 1 hour. Let stand 5 minutes before slicing.

- Yield: 6 servings

Come to Dinner Sweet and Sour Short Ribs

nonstick cooking spray
8-10 meaty short ribs
1 pound mushrooms, medium size, stems removed
2 large Spanish onions, sliced
3 (13¾-ounce) cans beef broth
2 cups dry white or red wine (a sauvignon blanc or a Beaujolais are good)
½ teaspoon dried thyme or 2 teaspoons of fresh thyme (2 sprigs)
1 large bay leaf or 2 small bay leaves
salt
pepper
¼ cup cider vinegar
¼ cup brown sugar
¼ cup ketchup
fresh parsley sprigs

For a more mellow flavor, add herbs earlier in the cooking process. If a strong flavor is required, sprinkle them in just prior to serving.

• Heat a Dutch oven on high heat until a drop of water evaporates at once. Lower heat to medium/high and spray interior with nonstick cooking spray. Brown short ribs on all sides, in as many batches as necessary and adjusting heat as necessary. Remove ribs from pan.

• Sauté mushrooms. Remove mushrooms with a slotted spoon and pour off any fat from pan.

• Place ribs back in the roasting pan. Cover with onions. Pour broth and wine over ribs and onions. Add water if needed to completely cover. Add thyme and bay leaf, salt, and pepper. Bring to a boil. Lower heat and simmer for 1 hour.

• Stir in vinegar and sugar. Simmer for an additional hour.

(recipe continued on next page)

(Come to Dinner Sweet and Sour Short Ribs, continued)

- Stir in ketchup and mushrooms and adjust seasonings. Cover and simmer for 20 minutes. Remove bay leaf.

- Can be served over noodles or rice. Garnish with parsley. Best made early in the day or the day before so you can remove a lot of fat. After the final simmer, separate solids from liquid. Refrigerate and then skim the solid fat from the surface of the liquid. Recombine to heat and serve.

- Yield: 6 servings

Steak à la Madeira

Let your palate be your guide.

7 **tablespoons butter, divided**
4 **small steaks (New York shell steaks,**
 4 to 6-ounces each)
¼ **cup chopped shallots**
½ **pound mushrooms, sliced (2 cups)**
1 **garlic clove, minced**
1 **teaspoon flour**
¼ **cup Madeira wine**
1 **teaspoon Dijon mustard**
 salt
 pepper to taste

- Trim fat from steaks and cut edges to prevent curling.

- Melt 4 tablespoons of the butter in a frying pan. Add steaks to the pan and sauté (approximately 6 minutes on each side, depending on thickness). Remove steaks, add salt and pepper to taste and keep warm.

- Add remaining butter to frying pan and cook shallots, mushrooms and garlic about 5 minutes. Add flour and stir constantly to mix. Add wine and mustard, stir until sauce begins to thicken. Serve sauce over steaks.

- Yield: 4 servings

Calico Bean Bake

½ **pound lean bacon, sliced in ½-inch pieces**
½ **pound lean ground beef**
1 **medium onion, chopped (1 cup)**
½ **cup ketchup**
1 **teaspoon dry mustard**
2 **tablespoons white vinegar**
¼ **cup brown sugar**
2 **(16-ounce) cans pork and beans**
1 **(16-ounce) can kidney beans, drained**
1 **(16-ounce) frozen package small**
  green lima beans, defrosted

- Preheat oven to 350°.

- Brown bacon over low heat. Remove bacon, place on absorbent paper. Drain bacon grease from skillet.

- Brown beef over low heat and drain. Add onions to beef and continue sautéing until soft.

- Mix beef, bacon, and onion in a large bowl. Add ketchup, mustard, vinegar, and brown sugar. Mix well. Carefully mix in pork and beans, kidney beans, and lima beans.

- Bake uncovered in a large casserole dish for 40 minutes. If there appears to be too much liquid, pour some off during the baking process. Cover with foil if top is getting dry or burned. Ingredients should be bubbling and hot.

- This recipe is easily doubled, tripled or even more for a large crowd. Just increase baking dish size and cooking time. This can also be cooked in a crock pot. Just follow all preparation directions as above. Instead of baking, pour into crock pot and cook over low heat setting for 8 to 10 hours, checking periodically.

- Yield: 10 servings

- Per serving: 356 Calories • 22% Fat

HA

Healthy Alternative Calico Bean Bake
Use ½-pound of ham cubes instead of the bacon. Cooper tested for excellence. Per serving: 322 Calories • 8% Fat

Mexican Lasagne

This recipe freezes and reheats beautifully.

1 **pound ground beef**
nonstick cooking spray
1 **medium onion, chopped**
1 **(14½-ounce) can stewed tomatoes**
1 **(6-ounce) can tomato paste**
1 **package Mexican seasoning**
8 **(8-inch) flour tortillas**
1 **(8-ounce) package cream cheese**
1 **(4-ounce) can sliced green chilies, drained**
4 **ounces Monterey Jack cheese, shredded**
(1 cup)

- Brown ground beef and drain.

- Spray a large skillet with nonstick cooking spray. Sauté onions until golden brown. Add ground beef, stewed tomatoes, tomato paste, and Mexican seasoning. Cover and simmer for 20 minutes, stirring occasionally.

- Place one-third of the sauce in the bottom of an 8 x 11-inch baking dish.

- Lay out tortillas on a counter. Divide the cream cheese into 8 cubes, spreading 1 cube on half of one side of each tortilla (half the circle). Then divide the can of diced green chilies on each tortilla on top of the cream cheese. Fold each tortilla in half and place over sauce in pan.

- Pour remaining sauce over tortillas. Sprinkle with cheese.

- Bake 30 minutes at 350°.

- Yield: 8 servings

- Per serving: 387 Calories • 52% Fat

"Mexican weather report: Chile today — Hot Tamale."

— Children's Joke

Healthy Alternative Mexican Lasagne

1 **pound extra lean ground beef**
  nonstick cooking spray
1 **medium onion, chopped**
1 **(14½-ounce) can stewed tomatoes**
1 **(6-ounce) can tomato paste**
1 **package Mexican seasoning**
8 **(8-inch) flour tortillas**
4 **ounces (½ package) low-fat cream cheese,**
  divided into 8 cubes
1 **(15-ounce) can kidney beans, drained**
¼ **cup water**
1 **(4-ounce) can sliced green chilies, drained**
2 **ounces Monterey Jack cheese, shredded**
  (½ cup)

- Brown ground beef and drain.

- In a large skillet sprayed with nonstick cooking spray, brown onions. Add ground beef, stewed tomatoes, tomato paste and Mexican seasoning. Cover and simmer for 20 minutes, stirring occasionally.

- Place one-third of the sauce in the bottom of an 8 x 11-inch baking dish.

- Lay out tortillas on counter. Spread a cream cheese cube on half of each tortilla.

- Purée can of beans with water. Spread 2 heaping tablespoons of puréed beans on other half of each tortilla.

- Place ⅛ of the can of green chilies on top cream cheese.

- Fold each tortilla in half and place over sauce in pan. Pour remaining sauce over tortilla. Sprinkle with cheese.

- Bake 30 minutes at 350°.

- Yield: 8 servings

- Per serving: 311 Calories • 27% Fat

Texas Stew

A great informal low-fat supper dish.
Serve with a green salad and crusty bread.

2 **tablespoons olive oil**
2 **pounds lean chuck, cubed**
1 **(13¾-ounce) can beef broth**
1 **cup hot water**
1 **(8-ounce) jar picante sauce**
1 **medium onion, cut into ½-inch wedges**
1 **(16-ounce) can whole tomatoes, drained and chopped**
1 **(10-ounce) package frozen corn**
3 **medium carrots, cut into ½-inch pieces**
2 **medium zucchini, cut into 1-inch pieces**
2 **tablespoons flour**
½ **cup cold water**

Never cook stews to a boil. The ingredients may toughen if cooked at a boil.

- Heat oil in a large pot, brown meat in batches.

- Add broth, hot water, picante sauce, and onion. Cover and simmer 1 hour or until meat is tender.

- Add tomatoes, corn, carrots, and zucchini. Cover and simmer an additional 25 minutes until the vegetables are tender.

- Put flour in a separate bowl. Gradually add cold water, mixing with a whisk until smooth. Add to stew. Heat and stir for 1 minute or until thickened. Season to taste.

- Yield: 8 servings

Moussaka

2-3 large eggplants, "stripe" peeled and sliced
   lengthwise into ½-inch slices
   salt
 1 cup oil, divided
 1 medium onion, chopped (½ cup)
 2 pounds ground beef
 2 tablespoons parsley, minced
 ½ cup (1 stick) butter
 ¼ teaspoon cinnamon
 1 tablespoon tomato paste
 ¼ teaspoon salt
 ½ cup water
 3 large eggs, beaten plus 7 large eggs,
   beaten
 2 ounces feta cheese, crumbled (½ cup)
   nonstick cooking spray
 ¾ cup grated Kefaloteri cheese (Parmesan
   cheese can be substituted)

- Advance preparation: salt eggplant and put in a colander. Place a heavy weight on top of the eggplant slices. This may have to be done in batches.

- An hour later, rinse eggplant slices under cold water. Squeeze each slice to remove water and lay flat on paper towels.

- Heat 2 tablespoons of oil in a skillet, sauté onions until soft. Add meat and brown lightly. Add parsley, butter, cinnamon, tomato paste, ¼ teaspoon salt, and ½ cup water. Mix and cook for 45 minutes.

- Remove from heat. Add three beaten eggs and feta cheese.

- In a separate skillet, fry eggplant in oil until golden brown. Place on absorbent paper.

- Spray a 9 x 12-inch pan with nonstick cooking spray.

(recipe continued on next page)

(Moussaka, continued)

- To assemble: place a layer of eggplant on the bottom. Cover with half of the meat mixture, then another layer of eggplant and the remaining meat mixture. Finish with eggplant layer (some eggplant may be remaining). Pour 7 beaten eggs over top. Sprinkle with grated cheese.

- Bake 45 minutes at 350°.

- Yield: 8 servings

- Per serving: 634 Calories • 74% Fat

Greek Menu

Skordelia

Greek Spinach Pie

Avgolemono Soup

Moussaka

Fife Zinfandel

Angela Pia

HA
Healthy Alternative
Moussaka

Here's a fabulous variation that honors tradition and taste. The secret is roasting vegetables. Roasting caramelizes the vegetable, giving it a wonderful taste and texture. The good news is, not only is it almost one-half the fat of the original recipe, but it is also less work. You don't need to stand over a hot frying pan, juggling tongs, plates and absorbent paper, or clean the oil splattered onto your kitchen wall.

 2-3 **large eggplants, peeled and sliced lengthwise into ½-inch thick slices nonstick cooking spray**
 1 **teaspoon oregano**
 ½ **teaspoon black pepper**
 1 **medium onion, chopped**
 2 **pounds extra lean ground beef**
 2 **tablespoons minced parsley salt to taste**
 ¼ **teaspoon cinnamon**
 1 **tablespoon tomato paste**
 ½ **cup water**
 2 **(8-ounce) containers egg substitute, divided**
 4 **ounces feta cheese (1 cup)**
 2 **tablespoons grated Parmesan cheese**

- Preheat oven to 450°.

- Spray both sides of sliced eggplant with nonstick cooking spray. Sprinkle with oregano and black pepper. Roast in oven for 30 minutes.

- While eggplant is roasting, spray a nonstick skillet with nonstick cooking spray. Sauté onions until soft. Add meat and brown lightly. Add parsley, salt, cinnamon, tomato paste, and water. Mix and cook for 45 minutes. Remove meat mixture from heat.

(recipe continued on next page)

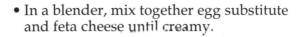

(Healthy Alternative Moussaka, continued)

To avoid a watery eggplant casserole, remove excess moisture by salting eggplant slices and draining them on a rack prior to using. Rub slices with lemon juice to prevent discoloration.

- In a blender, mix together egg substitute and feta cheese until creamy.
- Add three-fourths cup of the egg mixture to the meat mixture.
- Reduce oven temperature to 350°.
- Spray a 9 x 12-inch pan with nonstick cooking spray.
- To assemble: place a layer of eggplant on the bottom of the pan. Cover with half of the meat mixture, then another layer of eggplant and the remaining meat mixture. Finish with an eggplant layer (you may have eggplant leftover). Pour the remaining egg mixture over top. Sprinkle with Parmesan cheese.
- Bake 45 minutes.
- Yield: 8 servings
- Per serving: 207 Calories • 36% Fat

Happy Birthday Lamb

*For delicious lamb, do not overcook. The roast
is most succulent when rare or medium rare.*

1 **(6 to 7-pound) boned, rolled leg of lamb**
1 **teaspoon salt**
½ **teaspoon white pepper**
1 **teaspoon seasoned salt**
1 **teaspoon dried marjoram**
½ **teaspoon dried mustard**
⅛ **teaspoon ground cardamom**
2 **garlic cloves, sliced into slivers**
1½ **teaspoons dried thyme**
1 **teaspoon dried sage**
1 **orange, sliced into 8 slices and then cut
   into half moons
   fresh mint**

- Preheat oven to 325°.

- Combine salt, pepper, seasoned salt, marjoram,
  mustard, and cardamom. Rub into surface of
  lamb.

- Cut sixteen slashes about ½-inch deep (or deep
  enough for orange moons) into the surface of
  the lamb.

- Toss garlic in combined thyme and sage. Insert
  into slits along with orange moons.

- Place in roasting pan, fat side down. Place meat
  thermometer in center of thickest portion of
  meat.

- Roast uncovered about 2½ hours or until meat
  thermometer registers 170° to 175° (well done is
  180°).

- Garnish with mint leaves.

- Yield: 10 servings

Herb and Garlic Marinated Leg of Lamb

Beef and pork are not the only meats that are great tasting on a barbecue. Put a little excitement into your barbecuing—try lamb.

  1 **cup olive oil**
  1 **onion, sliced**
  ⅓ **cup dry white wine**
  ⅓ **cup fresh lemon juice**
  ⅓ **cup fresh parsley, chopped**
  3 **garlic cloves, minced**
1½ **tablespoons dried rosemary**
  2 **teaspoons Dijon mustard**
  ½ **teaspoon salt**
  ½ **teaspoon ground pepper**
  ¼ **teaspoon dried red pepper flakes**
  1 **(5 to 6-pound) leg of lamb, boned, butterflied and trimmed**

• To marinate lamb: a day in advance, combine oil, onion, wine, lemon juice, parsley, garlic, rosemary, Dijon mustard, salt, pepper, and red pepper flakes. Place lamb in a large roasting pan. Pour marinade over lamb. Cover, refrigerate and marinate overnight, turning at least once.

• When ready to cook: prepare barbecue grill with hot coals.

• Place lamb on grill and barbecue for 15 to 30 minutes per side. How do you know lamb is done? When tested with a two prong fork, juices should run pink not red.

• Yield: 10 servings

Olive oil can go rancid quickly in warm weather. Store in a cool, dark spot but not in the refrigerator. Only buy in a size you will use in two months.

Old Fashioned Lamb Shanks

Variety is so nutritious!...Three ounces of cooked lamb provides about 30% of the US RDA for zinc, niacin and B12.

1 (8-ounce) can tomato sauce
¼ cup brown sugar
1 cup white wine
1 large onion, sliced
1 teaspoon dill weed
½ teaspoon dried oregano
1 teaspoon dried rosemary
1 large garlic clove
1½ teaspoons salt
⅛ teaspoon pepper
4 lamb shanks (look for meaty shanks)

- Preheat oven to 300°.

- In a bowl, mix tomato sauce, brown sugar, wine, onion, dill weed, oregano, rosemary, clove, salt, and pepper.

- Place lamb in a roaster and pour sauce over lamb.

- Cover and cook for 3 hours. Remove cover and cook uncovered for 30 minutes.

- Pour sauce into another pan. Reduce by one-half over high heat.

- To serve: place meat on a serving platter and pour sauce over meat.

- Yield: 4 servings

Pork Chops Baroque

This recipe is prepared a day in advance.

¼ **cup dark raisins**
¼ **cup golden raisins**
¾ **cup brandy**
8 **(1-inch thick) pork loin chops**
  (4 pounds)
3 **tablespoons olive oil**
1 **(16-ounce) can white onions**
3 **tablespoons brown sugar**
1 **(6-ounce) can tomato paste**
⅓ **cup water**
3 **tablespoons red wine vinegar**
¾ **teaspoon dried thyme**
½ **teaspoon salt**
¼ **teaspoon pepper**

- Simmer raisins and brandy in a small saucepan over low heat for 1 minute. Cover and set aside.

- Sauté pork chops in batches in olive oil until browned. Remove from skillet and place in a 13 x 9-inch baking dish.

- Sauté onions in same skillet until lightly browned. Sprinkle onions with sugar, stirring constantly, until sugar melts. Stir in the raisin mixture, tomato paste, water, red wine vinegar, thyme, salt, and pepper. Bring to a boil, stirring to loosen browned particles of chops. Pour mixture over chops, cover with aluminum foil.

- Preheat oven to 350°.

- Bake for 1½ hours. Remove from oven and refrigerate overnight.

- Day of serving: bake covered at 350° for 30 minutes. Check to be sure liquid hasn't been completely absorbed. Add liquid if needed.

- Yield: 8 servings

- Per serving: 347 Calories • 41% Fat

Healthy Alternative Pork Chops Baroque

Simple changes: trim all visible fat from the pork chops. Use nonstick cooking spray and a nonstick skillet instead of oil. Per serving: 275 Calories • 23% Fat

Herbed Pork Roast with Roasted Redskin Potatoes

1 (2-pound) center cut, boneless roast of pork or 2 pounds of pork tenderloins
⅓ cup olive oil
2 garlic cloves, minced
2 teaspoons dried rosemary
2 teaspoons dried thyme
½ teaspoon salt
¼ teaspoon pepper
2½ pounds small redskin potatoes, quartered (4-5 cups)

- Preheat oven to 375°.

- Combine olive oil, garlic, rosemary, thyme, salt, and pepper in a large bowl.

- Place meat in a shallow baking pan. Coat meat with 3 tablespoons of seasoning mixture.

- Toss potatoes with remaining seasoning mixture. Arrange potatoes around meat.

- Roast 35 to 40 minutes until meat thermometer registers 155°, turning potatoes after 20 minutes. If potatoes are not browned or crispy, broil for 5 minutes.

- Yield: 8 servings

- Per serving: 388 Calories • 42% Fat

HA

Healthy Alternative Herbed Pork Roast with Roasted Redskin Potatoes

This dish is flavorful and succulent without added oil. After the meat and potatoes are placed in a roasting pan, spray the potatoes with nonstick cooking spray. Sprinkle the herbs over the pork roast and the potatoes. A fabulous, tasty juice forms from the pork roast. Per serving: 314 Calories • 23% Fat

According to ancient Chinese legend, it was a clumsy peasant boy, Bo-Bo, who, in burning down his father's pigsty, first tasted the joys of cooked pork. Today, it is "the other white meat!"

Tangy Pork

1 (4-pound) rolled and tied boneless pork loin
½ teaspoon salt
½ teaspoon garlic salt
2½ teaspoons chili powder, divided
1 cup apple jelly
1 cup ketchup
2 tablespoons vinegar

- Preheat oven to 325°.

- Rub roast with salt, garlic salt, and 1 teaspoon chili powder.

- Roast for 2 hours.

- Combine remaining chili powder, jelly, ketchup, and vinegar in saucepan and simmer.

- Brush on roast 15 minutes before roast is done. Mix ½ cup drippings from the bottom of the pan with sauce and serve with roast.

- Yield: 12 servings

Once upon a time, there were no tomatoes in ketchup. Originally a seasoning made from the brine of pickled fish, "ketsiap" was first brought to England from the Orient by sailors in the seventeenth and eighteenth centuries.

Elegant Stuffed Eggplant

1 medium eggplant (1 pound)
4 ounces bulk pork sausage, crumbled (1 cup)
1 tablespoon oil
1 small onion, chopped
1 small green pepper, chopped
1 garlic clove, minced
⅓ cup seasoned bread crumbs
2 tablespoons grated Parmesan cheese
½ teaspoon salt
1 cup marinara sauce

- Halve eggplant lengthwise. Scoop out pulp, leaving ½-inch shell. Chop pulp coarse.

- Heat oil in a medium skillet, sauté sausage over medium heat, for 3 minutes. Add onion, pepper, garlic and eggplant pulp. Sauté 5 minutes or until onion is tender. Stir in crumbs, Parmesan cheese, and salt. Spoon mixture into eggplant halves.

- Pour marinara sauce into skillet. Add eggplant halves, cover and simmer for 15 to 20 minutes or until eggplant shells are tender.

- To serve: place on serving dishes, spoon sauce over top. Add additional grated Parmesan cheese if desired.

- Yield: 2 servings

- Per serving: 436 Calories • 60% Fat

Eggplant is becoming increasingly popular. For a long time it was seen only on European-style menus, but it is much more widely used today. Eggplants should be firm, heavy in relation to size, with a uniformly dark, rich purple color.

Healthy Alternative
Elegant Stuffed Eggplant

*Turkey sausage, sweet Italian or hot, makes
a delicious replacement for pork sausage.
Even better news, turkey sausage contains
half the fat of regular sausage.*

1 **medium eggplant (1 pound)**
4 **ounces "Hot" turkey sausage, crumbled
   (1 cup)**
   nonstick cooking spray
1 **teaspoon olive oil**
1 **small onion, chopped**
1 **small green pepper, chopped**
1 **garlic clove, minced**
1 **cup cornflakes, crumbed (⅓ cup)**
2 **tablespoons grated Parmesan cheese**
2 **cups marinara sauce, divided**

- Halve eggplant lengthwise. Scoop out pulp, leaving ½-inch shell. Chop pulp coarse.

- Spray a medium skillet with nonstick cooking spray. Over medium heat, sauté sausage for 3 minutes. Add oil, onion, pepper, garlic, and eggplant pulp. Sauté 5 minutes or until onion is tender. Stir in crumbs and 1 cup of the marinara sauce.

- Spoon mixture into eggplant halves. Pour remaining 1 cup marinara sauce into a baking dish. Add eggplant. Seal baking dish with plastic wrap and then cover with aluminum foil.

- Bake for 25 minutes or until eggplant shells are tender.

- To serve: place on serving dishes, spoon sauce over top. Sprinkle with Parmesan cheese.

- Yield: 2 servings

- Per serving: 318 Calories • 38% Fat

Italian Veal Stew

1½ pounds veal, cut into 1½-inch cubes
¾ cup dry red wine
¼ cup flour
2 tablespoons unsalted butter
2 tablespoons olive oil
½ pound HOT Italian sausage, cut into ½-inch slices
1 medium onion, chopped (1 cup)
1 garlic clove, minced
1 (16-ounce) can plum tomatoes (or 5 ripe tomatoes, peeled)
1 cup chicken stock
1 tablespoon fresh basil or 1 teaspoon dried basil
½ teaspoon dried rosemary, crushed
salt
pepper
juice from ½ small lemon (1 tablespoon)
1 large red bell pepper, cut into ⅛-inch slices
1 large green bell pepper, cut into ⅛-inch slices
½ pound mushrooms, sliced
¼ cup chopped fresh parsley
1 teaspoon grated lemon peel

- A day in advance; pour wine over veal and marinate veal for 1½ hours in the refrigerator. Drain and reserve marinade.

- Pat meat dry, lightly dust with flour. Sauté in butter and oil in a deep heavy Dutch oven until lightly browned. Remove veal and set aside.

- In same pan, brown sausage and set aside.

Healthy Alternative Italian Veal Stew

Brown the veal cubes in 1 tablespoon of oil in a nonstick skillet, sprayed with nonstick cooking spray. Use turkey sausage instead of the regular Italian sausage. Amazing, but true, the turkey sausage is hard to distinguish from the "real stuff" in our Healthy Alternative Italian Veal Stew.
Per serving: 276 Calories • 47% Fat

(recipe continued on next page)

(Italian Veal Stew, continued)

- Sauté onions and garlic until lightly browned (don't let garlic burn as it will become bitter). Add reserved marinade, tomatoes, stock, basil, and rosemary to the pan. Stir and scrape up brown bits. Boil 5 minutes.

- Return veal and sausage to the pan. Add salt, pepper, and lemon juice. Reduce heat and simmer covered for 1 hour. Cool. Refrigerate overnight.

- Take out of refrigerator and remove fat from surface.

- Reheat. Add peppers and mushrooms and simmer 30 minutes.

- To serve: garnish with parsley and lemon peel. Serve over wide noodles with a green salad.

- Yield: 6 servings

- Per serving: 382 Calories • 57% Fat

"The Excellent and Approved Receipts from a Choice Manuscript of Sir Thomas Mayerne Knight", London (1658), was among the first English cookbooks to sanction veal as a suitable food. Since Saxon times, killing a healthy calf had been considered wanton and typical of the odious behavior of conquering Normans.

Simply Stroganoff

4 **pounds veal cubes**
½ **cup butter, divided**
½ **teaspoon salt**
⅛ **teaspoon pepper**
3 **(10¾-ounce) cans cream of mushroom soup (undiluted)**
3 **large onions, sliced (3 cups)**
¼ **cup water**
½ **teaspoon seasoned salt**
¼ **teaspoon hot sauce**
¼ **cup dry sherry**
1 **cup low-fat sour cream**

- Preheat oven to 375°.

- Heat ¼ cup of the butter in a skillet. Brown veal cubes in skillet one half at a time. Place meat in roasting pan. Add salt and pepper. Cover with cream of mushroom soup.

- Heat ¼ cup of the butter and sauté onion in skillet until soft and lightly browned. Spoon on top of veal.

- Add ¼ cup water, seasoned salt, and hot sauce to the skillet. Heat and stir to deglaze pan. Pour over meat and onion.

- Bake covered for 45 minutes. Uncover and add sherry. Bake an additional 35 minutes. Add sour cream and mix lightly. Bake 10 more minutes, just until heated through.

- Serve over noodles.

- Yield: 12 servings

- Per serving: 504 Calories • 42% Fat

HA
Healthy Alternative
Simply Stroganoff

4 pounds veal cubes
  nonstick cooking spray
½ teaspoon salt
⅛ teaspoon pepper
3 (10¾-ounce) cans low-fat cream of
  mushroom soup (undiluted)
3 large onions, sliced (3 cups)
½ cup vegetable broth, divided
½ teaspoon seasoned salt
¼ teaspoon hot sauce
¼ cup dry sherry
1 cup low-fat sour cream

- Preheat oven to 375°.

- Spray a large skillet with nonstick cooking spray. Brown veal cubes in skillet one half at a time. Place meat in large roaster. Add salt and pepper and cover with low-fat cream of mushroom soup.

- Heat ¼ cup of the vegetable broth in a skillet and sauté onion until soft and lightly browned. Spoon on top of veal.

- Add remaining vegetable broth, seasoned salt, and hot sauce to skillet. Heat and stir to deglaze pan. Pour over meat and onion.

- Bake covered for 45 minutes. Uncover and add sherry. Bake an additional 35 minutes. Add low-fat sour cream and mix lightly. Bake 10 more minutes, just until heated through.

- Serve over noodles.

- Yield: 12 servings

- Per serving: 398 Calories • 30% Fat

Veal Alla Romano

1 cup plus 1 tablespoon of flour
1 teaspoon rosemary
1 teaspoon dill weed
1 tablespoon paprika
1 teaspoon salt
½ teaspoon pepper
1 pound veal, cut into 1-inch cubes
12 tablespoons (1½ sticks) butter, divided
2 garlic cloves, minced
¾ cup rosé wine
1 medium onion, diced
2 carrots, pared and diagonally sliced
1 celery stalk, sliced
½ cup beef broth
½ cup water
¼ cup vegetable juice
1 bay leaf
1 teaspoon tarragon

- Preheat oven to 350°.

- Combine 1 cup of the flour, rosemary, dill weed, paprika, salt, and pepper in a plastic bag. Add veal cubes to flour mixture and shake to coat.

- In a skillet, melt 4 tablespoons of the butter. Add garlic and sauté until slightly browned. Add veal cubes and brown on all sides. Transfer meat to a 1-quart casserole.

- Deglaze skillet with wine and add to casserole.

- In a separate pan, melt 4 tablespoons of the butter. Sauté onions until lightly browned. Add to casserole.

- To the casserole, add the carrots, celery, beef broth, water, vegetable juice, bay

Healthy Alternative Veal Alla Romano
Substitute 2 tablespoons of olive oil for the butter and sauté onions in ¼ cup of beef broth.
Per serving: 270 Calories • 38% Fat

(recipe continued on next page)

(Veal Alla Romano, continued)

leaf, and tarragon. Cover and bake for 1 hour and 30 minutes.

- To make gravy, melt remaining 4 tablespoons of the butter in a small skillet. Stir in 1 tablespoon of flour and mix until thickened. Stir into casserole. Season to taste.

- Serve over noodles or rice.

- Yield: 4 servings

- Per serving: 532 Calories • 70% Fat

All cuts of veal are generally considered lean. How to brown veal with as little fat as possible is a neat trick. The secret is the right skillet and the right HEAT. Spray a nonstick skillet with nonstick cooking spray and heat to smoking. Brown the veal in batches.

A Taste of Tuscany

Layered Shrimp Spread

Warm Spinach-Arugula-Basil Salad with Pinenuts and Roasted Pepper

Veal Alla Romano

Garlic Bread

Columbia Crest Merlot

Mocha "Good" Ice Cream Pie

Veal Stew Marsala

A hearty, economical, and low-fat one-dish supper that will warm the soul on even the most blustery winter evening.

2 **pounds veal cubes**
¼ **cup flour**
2 **tablespoons olive oil**
1 **(13¾-ounce) can chicken broth**
2 **pounds small white boiling onions**
2 **medium onions, finely chopped (1½ cups)**
1 **teaspoon fines herbes**
  salt
  pepper to taste
5 **garlic cloves, minced**
2 **carrots, cubed (1 cup) or 12 baby carrots**
3 **celery stalks, chopped**
1 **pound button mushrooms**
½ **cup dry Marsala wine**
½ **cup sweet Marsala wine**

- Preheat oven to 325°.

- Dredge veal in flour. In small batches, brown cubed veal in olive oil. Place in an ovenproof casserole dish.

- Add chicken broth, onions, and garlic. Add fines herbes and season to taste with salt and pepper. Cover and cook for 1 to 1½ hours.

- Add carrots and celery. (Baby carrots make a nice presentation in stew.)

- Cook for 1 hour more. Add mushrooms and wine. (The flour from dredging should provide enough for thickening.)

- Serve over noodles.

- Yield: 6 servings

Prosciutto & Provolone Sandwiches

1 tablespoon olive oil
1 red onion, thinly sliced
2 tablespoons fresh pesto or ready made
½ cup mayonnaise
1 large round Portuguese or sourdough
    bread, sliced in half horizontally
½ pound prosciutto, thinly sliced
¼ pound provolone cheese, thinly sliced

- Preheat oven to 350°.

- Heat olive oil in a skillet. Sauté onions until slightly softened, but not overcooked.

- Combine pesto and mayonnaise. Spread both sides of sliced bread with pesto mix. Place prosciutto, provolone, and onions on bottom half of bread. Top with top half of bread. Cut into four wedges. Wrap each in aluminum foil.

- Bake 10 to 15 minutes, until cheese starts to melt. Serve warm.

- Yield: 4 servings

- Per serving: 780 Calories • 48% Fat

"Life itself is the proper binge."
— *Julia Child*

Healthy Alternative Vegetable Provolone Sandwiches

Saturday afternoon sandwich treat.

1 **red onion, thinly sliced**
1 **small yellow zucchini, sliced into ¼-inch slices**
1 **small green zucchini, sliced into ¼-inch slices**
½ **red bell pepper, julienned**
1 **small eggplant, sliced horizontally into ¼-inch slices**
  nonstick cooking spray
2 **tablespoons fresh pesto or ready made**
¼ **cup low-fat mayonnaise**
1 **large round Portuguese or sourdough bread, sliced in half horizontally**
¼ **pound provolone cheese, thinly sliced**

- Preheat oven to 350°.

- Arrange onions, zucchini, red bell pepper, and eggplant on a cookie sheet. Spray with nonstick cooking spray. Bake for 25 minutes until browned. Set aside.

- Combine pesto and low-fat mayonnaise.

- Spread both sides of sliced bread with pesto mix. Place vegetables on bottom half of bread. Top with provolone. Cover with top half of bread. Cut into four wedges. Wrap each in aluminum foil.

- Bake for 10 to 15 minutes, until cheese starts to melt. Serve warm.

- Yield: 4 servings

- Per serving: 495 Calories • 14% Fat

Apple Cider, Onion & Raisin Chutney

This condiment freezes well.

3 cups apple cider
¼ cup cider vinegar
1 (10-ounce) package frozen pearl onions
½ cup raisins
¼ cup light brown sugar, packed
  pinch ground cloves or cinnamon
½ cup chopped apples (optional)

- Mix all ingredients in a large sauce pan and simmer, stirring occasionally until it is reduced to a syrup consistency. If desired, add chopped apples.

Cranberry-Orange Chutney

1 pound fresh or frozen cranberries
1½ cups light brown sugar, packed
¾ cup red wine vinegar
⅓ cup raisins
1 orange, unpeeled, thinly sliced, and seeded
1 pear, pared, cored, and diced
2 tablespoons grated fresh ginger
1 cup chopped walnuts
½ teaspoon curry powder
¼ teaspoon dry mustard
¼ teaspoon allspice

- Combine all ingredients in a large sauce pan. Bring to a boil over medium heat. Simmer uncovered until thickened, stirring frequently. Pour into jars and store in refrigerator for one week before serving.

- Yield: 5 cups

Stuffed Italian Sandwich

*This is a great dish when hungry boys come home
from a Saturday afternoon touch football game.*

> 1 **cup oil-cured Sicilian olives, chopped**
> 1 **cup Kalamata olives, chopped**
> 3 **anchovies packed in oil**
> ½ **cup marinated artichoke hearts, drained**
> ½ **cup marinated whole pimentos, drained**
> 2 **garlic cloves, minced**
> ½ **cup mixed chopped basil, parsley and**
>   **fennel leaves**
> 1 **tablespoon extra virgin olive oil**
> ½ **pound Genoa salami, thinly sliced**
> ½ **pound prosciutto, thinly sliced**
> ½ **pound capicola, thinly sliced**
> ½ **pound mozzarella cheese, sliced**
> ½ **pound provolone cheese, sliced**
> 1 **2-pound round loaf Italian bread**
>   **(9 to 10-inch diameter)**

- Place the olives, anchovies, artichokes, and
  pimentos in a food processor and pulse to
  coarsely chopped. Transfer the mixture to a
  bowl.

- Add the garlic, herbs, and olive oil. Mix well.
  Cover and let stand at room temperature for 1
  hour.

- With a bread knife, cut ½-inch slice off the top
  of the bread and set aside. With your fingers,
  hollow out the inside of the bread, leaving a
  ½-inch wall and base.

- To assemble: place one-half of the marinated
  salad in the hollowed-out bread, spreading it as
  evenly as possible. Then place alternating
  layers of the meats and cheese on the top of the
  salad until all the ingredients are used. Press
  down each layer with your hand as you add it.
  Spread the remaining salad evenly on top of
  the last layer. Replace the bread top.

(recipe continued on next page)

(Stuffed Italian Sandwich, continued)

- Wrap loaf tightly in foil and place a three-pound weight on top
- Refrigerate the loaf for at least 6 hours or overnight.
- Remove the weight and foil, cut the loaf into wedges and serve.
- Yield: 8-10 servings

Pepper Relish

Serve with beef, pork or chicken.

3 **large peppers (2 green & 1 red)**
3 **medium onions**
¾ **cup sugar**
¾ **cup vinegar**
1 **tablespoon mustard seed**
2-3 **crumbled cloves**

- Coarsely chop peppers and onions in blender in scalding water. Drain.
- Mix peppers, onions, sugar, vinegar, mustard seed, and crumbled cloves in saucepan. Bring to a boil and simmer 10 minutes.
- Spoon into jars. After 10 minutes, add juice to cover (relish soaks up juice). Freezes well.
- Yield: 2 pints

Hot Fruit Compote

½ cup each of prunes, pears, peaches,
  pineapple
1½ cups applesauce
 1 teaspoon cinnamon
½ teaspoon ginger
½ teaspoon nutmeg
  juice of ½ lemon and its peel, chopped

- Combine fruits with applesauce in a casserole.
  Add cinnamon, ginger, and nutmeg. Add
  lemon juice and peel. Mix.

- Place covered in a 250° oven for at least 1 hour,
  longer if desired, before serving. Other fruits
  can be substituted and either fresh or canned
  fruits may be used.

- Yield: 6 servings

Cranberry Relish

Serve with turkey, chicken or pork.

 1 quart fresh cranberries
 2 whole oranges
 2 whole apples, cored but not peeled
 1 lemon, seeded
 2 cups sugar
½ teaspoon cinnamon
½ teaspoon nutmeg
 1 cup chopped nuts (optional)

- Coarsely grind cranberries, oranges, apples and
  lemon. Stir in sugar, cinnamon and nutmeg.
  Simmer for 5 to 10 minutes in a saucepan. Stir
  in nuts. Refrigerate overnight to allow the
  flavors to blend.

- Yield: 12 servings

Rich Raisin Sauce for Ham

Serve with baked ham, ham steak, or pork. Fabulous!

> 1 cup raisins
> 1 cup white wine
> ¼ cup orange marmalade
> 1 cinnamon stick
> 3 tablespoons lemon juice
> ½ teaspoon nutmeg
>   pepper
> 1 cup mayonnaise

- In a bowl, soak the raisins in the wine for 24 hours.

- Transfer the mixture to a sauce pan and heat it. Add the marmalade and the cinnamon stick and simmer the mixture over low heat, stirring until the marmalade is melted. Discard the cinnamon stick and add the lemon juice, nutmeg, and pepper.

- Remove from heat and let stand for 5 minutes. Stir in the mayonnaise.

- Chill and serve.

- Yield: 2 cups

"Cooking is like love — is should be entered into with abandon or not at all."
— Anonymous

Annapolis Crab Cakes

Serve with a dry California chenin blanc.

1 pound fresh crabmeat (backfin preferred)
1 large egg, beaten
1 tablespoon mayonnaise
dash Worcestershire sauce
1 teaspoon salt
½ teaspoon Old Bay seasoning
1 teaspoon dry mustard
¾ cup fresh bread crumbs
oil for frying

- Pick through crabmeat and remove any cartilage. Try to keep the pieces of crab as large as possible.

- Line a baking sheet with wax paper.

- Mix egg, mayonnaise, Worcestershire sauce, salt, Old Bay seasoning, and mustard in a large bowl. Gently add bread crumbs and crab.

- Shape the mixture into four large crab cakes. Place the crab cakes on baking sheet. Cover with plastic wrap and refrigerate for 2 hours or longer.

- Remove from refrigerator and sauté the crab cakes in ¼-inch of oil in a frying pan for about 3 to 6 minutes, depending on size, until golden brown. Drain on paper towels.

- Yield: 4 servings

- Per serving: 330 Calories • 57% Fat

As a lovely touch for a fish dish, make lemon or lime twists. Just cut into a citrus slice from the edge to the center, then twist in opposite directions.

HA
Healthy Alternative
Annapolis Crab Cakes

*These tasty low-fat crab cakes
will delight your family and friends.*

1 **pound fresh crabmeat (backfin preferred)**
  nonstick cooking spray
¼ **cup egg substitute**
1 **tablespoon low-fat mayonnaise**
  dash Worcestershire sauce
1 **teaspoon salt**
½ **teaspoon Old Bay seasoning**
1 **teaspoon dry mustard**
2 **cups cornflakes, crumbled (⅔ cup)**

- Pick through crabmeat and remove any cartilage. Try to keep the pieces of crab as large as possible.

- Spray a baking sheet with nonstick cooking spray.

- Mix egg substitute, low fat mayonnaise, Worcestershire sauce, salt, Old Bay seasoning, and mustard together. Gently add cornflake crumbs and crab.

- Shape the mixture into four large crab cakes. Place the crab cakes on a baking sheet. Cover with plastic wrap and refrigerate for 2 hours or longer.

- Remove from refrigerator and broil 6 inches from flame for 5 minutes on each side until golden brown.

- Yield: 4 servings

- Per serving: 161 Calories • 12% Fat

Crab Casserole

nonstick cooking spray
2 pounds fresh crabmeat (backfin preferred)
4 slices bread, crusts removed
1 cup (2 sticks) butter, divided
4 cups whole milk
¾ cup flour
salt
pepper
hot sauce to taste
Worcestershire sauce to taste

- Preheat oven to 350°.

- Spray a casserole dish with nonstick cooking spray.

- Pick through crabmeat and remove cartilage.

- To make topping: make bread crumbs from bread. Melt 4 tablespoons of the butter and mix into bread crumbs. Set aside.

- Melt the remaining butter in a saucepan. Mix in flour. With a whisk, stir in milk until thickened. Season to taste. Sauce should be "hot" in flavor. Fold in crabmeat and place in a casserole dish.

- Bake until bubbly, about 15 to 20 minutes. Remove from oven and sprinkle with bread crumb topping. Bake an additional 5 to 10 minutes until topping is golden brown.

- Yield: 10 servings

- Per serving: 364 Calories • 62% Fat

Healthy Alternative Crab Casserole

A delicious low-fat cream sauce makes this crab casserole a hit!

nonstick cooking spray
2 pounds crabmeat (backfin preferred)
2 cups cornflakes, crumbled (⅔ cup)
2 teaspoons butter, melted
2 (12-ounce) cans evaporated skim milk
2 tablespoons cornstarch
salt
pepper
hot sauce to taste
Worcestershire sauce to taste

- Preheat oven to 350°.

- Spray a casserole dish with nonstick cooking spray.

- Pick through crabmeat and remove cartilage.

- To make topping: mix melted butter with cornflake crumbs. Set aside.

- Mix cornstarch with evaporated skim milk in a saucepan. Heat until thickened. Season to taste—sauce should be "hot" in flavor. Fold in crabmeat and place in casserole dish.

- Bake until bubbly, about 15 to 20 minutes. Remove from oven and sprinkle with cornflake topping. Bake an additional 5 to 10 minutes until topping is golden brown.

- Yield: 10 servings

- Per serving: 166 Calories • 14% Fat

Baked Crabmeat Remick

Feeding body and soul.

nonstick cooking spray
1 **pound crabmeat**
6 **bacon slices, cooked, drained, and crumbled**
1 **teaspoon dry mustard**
½ **teaspoon paprika**
½ **teaspoon celery salt**
few drops hot sauce
½ **cup chili sauce**
1 **teaspoon tarragon vinegar**
1¾ **cups mayonnaise**

- Preheat oven to 350°.

- Spray six shells with nonstick cooking spray.

- Pick through crabmeat and remove any cartilage. Pile crabmeat in shells.

- Top each with some crumbled bacon. Bake in oven for 10 minutes.

- Mix together mustard, paprika, celery salt, hot sauce, chili sauce, tarragon vinegar, and mayonnaise. Spread the warm crabmeat with the sauce and glaze under the broiler.

- Yield: 6 servings

- Per serving: 445 Calories • 78% Fat

Crabs are the second most popular shellfish in the United States (shrimp is first). The hard-shell, or blue, crab of the Atlantic, the Dungeness of the Pacific, and the Alaskan king crab are the most readily available.

Healthy Alternative
Baked Crabmeat Remick

Feeding body, soul and heart.

nonstick cooking spray
1 pound crabmeat
2 bacon slices, cooked, drained, and crumbled
1 teaspoon chicken bouillon granules
2 tablespoons cornstarch
1 cup evaporated skim milk
1 teaspoon dry mustard
½ teaspoon paprika
½ teaspoon celery salt
 few drops hot sauce
½ cup chili sauce
1 teaspoon tarragon vinegar
½ cup low fat mayonnaise

- Preheat oven to 350°

- Spray six shells with nonstick cooking spray.

- Pick through crabmeat and remove any cartilage. Pile crabmeat in shells and top each with some crumbled bacon.

- Make a velouté by dissolving bouillon granules and cornstarch in evaporated skim milk. Heat until thick. Add mustard, paprika, celery salt, hot sauce, chili sauce, tarragon vinegar, and mayonnaise.

- Spread about 2 tablespoons of sauce over each shell.

- Bake for 15 minutes. If topping is not bubbly and golden brown, glaze under the broiler.

- Yield: 6 servings

- Per serving: 188 Calories • 22% Fat

Mom Gandolfo's Spaghetti and Crabs

Italian soul food…Abbondanza!

2 (28-ounce) cans whole tomatoes, puréed
    in blender
2 (16-ounce) cans Italian-flavored salsa
4 garlic cloves
½ cup olive oil
2 (2-pound) bags frozen crabs, thawed,
    washed, fins removed (on the back side of
    the crabs), and broken in half
1 pound spaghetti # 9, cooked al dente

- Simmer tomatoes and salsa for ½ hour.

- In a large pan, sauté garlic in olive oil, until soft but not brown.

- Add crabs and mix until the crabs turn a reddish color.

- Add tomato sauce and simmer for an hour.

- To serve: remove crabs from pot and place on a serving dish. Put the cooked spaghetti in a separate large serving bowl. Pour sauce over spaghetti.

- Yield: 4 servings

"The trouble with eating Italian food is that five or six days later, you're hungry again."
— George Miller

Fisherman's Delight

nonstick cooking spray
½ **pound fresh crabmeat**
1 **(8½-ounce) can artichoke hearts (not marinated), drained**
½ **pound medium shrimp, cooked, peeled, and deveined**
2 **tablespoons plus 2 teaspoons butter**
½ **pound mushrooms, sliced**
2½ **tablespoons flour**
½ **teaspoon salt**
¼ **teaspoon pepper**
1 **cup heavy cream**
1 **tablespoon Worcestershire sauce**
2 **tablespoons dry sherry**
½ **cup grated Parmesan cheese**
lemon wedges
fresh parsley

- Preheat oven to 350°.

- Spray a 2-quart casserole dish with nonstick cooking spray.

- Pick through crabmeat and remove any cartilage.

- Arrange artichoke hearts, crabmeat, and shrimp on bottom of casserole dish.

- In a skillet, heat 2 tablespoons of butter and sauté mushrooms for 5 minutes. Add to casserole dish.

- Melt remaining 2 teaspoons of butter in a saucepan and whisk in the flour, salt, pepper, and cayenne pepper. Add heavy cream and whisk until smooth. Add Worcestershire sauce and sherry.

- Pour sauce over crab mixture and sprinkle with Parmesan. Bake for 30 minutes. Garnish with lemon wedges and parsley.

- Yield: 4 servings

- Per serving: 369 Calories • 60% Fat

Is there any easier way to remove cartilage from crabmeat? Spread the crabmeat on a baking sheet and bake in a 350° oven for 1 to 2 minutes (do not overbake). The cartilage will turn white and will be easier to remove. A helpful tip brought to you by the chefs at Cooper.

HA
Healthy Alternative
Fisherman's Delight

nonstick cooking spray
½ **pound mushrooms, sliced**
½ **pound fresh crabmeat**
1 **(8½-ounce) can artichoke hearts (not marinated), drained**
½ **pound medium shrimp, cooked, peeled, and deveined**
1 **teaspoon chicken bouillon granules**
2 **tablespoons cornstarch**
8 **ounces evaporated skim milk**
½ **teaspoon salt**
¼ **teaspoon pepper**
dash cayenne pepper
1 **tablespoon Worcestershire sauce**
2 **tablespoons dry sherry**
½ **cup grated Parmesan cheese**
lemon wedges
fresh parsley

- Preheat oven to 350°.

- Spray a 2-quart casserole dish with nonstick cooking spray.

- Place mushrooms on a large piece of aluminum foil and seal. Bake for 30 minutes.

- Pick through crab and remove any cartilage.

- Arrange artichoke hearts, crabmeat and shrimp on bottom of casserole dish. Add cooked mushrooms.

- Dissolve chicken bouillon granules and cornstarch in evaporated skim milk. Heat until thick. Whisk in salt, pepper, cayenne pepper, Worcestershire sauce, and sherry.

- Pour sauce over crab mixture and sprinkle with Parmesan.

(recipe continued on next page)

(Healthy Alternative Fisherman's Delight, continued)

- Bake for 30 minutes. Garnish with lemon wedges and parsley.
- Yield: 4 servings
- Per serving: 193 Calories • 24% Fat

Fishing for Compliments

Eat to your heart's content.

1½ pounds fresh fish filet (flounder, orange roughy)
¾ cup salsa
2 tablespoons mayonnaise
2 tablespoons honey
2 tablespoons Dijon mustard

- Preheat oven to 450°.
- Cut fish into bite size portions. Put in baking dish and bake uncovered 4 to 6 minutes (until fish is flaky). Remove from oven and drain liquid.
- Mix salsa, mayonnaise, honey, and mustard in a bowl. Spoon over fish.
- Return fish to oven for 2 to 3 minutes, until heated through.
- Serve with rice and a colorful vegetable.
- Yield: 6 servings

Grilled Marinated Bluefish

      2 **large or 4 medium bluefish filets**
        milk
      ½ **cup lemon juice**
      ½ **cup soy sauce**
      3 **tablespoons ketchup**
      1 **large scallion, minced**
    3-4 **garlic cloves**
      ½ **teaspoon pepper**

- Soak filets in milk overnight. Next day, drain and pat dry.

- Combine remaining ingredients and marinate bluefish for several hours.

- Grill over medium coals (or broil) for 10 minutes per inch thickness of fish.

- Yield: 4 servings

Baked Shad

A special recipe to celebrate shad season.

      1 **(1-pound) shad filet**
        salt
        pepper
      2 **slices bacon**
        lemon wedges

- Preheat oven to 375°.

- Place shad in a baking dish, sprinkle with salt and pepper. Top with bacon slices.

- Bake about 35 minutes or until bacon is crisp. Serve with lemon wedges. Boiled new potatoes and fresh Jersey asparagus are a nice accompaniment

- Yield: 2 servings

Orange Roughy Marrakech

For a Middle Eastern change of pace.

1 **pound orange roughy, cut into 4 pieces**
nonstick cooking spray
1 **tablespoon grated fresh ginger, divided**
¼ **cup orange juice**
1 **cup white wine**

- Spray skillet with nonstick spray. Sprinkle ½ teaspoon of the ginger on bottom of pan.

- Place fish in skillet. Sprinkle remaining ginger on top of fish. Pour orange juice and wine along the sides.

- Sauté fish approximately 8 minutes. Sauce will thicken slightly. Excellent on rice.

- Yield: 4 servings

Peeled and sliced fresh ginger root keeps well in pale dry sherry. Refrigerate and use as needed.

𝔸rabian 𝔑ights 𝔇elights

Roasted Spring Garlic

Orange Roughy Marrakech

Scattered Confetti Rice Salad

Middle Eastern Flat Bread

*Robert Mondavi
Chardonnay Reserve*

Peanut Brittle Cheese Cake

Savory Baked Salmon Dill-Jonnaise

Combining the light bite of a good Dijon mustard with the piquancy of dill weed, this modified dijonnaise sauce-marinade wonderfully compliments the flaky soft fullness of a fine Norwegian salmon filet. Serve it with a light and dry white wine…we'd recommend a Pinot Grigio or an Est! Est! Est!!

nonstick cooking spray
1 **(2-pound) salmon filet**
  juice of 2 lemons, strained
2 **tablespoons extra-virgin olive oil**
½ **cup dry white wine**
1 **tablespoon balsamic vinegar**
4 **tablespoons Dijon mustard**
1 **teaspoon prepared horseradish**
1 **teaspoon garlic powder**
2 **teaspoons dill weed**
1 **teaspoon finely chopped parsley**
3 **tablespoons capers, drained and rinsed**

Keep the flavor of your mustard fresh by placing a thin slice of lemon under the lid of the jar.

- Lightly spray a broiler pan with nonstick cooking spray.

- Thoroughly rinse and pat dry the salmon, place it skin side down on broiler pan.

- Combine the lemon juice, olive oil, wine, vinegar, mustard, horseradish, garlic powder, dill weed, parsley, and capers in a small bowl. Whisk vigorously until smooth.

- Baste salmon filet with about one-quarter of the sauce. Refrigerate basted salmon for at least 30 minutes after basting.

- Preheat oven to 450°.

(recipe continued on next page)

(Savory Baked Salmon Dill-Jonnaise, continued)

- Remove salmon from refrigerator. Bake on the middle rack of the oven. Baste once with one-quarter of the sauce. Baking time is approximately 10 minutes per inch of thickness of salmon filet.

- When finished baking, turn filet over carefully and remove skin by scraping with a dull knife edge. Turn filet right side up again, divide into six portions and place on dinner plates. Heat reserved sauce in microwave oven for 3 minutes, and spoon over filet portions.

- Yield: 6 servings

Salmon Steak Supreme

A dinner party treat, yet simple enough to make everyday.

2 salmon steaks (about ½-pound each and 1-inch thick)
Dijon mustard
dried dill weed
honey

Don't avoid this fabulous recipe because salmon is a "fatty" fish. Salmon contains a heart protective type of fat.

- Preheat oven to 350°.

- Line glass baking dish with foil.

- Rinse salmon steaks and pat dry. Place steaks on foil. Spread with mustard and sprinkle with dill. Drizzle with honey.

- Bake 20 to 30 minutes.

- Yield: 2 servings

Boca Raton Shrimp

*Serve this, and your friends might think
there is a chef hiding in your kitchen.
No one need know how easy it is.*

4 tablespoons butter
½ pound large shrimp, peeled and deveined
2 tablespoons shallots, minced
½ dry white wine
¼ cup Pernod
½ cup minced scallions

- Heat the butter in a skillet until foaming. Add the shrimp and sauté, stirring until pink (about 3 minutes). Transfer shrimp with a slotted spoon to a plate and keep warm.

- Add shallots to skillet and sauté over low heat for 1 minute. Add the wine and reduce it over high heat to about ¼ cup. Add the Pernod and scallions and cook 1 minute.

- Return shrimp and heat 1 minute. Serve over rice.

- Yield: 2 servings

"We have observed in France that those who live almost entirely on shellfish and fish...are more ardent in love than others."
— *Dr. Nicholas Venette*

Shrimp Orleans

If you don't have a cup of seafood stock in your refrigerator, use one of the new and great tasting cans of vegetable broth from your grocery store.

1 tablespoon paprika
¼ teaspoon cayenne
1½ teaspoons onion powder
1½ teaspoons garlic powder
½ teaspoon pepper
½ teaspoon dried oregano
½ teaspoon dried thyme
½ teaspoon white pepper
2 tablespoons olive oil
1 pound medium shrimp, peeled and deveined
2 large onlons, chopped (2 cups)
1 large green pepper, chopped (1 cup)
1 large rib celery, chopped (½ cup)
1½ cups white wine
6 medium garlic cloves, minced
4 medium tomatoes, chopped (2 cups)
1 cup seafood stock or vegetable broth
6 cups cooked rice

- Combine paprika, cayenne, basil, onion powder, garlic powder, pepper, oregano, thyme, and white pepper in a bowl.

- Sprinkle half of seasoning mixture over shrimp and set aside.

- Preheat a 10-inch skillet with olive oil. Sauté onions, green pepper, and celery. Add remaining seasoning mix to vegetables and cook until vegetables brown. Add wine and garlic to mixture, stir to clear bottom of skillet. Cook vegetables until soft and pan is dry. Add tomatoes and seafood stock and bring to a boil.

- Add shrimp and cook until shrimp is pink and plump (about 4 minutes).

- Serve over rice.

- Yield: 4 servings

Shrimp & Pea Skillet

1½ **pounds shrimp, peeled, and deveined**
1 **(8-ounce) can water chestnuts, drained and sliced**
¼ **cup vegetable oil**
1 **(10-ounce) package frozen green peas**
1 **(4-ounce) can sliced mushrooms, undrained**
1½ **teaspoons salt**
¼ **teaspoon pepper**
1 **tablespoon soy sauce**
1 **tablespoon cornstarch**
½ **cup water**

- Heat oil in a large skillet over medium heat. Sauté shrimp until pink.

- Add water chestnuts, peas, mushrooms, and mushroom liquid. Sprinkle with salt, pepper, and soy sauce. Cover and simmer 4 to 5 minutes.

- Mix cornstarch with water and add to shrimp mixture. Cook, mixing well, until sauce is clear and thickens. Cook an additional 2 minutes. Serve over rice.

- Yield: 6 servings

- Per serving: 236 Calories • 40% Fat

HA

Healthy Alternative Shrimp & Pea Skillet

Use 2 tablespoons of oil to stir fry. Cooper-tested and rated: "Can't tell the difference from the original!"
Per serving: 195 Calories • 27% Fat

Shrimp Sizes:

Jumbo	10 per pound
Large	10 - 25 per pound
Medium	25 - 40 per pound
Small	40 - 60 per pound

Shrimp Plaka Style—
Greek (Garides à la Plaka)

Fabulous!

2 pounds extra large shrimp, peeled and
   deveined
½ cup olive oil
½ dry white wine
¼ cup lemon juice
5 garlic cloves, minced
1 teaspoon dried oregano
3 tablespoons finely chopped parsley
   salt
   pepper

• Preheat oven to 375°.

• Arrange shrimp in a shallow dish.

• Combine olive oil, wine, lemon juice, garlic,
oregano, parsley, salt, and pepper. Pour over
shrimp.

• Bake 15 minutes or until shrimp turn pink.

• Yield: 6 servings

*Serve with lots of hot crusty bread, a huge green
salad, simply dressed, and a decadent dessert
such as Midnight Lace Cake.*

Shrimp Scampi and Bell Pepper

2 pounds large unpeeled shrimp
3 tablespoons butter
1 large red pepper, chopped
8 medium garlic cloves, crushed
½ cup dry white wine
¼ cup minced parsley
   juice of 1 large lemon (¼ cup)
½ teaspoon salt
¼ teaspoon pepper
   paprika
1 pound of angel hair pasta, cooked al dente

- Peel shrimp leaving tails intact. Starting at tail end, butterfly underside of each shrimp, cutting to but not through the back of shrimp. Arrange shrimp, cut side up, in a large dish that the shrimp can be broiled in.

- Melt butter in a small skillet. Add bell pepper and garlic. Sauté 2 minutes.

- Remove from heat. Stir in wine, parsley, lemon juice, salt, and pepper.

- Spoon wine mixture evenly over shrimp. Sprinkle with paprika. Broil 6 minutes until shrimp is pink.

- Serve over angel hair pasta.

- Yield: 6 servings

Shrimp Scampi with Wine

Mama Mia! That's good.

2 tablespoons butter
juice of 1 large lemon
1 (16-ounce) can stewed tomatoes
2 cups white wine
1 (8-ounce) can tomato sauce
12 garlic cloves, minced (2 tablespoons)
3 tablespoons dried parsley
salt
pepper
1 pound medium shrimp, peeled, and deveined
1 pound linguini pasta, cooked al dente
lemon slices
sprig of fresh parsley

- Melt the butter in a large skillet. Add lemon juice, tomatoes, wine, tomato sauce, garlic, parsley, salt, and pepper. Boil until mixture decreases to half of its volume.

- Reduce heat to medium and add shrimp. Cook for approximately 5 minutes until shrimp turns pink. Remove shrimp and boil sauce for an additional 5 minutes.

- To serve: place the pasta on a flat serving dish. Pour the sauce over the pasta and toss. Arrange the shrimp on top of the pasta. Garnish with lemon and parsley. Serve immediately.

- Yield: 4 servings

Citron Oriental Swordfish

For a real treat, serve leftover Citron Oriental Swordfish on a plate of spring mix salad greens and top with Poppy Seed Dressing.

8 (5 to 6-ounce) swordfish steaks
½ cup soy sauce
1 teaspoon grated lemon peel
   juice from 1 large lemon (¼ cup)
1 garlic clove, minced
2 teaspoons Dijon mustard
½ cup vegetable oil
   lemon wedges
   parsley

- In advance: marinate fish in soy sauce, lemon peel, lemon juice, garlic, mustard, and oil. Prick the steaks with a fork, so the marinade can penetrate. Cover and refrigerate for 1 to 3 hours, turning occasionally.

- If broiling in oven: broil fish in marinade 5 to 6 minutes on each side (thicker fish may need longer).

- If grilling, cook over moderately hot coals, basting regularly with marinade. Garnish with lemon wedges and parsley.

- Yield: 8 servings

"It's all right to drink like a fish — if you drink what a fish drinks."
— *Mary Pettibonre Poole*

Swordfish with Parmesan Crust

1 cup plus 2 tablespoons flour
¼ teaspoon salt
⅛ teaspoon pepper
3 egg whites
2½ cups grated Parmesan cheese
¼ cup milk
4 (6 ounce, 1-inch thick) swordfish steaks
2 tablespoons dry white wine
2 tablespoons lemon juice
½ cup (1 stick) butter, cut into 8 pieces
1 teaspoon fresh, chopped parsley
1½ teaspoons capers, drained

- Mix flour, salt, and pepper.

- In a separate bowl mix egg whites and milk.

- Dredge fish in flour mixture, dip in egg mixture and then coat with Parmesan cheese.

- Place on a baking sheet and refrigerate for at least 1 hour.

- Preheat oven to 350°.

- Remove from refrigerator and bake 6 to 9 minutes.

- To prepare sauce: boil wine and lemon juice in small saucepan. Reduce to 2 tablespoons. Put on low heat. Whisk in butter, a piece at a time, just until melted. (Do not boil). Stir in capers and parsley.

- Yield: 4 servings

- Per serving: 880 Calories • 48% Fat

Healthy Alternative Swordfish with Parmesan Crust

Try our Cooper-tested heart healthy
"Parmesan Crust". The crust is so good it's worth
repeating on other types of fish or on a chicken cutlet.

- 1 **cup plus 2 tablespoons flour**
- ¼ **teaspoon salt**
- ⅛ **teaspoon pepper**
- ¾ **cup egg substitute**
- ½ **cup skim milk, divided**
- 3 **cups cornflakes, crumbled (1 cup crumbs)**
- ½ **cup grated Parmesan cheese**
- 4 **(6-ounce, 1-inch thick) swordfish steaks**
- 1 **teaspoon cornstarch**
- ½ **teaspoon chicken bouillon granules**
- 1 **teaspoon butter**
- 1 **teaspoon fresh, chopped parsley**
- 6 **sun dried tomatoes, julienned**

- Mix flour, salt, and pepper.

- In a separate bowl, mix egg substitute and ¼ cup skim milk.

- In another bowl, mix cornflake crumbs and Parmesan cheese.

- Dredge fish in flour mixture, dip in egg mixture and then coat with Parmesan cheese mixture.

- Place on a baking sheet and refrigerate for at least 1 hour.

- Preheat oven to 350°.

- Remove from refrigerator and bake 6 to 9 minutes.

- To prepare sauce: dissolve cornstarch and chicken bouillon granules in remaining ¼ cup skim milk. Heat until thick. Whisk in butter and add parsley and sun dried tomatoes.

- Yield: 4 servings

- Per serving: 582 Calories • 18% Fat

Gram's Old Fashioned Applesauce Cake

This is a cozy fireside kind of winter dessert.

nonstick cooking spray
1 cup (2 sticks) margarine, softened, or shortening
2 cups sugar
3 cups flour, sifted
1 tablespoon cinnamon
1½ teaspoons nutmeg
½ teaspoon ground cloves (optional)
½ teaspoon salt
1 tablespoon baking soda
2½ cups applesauce
2 tablespoons dark corn syrup
1 cup raisins

Butter Icing
4 tablespoons butter
2 cups confectioners' sugar, sifted
¼ teaspoon vanilla

- Preheat oven to 350°.

- Spray loaf pan with nonstick cooking spray.

- With an electric mixer, cream shortening and sugar.

- Sift flour, cinnamon, nutmeg, cloves (optional), salt, and baking soda.

- Add flour mixture to shortening, alternating with applesauce. Beat well after each addition. Add corn syrup and raisins.

- Bake about 40 to 45 minutes.

- To make butter icing: with an electric mixer, mix butter, confectioners' sugar, and vanilla, until well blended.

- Frost when cool.

Much Requested Apple Cake

nonstick cooking spray
2 teaspoons cinnamon
4 teaspoons sugar
4 medium apples, peeled, cored and sliced
4 large eggs
1 cup vegetable oil
2 cups sugar
3 cups flour
1 teaspoon salt
3 teaspoons baking powder
½ cup orange juice
1 teaspoon vanilla
confectioners' sugar

- Preheat oven to 350°.

- Spray a 10-inch tube pan with nonstick cooking spray and dust with flour.

- Mix the cinnamon and sugar. Toss apples with cinnamon and sugar mixture. Set aside.

- With mixer, beat the eggs. Gradually add the oil and beat in sugar.

- In a separate bowl, sift the flour, salt, and baking powder.

- Add the flour mixture and the orange juice alternately to the egg mixture, beating after each addition. Beat in the vanilla. Batter will be thick.

- Pour one-third of the batter into the prepared pan. On top of the batter, layer one-half of the apple mixture. Repeat this process a second time. The final layer will be the remaining one-third of the batter.

(recipe continued on next page)

(Much Requested Apple Cake, continued)

- Bake for 1 hour or until toothpick inserted in the center comes out clean. Cool in pan for 10 minutes on a cooling rack. Loosen cake from pan and cool, top side up.

- After cooling, cake may be dusted with confectioners' sugar.

Bailey's Ice Cream Cake

1½ cups cookie crumbs (chocolate sandwich cookies are good)
  4 tablespoons butter, softened
  1 quart butter pecan ice cream, softened
  1 cup Bailey's Irish Cream, divided
10 chocolate-covered English toffee bars, chopped
  1 quart coffee ice cream, softened
  1 cup toasted pecans
  1 jar fudge sauce
  2 tablespoons Bailey's Irish Cream
  1 cup heavy cream, whipped

- Mix cookie crumbs with butter and put in the bottom of a 9-inch springform pan.

- Mix butter pecan ice cream with ½ cup of the Bailey's Irish Cream. Put in pan. Sprinkle with the chocolate-covered English toffee bars. Freeze for ½ hour.

- Mix coffee ice cream, the remaining ½ cup Bailey's Irish Cream, and pecans. Put in pan and freeze.

- Mix chocolate fudge sauce with the 2 tablespoons of Bailey's Irish Cream. Heat just to pouring consistency.

- To serve: unmold and spread with whipped cream. Slice and pour on flavored fudge sauce.

Maine Blueberry Cake

A true blue delight.

nonstick cooking spray
½ **cup (1 stick) butter**
1¼ **cups sugar, divided**
1 **large egg**
2 **cups flour**
2½ **teaspoons baking powder**
½ **teaspoon salt**
½ **cup milk**
2 **cups blueberries**
juice and grated peel of 1 lemon

- Preheat oven to 350° degrees.

- Spray an 8 x 12-inch pan with nonstick cooking spray.

- Cream the butter and ½ cup of the sugar. Add egg and beat.

- In a separate bowl, mix flour, baking powder, and salt.

- Add the dry ingredients to the creamed butter; alternating with milk. Fold in the blueberries.

- Bake for 40 to 50 minutes.

- To make the topping: mix juice and grated peel of lemon with the remaining ¾ cup of sugar.

- Spread on hot cake and bake an additional 5 minutes. Cool and serve.

Blueberries belong to the "Vaccinium" genus, and there are many varieties of them. In their wild state, blueberries are found from the northern tip of Alaska down to Florida.

Happy Husband Cake

He said, "Oh man, was that good!"

2 cakes German sweet chocolate
4 tablespoons sugar
6 tablespoons water
4 large eggs, separated
3 packages lady fingers
Topping
    ½ pint heavy cream
    2 tablespoons confectioners' sugar

- Melt chocolate and sugar in top of double boiler.

- Beat egg yolks. Add to chocolate mixture, cook until mixture thickens. Set aside and cool.

- With an electric mixer, beat egg whites until they stand in stiff peaks; fold into chocolate mixture.

- Separate lady fingers and stand in a single layer around sides of an angel food cake pan. Crumble remaining lady fingers. Cover the bottom of the pan with a layer—about one-quarter of the crumbled lady fingers.

- Pour cooled chocolate mixture over crumbled lady fingers, then add more lady fingers, more chocolate, repeating layers, ending with crumbled lady fingers on top.

- Cover and refrigerate overnight.

- To make topping: whip heavy cream and add confectioners' sugar.

- To serve: turn out cake on plate and ice with sweetened whipped cream.

Chocolate Truffle Torte

This cake will keep up to 2 weeks in the refrigerator, tightly covered. Served at room temperature, this cake is like a creamy truffle; chilled it's like a fudge.

nonstick cooking spray
16 ounces bittersweet (or semi-sweet) chocolate, coarsely chopped
1 cup (2 sticks) unsalted butter
6 large eggs
confectioners' sugar

- Heat oven to 425°.

- Spray an 8-inch springform pan with nonstick cooking spray. Line bottom of pan with waxed paper. Spray waxed paper with nonstick cooking spray. Wrap outside of pan with a double layer of heavy duty foil.

- Melt chocolate and butter in a double boiler on low heat. Stir occasionally until melted and smooth.

- Break eggs into heavy large mixing bowl set over simmering water. Stir constantly, to prevent scrambling, until eggs are warm to the touch (about 3 minutes). Remove from heat and beat with electric mixer 5 to 7 minutes, until triple in volume and soft peaks form when beaters are lifted.

- Fold half the eggs into the melted chocolate until partially incorporated; then fold in remaining eggs just until blended.

- Pour into prepared pan and smooth top with spatula. Place in a larger pan and add hot water up to two-thirds of the side of springform pan. Bake 5 minutes. Cover loosely with lightly buttered foil and bake 35 minutes longer.

(recipe continued on next page)

(Chocolate Truffle Torte, continued)

- Remove pan to wire rack and cool 45 minutes. Cover and refrigerate until very firm (3 hours).

- To serve: unmold on a flat plate lined with plastic wrap. Run a thin metal knife or spatula around edge of cake; remove pan sides. Place lined plate on cake and carefully invert. Remove pan bottom and peel of paper. Turn cake onto serving plate and remove plastic wrap. Cover with a doily. Sprinkle confectioners' sugar over doily to form a beautiful pattern. Carefully remove doily.

French Chocolate Cake

4 large eggs
1 cup sugar
7 ounces semi-sweet chocolate, melted
¾ cup plus 2 tablespoons (1¾ sticks) butter
1 cup flour
1 teaspoon baking powder
½ cup hazelnuts, chopped
1 teaspoon vanilla
  fresh or frozen raspberries

- Preheat oven to 425°.

- Spray a tart pan with nonstick cooking spray.

- With an electric mixer, in a large bowl, beat eggs and sugar until light.

- Mix chocolate and butter together. Add to egg mixture. Mix in flour and baking powder. Fold in hazelnuts and vanilla.

- Pour into tart pan and bake 15 minutes.

- Serve with fresh or frozen raspberries.

Jersey Fresh Fruit Cake

nonstick cooking spray
3 cups flour
1½ teaspoons baking soda
1½ teaspoons baking powder
1 cup butter (2 sticks), softened
2¾ cups sugar, divided
¼ teaspoon salt
4 large eggs
2 teaspoons vanilla
⅓ cup orange juice
2 mashed bananas
1-2 tablespoons ground cinnamon
4 large peaches, peeled, stoned and thinly sliced
1 cup fresh blueberries
1 cup raisins
4 ounces nuts, chopped (1 cup)
confectioners' sugar

- Preheat oven to 350°.

- Spray 10-inch tube or bundt pan with nonstick cooking spray.

- Combine flour, baking soda, and baking powder. Set aside.

- With an electric mixer, cream butter and 2½ cups of the sugar in a large bowl. Add salt, eggs, vanilla, orange juice, and bananas.

- Add dry ingredients and beat 2 minutes or until very thick.

- Combine the remaining sugar and cinnamon. Toss with peaches, blueberries, raisins, and nuts.

- Fill prepared pan with alternating layers of batter and fruit mixture, beginning and ending with batter. Bake 1¼ to 1½ hours or until

(recipe continued on next page)

(Jersey Fresh Fruit Cake, continued)

toothpick inserted in center comes out clean. Cool in pan on wire rack for 10 to 20 minutes. Remove from pan to complete cooling.

• Dust with confectioners' sugar.

Brandied Date and Nut Torte

Make one or two days ahead and cover with aluminum foil and refrigerate—it mellows.

This recipe sounds weird when you read it and it looks weird when you mix it up but it does work. This makes a special holiday dessert.

   8 **ounces dates, chopped (1¼ cups)**
   3 **ounces walnuts, chopped (¾ cup)**
   2 **teaspoons baking powder**
  18 **squares graham crackers, broken in pieces, not crumbs**
   2 **large eggs, beaten**
   1 **cup sugar**
   ½ **cup vegetable oil**
   1 **cup milk (optional: for a richer taste use ⅓ cup brandy and ⅔ cup milk)**
     pinch salt

• Preheat oven to 350°.

• Combine dates, walnuts, baking powder, and crackers and press into a pie plate or square pan.

• Mix eggs, sugar, oil, and milk. Pour over date mixture.

• Bake 30 to 40 minutes until set and golden brown.

• Serve with whipped cream.

Midnight Lace Cake

Life is short; eat dessert first.

nonstick cooking spray
3 cups flour, sifted
1½ cups cocoa
2 teaspoons baking powder
3 teaspoons baking soda
1 teaspoon salt
1 pound (4 sticks) butter, melted
1 teaspoon vanilla
3 cups sugar
4 extra large eggs at room temperature, beaten
1 cup hot coffee
1 cup milk
confectioners' sugar

- Spray a 13 x 9-inch glass baking dish with nonstick cooking spray.

- Preheat oven to 325°.

- Mix flour, cocoa, baking powder, baking soda, and salt.

- Combine melted butter, vanilla, sugar, and eggs.

- In a separate bowl, combine hot coffee and milk.

- Slowly add the butter mixture, alternating with the coffee mixture to the dry ingredients. Pour into the dish.

- Bake 1½ hours.

- Dust with confectioners' sugar if desired.

Oatmeal Cake

1¼ cups boiling water
1 cup quick oats
½ cup (1 stick) butter, cut into pieces
1 cup sugar
1 cup brown sugar, packed
2 large eggs
1½ cups sifted flour
1 teaspoon baking soda
1 teaspoon baking powder
1 teaspoon cinnamon

Topping

½ cup (1 stick) butter
½ cup evaporated milk
1 cup sugar
½ cup chopped walnuts
½ cup coconut
1 teaspoon vanilla

- Preheat oven to 350°.

- Mix boiling water, quick oats, and butter. Cover and let stand 20 minutes.

- Combine sugar, brown sugar, and eggs. Add flour, baking soda, baking powder, and cinnamon. Stir in oatmeal mixture and blend well.

- Spoon into a 13 x 9-inch pan.

- Bake 35 minutes or until a toothpick inserted in the center comes out clean.

- To make topping: simmer butter and milk for 10 minutes. Add sugar, nuts, coconut, and vanilla. Pour over hot cake.

Sour Cream Marbled Pound Cake

butter
sugar
6 ounces semi-sweet chocolate
1 cup (2 sticks) butter
2½ cups sugar
6 large eggs
3 cups sifted flour
¼ teaspoon baking powder
1 cup sour cream
2 teaspoons vanilla
1 tablespoon almond extract
confectioners' sugar

- Preheat oven to 325°.

- Butter a bundt or 10-inch tube pan. Add a large scoop of sugar to the pan and rotate it until all the interior surfaces are generously coated. Gently tap out excess, but allow as much sugar as possible to adhere, for this is what forms the good outer crust.

- Melt chocolate in the top of a double boiler.

- With an electric mixer, cream the butter and sugar until the mixture is very thick and pale, at least 6 minutes. Beat in the eggs one at a time, beating a full minute after each addition.

- Sift the flour and baking soda.

- With the mixer running at low speed, add the dry ingredients alternating with the sour cream. Add the vanilla and almond extract. Remove bowl from the mixer, give a final stir with a spatula to catch any ingredients remaining at the bottom of the bowl. Pour slightly over half of the batter into the pan.

- Add the melted chocolate to the remaining batter and stir until blended. Spoon the

(recipe continued on next page)

(Sour Cream Marbled Pound Cake, continued)

chocolate batter onto the white and, with each spoonful, cut down and swirl the chocolate through.

• Place cake in oven and bake for 1 hour, or until a tester inserted in the center of the cake comes out clean.

• Remove and cool briefly on a rack before unmolding. Run a knife around the edge of the cake and turn it onto a serving platter.

• Dust with confectioners' sugar before serving.

Mother's Day Dinner

Cold Tomato Cream

Chicken with Basil Cream Sauce

Spring Asparagus

Not-so-Plain Jane Rice

Moët and Chandon Champagne

Sour Cream Pound Cake

Walnut Pumpkin Cake

Crust
- butter
- 1 (6-ounce) package zwieback crackers, crushed
- ¼ cup sugar
- 6 tablespoons butter, melted

Cake
- 3 (8-ounce) packages cream cheese, softened
- ¾ cup sugar
- ¾ cup light brown sugar, firmly packed
- 5 large eggs
- 1 (16-ounce) can pumpkin
- 1 teaspoon pumpkin pie spice
- ½ teaspoon nutmeg
- ¼ cup heavy cream

Topping
- 6 tablespoons butter, softened
- 1 cup light brown sugar, firmly packed
- 1 cup coarsely chopped walnuts

Garnish
- ½ cup heavy cream, whipped
- pecan halves

- To make crust: coat the bottom and sides of a 9-inch springform pan with butter. Blend zwieback crumbs, sugar and melted butter. Press firmly onto bottom and sides of the springform pan. Chill.

- Preheat oven to 325°.

- To make cake: beat cream cheese with electric mixer at medium speed until smooth. Gradually add sugar and brown sugar, beating until well mixed.

- Beat in eggs one at a time until mixture is light and fluffy.

- Beat in pumpkin, spices, and heavy cream at low speed. Pour mixture into pan.

(recipe continued on next page)

(Walnut Pumpkin Cake, continued)

- Bake for 1 hour and 35 minutes.

- To make topping: mix butter and brown sugar until crumbly. Stir in walnuts.

- Remove cake from oven and sprinkle with walnut topping. Bake an additional 10 minutes. Remove from oven and cool. When cake has cooled, refrigerate several hours.

- To serve: frost with whipped cream and garnish with a few pecan halves.

Father's Day Dinner

Repartee

*Tomatoes with
Fresh Tomato Dressing*

Entrecôte au Poivre

Corn Pudding Delicious

Tyrrell's Cabernet Merlot

Walnut Pumpkin Cake

Peanut Brittle Cheese Cake

How sweet it is!

1 cup graham cracker crumbs
4 tablespoons unsalted butter, melted
**4 (8-ounce) packages of cream cheese,
softened**
1 cup sugar
3 large eggs
¼ cup milk
2 tablespoons flour
1 teaspoon vanilla
½ pound peanut brittle, coarsely chopped
1 cup sour cream
fresh raspberries

- Preheat oven to 350°.

- To make crust: in a bowl, mix graham cracker crumbs and butter. Press into bottom of a 9-inch springform pan. Bake crust for 10 minutes.

- Increase oven temperature to 400°.

- In a large bowl, with mixer at high speed, beat cream cheese, sugar, eggs, milk, flour, and vanilla for 2 minutes. Stir in half the brittle and pour over crust in pan.

- Bake 15 minutes. Reduce heat to 300° and bake an additional 45 minutes.

- Cool completely on rack. Chill.

- To serve: spread sour cream over top and sides of cheese cake. Sprinkle with the finely chopped and larger pieces of brittle. Garnish with raspberries.

- For ease of slicing, warm the blade of your knife under hot water before slicing.

Beacon Hill Chocolate Cookies

nonstick cooking spray
1 cup chocolate chips
2 egg whites
⅛ teaspoon salt
½ cup sugar
½ teaspoon vinegar
½ teaspoon vanilla
½ cup flaked coconut
1 ounce walnuts, chopped (¼ cup)

- Spray cookie sheets with nonstick cooking spray.

- Preheat oven 350°.

- Melt chocolate in the top of a double boiler.

- Beat egg whites and salt until foamy. Gradually add sugar, beating well after each addition until well blended. Continue beating until mixture stands in stiff peaks.

- Add vinegar and vanilla and beat well. (Entire beating process takes about 10 minutes).

- Fold in coconut, nuts, and melted chocolate.

- Drop by rounded tablespoonfuls onto greased cookie sheet.

- Bake for 10 minutes.

- Yield: 2½-3 dozen

Important information for chocolate lovers: the fat in dark chocolate is healthier than the fat in milk chocolate.

Kindergarten Chocolate Chip Cookies

A lot of cookies for a lot of kids.

2 cups (4 sticks) butter
2 cups brown sugar, firmly packed
2 cups sugar
4 large eggs
2 teaspoons vanilla
5 cups quick cooking oats
4 cups flour
½ teaspoon salt
2 teaspoons baking soda
2 teaspoons baking powder
2 (12-ounce) packages chocolate chips
1 (8-ounce) chocolate bar, chopped
12 ounces walnuts, chopped (3 cups)

• Cream together butter and sugars. Add eggs and vanilla.

• Put oatmeal in blender and blend to a fine powder.

• Combine oats, flour, salt, baking powder, and baking soda. Add to butter mixture. Fold in chocolate chips, chopped chocolate, and walnuts.

• Refrigerate for about 1 hour.

• Preheat oven to 375°.

• Roll dough into balls and place 2 inches apart on cookie sheet.

• Bake 10 minutes.

• Yield: 9 dozen

To soften hardened brown sugar, add several drops of water to the package of brown sugar and microwave for about 15 seconds.

Chocolate Madeleines

This recipe uses "Dutch" cocoa, which is a special cocoa that has been processed to be less acid in taste, darker in color, and less likely to settle in the bottom of the cup.

butter, melted
4 large eggs, separated
½ cup sugar
½ cup Dutch cocoa
½ cup sifted flour
1 teaspoon baking powder
½ cup (1 stick) butter, softened
2 teaspoons almond extract
confectioners' sugar

*The botanical name for cocoa bean tree is **Theobroma cacao**. For all you chocolate lovers, this means "food for the gods".*

- Preheat oven to 425°.

- Brush madeleine molds with melted butter.

- Beat egg yolks, sugar, and cocoa together. Fold in flour and baking powder. Add ½ cup butter and almond flavoring. Batter will be very stiff.

- Beat egg whites until they form a stiff peak. Fold into dough. Spoon into molds (molds should be about two-thirds full).

- Bake about 10 minutes until risen and firm.

- Remove from pan and cool. Sprinkle with confectioners' sugar before serving. The madeleines should be stored in an air-tight container to prevent their becoming dry.

- Yield: 2 dozen

Chocolate Pecan Wafers

nonstick cooking spray
½ **cup (1 stick) butter, softened**
½ **teaspoon salt**
1 **teaspoon vanilla**
1 **cup sugar**
2 **large eggs**
3 **ounces unsweetened chocolate, melted**
¾ **cup flour**
3 **ounces pecans, chopped (¾ cup)**

- Preheat oven to 325°.

- Spray cookie sheets with nonstick cooking spray.

- Combine butter, salt, and vanilla. Mix in sugar and eggs. Blend in chocolate. Add flour and nuts. Mix well.

- Drop by half teaspoonfuls onto cookie sheet.

- Bake for 12 minutes.

- Yield: 3 dozen

When melting chocolate, it is important to keep moisture from coming in direct contact with the chocolate, because moisture will cause chocolate to stiffen.

Brown-edged Butter Cookies

Thin, crisp, buttery dropped cookies with delicious flavor!

½ **cup (1 stick) butter, softened**
⅓ **cup sugar**
½ **teaspoon vanilla**
1 **large egg**
¾ **cup sifted flour**
⅛ **teaspoon salt**

- Preheat oven to 350°.

- Cream butter, sugar, vanilla, and egg together until light and fluffy. Beat in flour and salt.

- Drop by half teaspoonfuls onto ungreased cookie sheet.

- Bake about 10 minutes until edges are golden brown. Cool on wire racks.

- Yield: 2 dozen

A great tip to help make this a crisp, light cookie: sift flour before measuring. Sift on a piece of wax paper and spoon into a measuring cup. The sifted flour will be lighter and make a crispier cookie.

Come to Tea

Chicken Almond Puffs

Our Favorite Banana Tea Loaf

**Lemon Tea Bread
with
Pennsylvania Lemon Butter**

Brown-edged Buttter Cookies

A Selection of Teas

Crunchy Jumble Cookies

This is a "surprise your company" cookie because they keep so well. Double this recipe and store in an air-tight container for a week to 10 days. If the guests don't show up , don't worry, put them in the freezer. They freeze beautifully.

nonstick cooking spray
1¼ cups flour
½ teaspoon baking soda
¼ teaspoon salt
½ cup butter, softened
1 cup sugar
1 teaspoon vanilla
1 large egg
2 cups crispy rice cereal
1 (6-ounce) package semi-sweet chocolate morsels
8 ounces pecans, chopped (2 cups)

- Preheat oven to 350°.

- Spray cookie sheet with nonstick cooking spray.

- In a small bowl, combine flour, baking powder, and salt.

- In a large bowl, combine butter and sugar. Beat until creamy. Add egg and vanilla. Mix well.

- Blend in flour mixture. Stir in crispy rice cereal, chocolate morsels, and nuts (some people prefer 1 cup raisins instead of the nuts). Drop by level teaspoonfuls onto cookie sheet.

- Bake 12 minutes. Cool on wire racks.

- Yield: 3 dozen

Date and Nut Bars

nonstick cooking spray
1 cup brown sugar, firmly packed
½ cup butter, melted
1 large egg
¾ cup flour
½ teaspoon baking powder
½ teaspoon salt
4 ounces pecans, chopped (1 cup)
6 ounces dates, chopped (1 cup)

- Preheat oven to 350°.

- Spray 9-inch square pan with nonstick cooking spray.

- Cream brown sugar, butter, and egg.

- Sift together flour, baking powder, and salt. Add to creamed mixture. Fold in nuts and dates.

- Bake about 20 minutes.

- Yield: 16 bars

When cutting sticky foods such as marshmallows or dried or candied fruits, dip kitchen shears into sugar or hot water periodically while cutting.

Pajama Party Coconut Dream Bars

Crust

- ½ **cup (1 stick) butter**
- ½ **cup brown sugar, firmly packed**
- 1½ **cups flour**
- 3 **large eggs**

Filling

- 1½ **cups brown sugar, firmly packed**
- 1¼ **cups flour**
- 1 **teaspoon baking powder**
- ¼ **teaspoon salt**
- 1½ **cups coconut**
- 1 **teaspoon vanilla**
- 2 **ounces walnuts, chopped (½ cup)**

- Preheat oven to 350°.

- To make crust: cream butter and brown sugar. Cut the creamed butter into the flour until mixture resembles coarse crumbs. Press into a 9 x 13-inch pan. Bake for 15 minutes.

- To make filling; beat eggs until light and foamy. Gradually add brown sugar and beat until thick.

- Sift flour, baking powder, and salt. Blend into egg mixture. Stir in coconut, vanilla, and nuts.

- Spread over crust and bake 20 to 25 minutes.

- Cool. Cut into squares with a wet knife.

- Yield: 20 squares

Great Scotts

½ cup (1 stick) butter
½ cup (1 stick) unsalted butter
1 cup brown sugar, firmly packed
1 cup sugar
2 large eggs
2 tablespoons milk
2 teaspoons vanilla
2 cups flour
1 teaspoon baking powder
1 teaspoon baking soda
½ teaspoon salt
2 cups quick cooking oats
1 (12-ounce) bag semisweet mini chocolate chips
4 ounces walnuts, chopped (1 cup)
nonstick cooking spray

- Cream butters, sugar, eggs, milk, and vanilla.

- Sift flour, baking powder, baking soda, and salt. Add to butter mixture. Stir in oats. Fold in chocolate chips and walnuts.

- Refrigerate for at least 30 minutes.

- Preheat oven to 350°. Spray cookie sheets with nonstick cooking spray.

- Roll dough into balls and flatten into rounded disks.

- Bake until the edges are browned, about 8 to 10 minutes. Be careful not to overbake.

- Yield: 4 dozen

Irish Lace Cookies

These cookies are as fragile as a china doll;
the edges break easily. Because they are so delicious,
they are deserving of special care. Store them in an
air tight tin between layers of waxed paper.

1 cup quick oatmeal
½ cup (1 stick) butter, melted
1 cup sugar
2 tablespoons flour
¼ teaspoon salt
¼ teaspoon baking powder
1 large egg, beaten
1 teaspoon vanilla

- Preheat oven to 325°.

- Spread aluminum foil on baking sheet.

- Sift together flour, sugar, baking powder, and salt. Add oatmeal, melted butter, egg, and vanilla. Mix well.

- Drop by half teaspoonfuls onto the foil-lined baking sheet, 4 inches apart.

- Bake about 10 minutes, or until lightly brown.

- Allow cookies to cool and then peel the cookie off the aluminum foil. (Cookies must be cooled to remove them easily.)

- Yield: 2-3 dozen

"Epicure: One who gets nothing better than the cream of everything, but cheerfully makes the best of it."

— Oliver Hereford

Toasted Oatmeal Cookies

Sugar and spice and everything nice.

¾ **cup (1½ sticks) butter, melted**
2½ **cups raw rolled oats (not quick oats)**
1 **cup flour**
1 **teaspoon cinnamon**
½ **teaspoon salt**
½ **teaspoon baking soda**
1 **cup brown sugar, firmly packed**
2 **large eggs**
1 **teaspoon vanilla**
4 **ounces walnuts, chopped (1 cup)**

- Preheat oven to 375°.

- Melt butter in medium skillet. Sauté oats, until golden brown. Remove from heat and cool.

- Sift flour, cinnamon, salt, and baking powder.

- With an electric mixer, combine sugar, eggs, and vanilla. Beat until light and fluffy. Stir in cooled rolled oats and flour mixture until well combined.

- Drop by slightly rounded teaspoonfuls onto ungreased cookie sheet.

- Bake about 10 to 12 minutes, or until golden brown. Remove to wire rack and cool.

- Yield: 4 dozen

Why use raw oats instead of quick oats? Raw oats are thicker and will give this cookie a chewier taste.

Ricotta Cookies

*Make a kid happy by sprinkling multi-colored
sprinkles on these iced cookies.*

1 cup (2 sticks) butter
2 cups sugar
3 large eggs
1 teaspoon baking soda
1 teaspoon vanilla
½ teaspoon salt
1 (16-ounce) container ricotta cheese
4 cups flour

Icing

1 box confectioners' sugar
½ cup (1 stick) butter, softened
1 large egg
1 teaspoon vanilla
2 tablespoons milk

- Preheat oven to 350°.

- Cream butter, sugar, and eggs. Add baking soda, vanilla, and salt.

- Alternately add ricotta cheese and flour until well mixed.

- Drop by rounded tablespoonfuls onto ungreased cookie sheet.

- Bake for 15 minutes.

- To make icing: mix confectioners' sugar, butter, egg, vanilla, and milk until smooth. Sprinkle chocolate sprinkles on the icing.

- Yield: about 6 dozen, depending on size

Snowy Almond Cookies

nonstick cooking spray
⅔ cup butter
⅓ cup sugar
1⅓ cups flour
⅛ teaspoon salt
1 teaspoon vanilla
4 ounces toasted almonds, chopped (1 cup)
confectioners' sugar

- Preheat oven 300°.
- Spray baking sheets with nonstick cooking spray.
- Cream butter and sugar until light and fluffy. Add flour, salt, vanilla, and almonds. Work lightly with fingertips.
- Shape into small balls, place on cookie sheet and flatten carefully with a fork.
- Bake 25 minutes.
- Cool. Roll in confectioners' sugar.
- Yield: 4 dozen

Toasting nuts deepens not only their color but also their flavor. Spread the nuts on a cookie sheet and toast in a 350° oven 3-5 minutes. Check them frequently as they burn easily.

Sour Cream Apple Pie

If an apple a day keeps the doctor away, we're ready.

- 1 **9-inch pie shell, unbaked**
- 6 **medium-sized apples, (preferably Granny Smith), peeled, cored and sliced**
- 2 **tablespoons flour**
- ¾ **cup sugar**
- ⅛ **teaspoon salt**
- 1 **large egg, beaten**
- 1 **cup sour cream**
- 1 **teaspoon vanilla**
- ⅛ **teaspoon nutmeg**

Topping
- ⅓ **cup sugar**
- ⅓ **cup flour**
- 1 **teaspoon cinnamon**
- 4 **tablespoons butter**

- Preheat oven to 400°.

- To make filling: sift together flour, sugar, and salt. Add egg, sour cream, vanilla, and nutmeg. Combine thoroughly. Fold in apple slices and spoon into the pie shell.

- Bake for 15 minutes. Reduce heat to 350° and bake for another 30 minutes.

- While pie is baking, make topping: mix together sugar, flour, and cinnamon. Cut in the butter to make crumbs.

- Take the pie out of the oven, sprinkle it with the topping, and put it back in the oven for an additional 30 minutes.

Black Jack Daniels Chocolate Pecan Pie

1 9-inch pie shell
2 large eggs
1 cup sugar
½ cup (1 stick) butter, melted
3-4 tablespoons bourbon
¼ cup cornstarch
4 ounces pecans, chopped (1 cup)
1 cup semi-sweet chocolate chips
whipped cream

- Preheat oven to 350°.

- With an electric mixer, beat eggs. Gradually add sugar to the eggs. Mix in butter and bourbon. Blend in cornstarch. Stir in nuts and chips. Pour into shell.

- Bake for 45 to 50 minutes.

- Serve warm garnished with whipped cream.

White House Pecan Pie

2 tablespoons butter
1 cup sugar
1 cup dark corn syrup
2 large eggs, beaten
1 teaspoon vanilla
4 ounces pecan halves (1 cup)
1 9-inch unbaked pie shell

- Preheat oven to 275°.

- With an electric mixer, cream butter, sugar, corn syrup, eggs, and vanilla. Beat well. Stir in pecan halves. Pour in pie shell.

- Bake for 45 minutes.

Double Good Summer Blueberry Pie

This is double good...whole fresh blueberries in a blueberry sauce.

¾ **cup sugar**
3 **tablespoons cornstarch**
⅛ **teaspoon salt**
¼ **cup water**
4 **cups blueberries, divided**
1 **tablespoon butter**
1 **tablespoon lemon juice**
1 **9-inch baked pie shell**
whipped cream

- Combine sugar, cornstarch, and salt in a saucepan. Add water and 2 cups of the blueberries.

- Cook over medium heat, stirring constantly with a wooden spoon until mixture comes to a boil, and is thickened and clear. Remove from heat and stir in butter and lemon juice. Cool.

- Place remaining 2 cups of blueberries in the pie shell, and top with cooked blueberry mixture.

- Chill and serve garnished with whipped cream.

"Everyone needs a touch of luxury, something grand and pampering."
— *Bill Blass*

Brandy Alexander Pie

Taste how dreamy a cream pie should be.

1 **envelope unflavored gelatin**
½ **cup cold water**
⅔ **cup sugar, divided**
⅛ **teaspoon salt**
3 **large eggs, separated**
¼ **cup brandy**
¼ **cup crème de cacao**
2 **cups heavy cream, whipped, divided**
1 **9-inch graham cracker crust**
  chocolate curls

Chocolate curling may sound like a sport or a new dance craze but for chocolate lovers it's another excuse to use chocolate. To garnish with chocolate curls: warm chocolate bar or chunk slightly. Draw a vegetable peeler blade along a smooth surface of chocolate.

- Sprinkle the gelatin over the cold water in saucepan. Add ⅓ cup of the sugar, salt, and egg yolks. Stir to blend.

- Heat the gelatin mixture over low heat, stirring until the gelatin dissolves and the mixture begins to thicken. Remove from heat and stir in the brandy and crème de cacao. Chill. Mixture will continue to thicken.

- With an electric mixer, beat the egg whites until they stand in stiff peaks. Gradually beat in the remaining sugar. Fold egg white mixture into the egg yolk mixture. Fold in one cup of the whipped cream. Turn into prepared crust.

- Chill several hours or overnight. Garnish with the remaining whipped cream and chocolate curls.

Pine Barrens Cranberry Pie

Pie crusts will be glossy if brushed
with a little milk before baking.

2 9-inch pie shells, one cut into lattice strips
1 (1-pound) bag fresh cranberries
½ cup brown sugar, firmly packed
½ cup molasses
1 tablespoon cornstarch
sugar

- Preheat oven to 425°.

- Put cranberries in a 9-inch pie shell.

- Mix brown sugar, molasses, and cornstarch together. Spoon mixture over cranberries.

- Cover cranberries with lattice strips. Sprinkle with a little sugar.

- Bake for 45 minutes. This pie is going to bubble over. To save clean up, place a cookie sheet on a rack below the pie.

Grease a measuring cup before measuring molasses or honey.

Snappy Lemon Pie

Your lips will pucker for more than just a kiss.

28 **ginger snap cookies**
⅓ **cup butter, melted**
3 **large egg yolks**
1 **(12-ounce) can sweetened condensed milk**
½ **cup fresh lemon juice**
   whipped cream and a few gingersnap
   crumbs

- Preheat oven to 350°.

- Place cookies in a blender, 4 to 5 at a time, and blend into crumbs.

- Put cookie crumbs in a bowl and add melted butter. Press into a 9-inch pie plate. Bake for 8 minutes. Cool.

- Reduce oven temperature to 325°.

- Beat egg yolks. Stir in milk and lemon juice. Pour into prepared pie crust and bake for 30 minutes. Cool.

- Keep refrigerated until ready to serve. Top with whipped cream and a few gingersnap crumbs.

A Southern Luncheon

Pumpkin Soup

Hot Chicken Salad
from Alabama

Assorted Rolls

Iced Tea

Snappy Lemon Pie

Macadamia Nut Cream Pie

A very beautiful, very romantic pie.

⅔ **cup sugar**
½ **cup flour**
½ **teaspoon salt**
2 **cups milk**
3 **large egg yolks**
2 **tablespoons butter, melted**
2 **teaspoons vanilla**
4 **ounces macadamia nuts, ground**
 (about 1 cup), divided
1 **9-inch pie shell, baked**
 whipped cream

- Mix sugar, flour, salt, and milk and cook in the top of a double boiler until mixture thickens (about 10 minutes). Remove from heat.

- In a separate bowl, beat eggs yolks. Gradually pour half of egg yolks into hot mixture and stir. When smooth, add the rest of the egg to the hot mixture and cook until thickened. Remove from heat.

- Add butter, vanilla, and ¾ cup of the ground macadamia nuts. Cool.

- Pour into crust. Cover with whipped cream and sprinkle lightly with the remaining ground nuts.

The macadamia nut is a large, light tan, unevenly round, creamy nut. It has a rich, sweet, and buttery flavor.

Mocha "Good" Ice Cream Pie

2 ounces (2 squares) unsweetened chocolate
2 tablespoons butter
2 tablespoons hot milk
⅔ cup sifted confectioners' sugar
1½ cups coconut
1 pint butter pecan or coffee ice cream, softened
2 teaspoons instant coffee
1 ounce pecans, chopped (¼ cup)
several whole pecans

• Butter a 9-inch pie plate.

• Melt chocolate and butter in top of double boiler. Add hot milk and sugar to chocolate mixture. Mix well. Stir in coconut. Press into bottom and sides of pie plate. Chill one hour.

• Stir ice cream to soften and thoroughly mix in coffee and chopped pecans. Spread into pie shell swirling top. Decorate with pecan halves and place in freezer until firm.

• Soften about 3 minutes before serving.

" 'How long does getting thin take?' Pooh asked anxiously."

— "Winnie the Pooh", A. A. Milne

Peach Custard Pie

"Ripe for the picking."

Crust
>   1 **cup flour**
>   1 **tablespoon sugar**
>   ½ **cup (1 stick) butter, softened**

Filling
>   5-6 **large ripe peaches, pitted, peeled and sliced**
>   1 **tablespoon plus 1 cup sugar**
>   3 **large eggs**
>   1 **teaspoon vanilla**
>   1 **cup milk**
>   **cinnamon**
>   **nutmeg**

- Preheat oven to 350°.

- Mix flour and sugar. With your hands, thoroughly incorporate butter into flour mixture. Pat into a deep 9-inch pie pan. Use heel of hand to pack into place.

- Place peaches in pie shell. Sprinkle 1 tablespoon of the sugar on peaches.

- Beat eggs until lemon colored, add remaining 1 cup of sugar and mix thoroughly. Add vanilla and milk, mix well. Pour over peaches. Sprinkle with cinnamon and nutmeg.

- Bake about 60 minutes or until custard is set.

To prevent soggy crust in custard pies or quiche, brush a little egg white on the uncooked shell and bake 10 minutes in preheated 425° oven. Pour in filling and bake according to recipe directions.

Deep Dish Rhubarb Pie

The dark, rich red stalks of rhubarb should be of medium thickness, firm, clean, and crisp. Rhubarb is available in late spring and early summer. If you are a little shy to buy fresh rhubarb, pick up a package of frozen rhubarb in the freezer section of your grocery store.

Rhubarb is a forgotten vegetable with a surprise nutritional bonus: ½ cup of rhubarb has as much calcium as ½ cup of milk.

- 1 **9-inch pie shell, unbaked**
- 1½ **tablespoons tapioca**
- 3 **tablespoons flour**
- 1½ **cups sugar**
- ⅛ **teaspoon salt**
- 3 **large eggs, beaten**
- 4½ **cups rhubarb, chopped**

Topping
- ½ **cup sugar**
- ¾ **cup flour**
- 5 **tablespoons butter, softened**

- Preheat oven to 450°.

- Spread tapioca on bottom of crust.

- To make filling: mix flour, sugar, salt, and eggs. Stir in rhubarb and pour into crust.

- To make topping: crumble together the sugar, flour, and butter. Sprinkle over top.

- Bake for ten minutes, then turn temperature down to 325° and bake for an additional hour.

Shoo Fly Pie

Crust
- 1½ **cups flour**
- ½ **teaspoon salt**
- ½ **cup vegetable shortening**
- 4-6 **tablespoons ice water**

Crumbs
- ¾ **cup flour**
- ½ **cup brown sugar**
- 2 **tablespoons vegetable shortening**
- ½ **teaspoon cinnamon**
- ¼ **teaspoon salt**
- ⅛ **teaspoon nutmeg**
- ⅛ **teaspoon ginger**
- ⅛ **teaspoon ground cloves**

Filling
- ½ **cup molasses**
- 1 **large egg yolk**
- ½ **teaspoon baking soda**
- ¾ **cup boiling water**
- **whipped cream**

- Preheat oven to 450°.

- To make crust: sift flour with salt. Cut in vegetable shortening with knives or fork. Add only enough water (4-6 tablespoons) to hold mixture together. Roll out on lightly floured board.

- Place the crust in a pie pan. Trim and crimp edges.

- To make crumbs: combine flour, sugar, salt, and spices. With a fork or two knives work in vegetable shortening. Sprinkle three-fourths of the crumbs on pie crust.

- To make filling: whisk together molasses, egg yolk, and baking soda that has been dissolved in boiling water. Pour filling over crumbs in pie crust. Top with crumbs.

- Bake until pie crust edges start to turn brown about 5 minutes. Reduce heat to 375° and bake an additional 20 minutes or until firm.

- Serve warm with whipped cream.

Angela Pia

A simple and a classic dessert.

2 (8-ounce) packages cream cheese, softened
4 large egg yolks
½ cup sugar
2 tablespoons dark rum
fresh or frozen raspberries, thawed

- Using an electric mixer, beat the cream cheese until it is smooth.

- In a separate bowl, beat the egg yolks vigorously. Add sugar and rum and beat the mixture hard for at least 5 minutes until it is thick and creamy.

- Combine the egg yolk and cream cheese mixtures and blend together.

- Put the mousse in individual stemmed glasses and top with raspberries. Chill at least one hour before serving.

- Yield: 6 servings

"No mean woman can cook well, for it calls for a light head, a generous spirit, and a large heart."
— Paul Gauguin

Brag about Brownies

nonstick cooking spray
½ **cup (1 stick) butter**
2 **squares unsweetened chocolate**
1 **cup sugar**
2 **large eggs**
½ **cup flour**
1 **teaspoon vanilla**
3 **ounces pecans, chopped (optional)**

- Preheat oven to 350°.

- Spray a 8 x 8-inch pan with nonstick cooking spray.

- In the top of a double boiler, melt butter and chocolate together. Pour into a mixing bowl.

- Stir in sugar. Add eggs, one at a time, beating after each egg. Add flour and vanilla. This is a good time to add nuts if you like your brownies with nuts.

- Bake for 25 to 30 minutes.

- Yield: 16 brownies

Chocolate and its brother, cocoa, are made from the beans of the cacao tree which is native to the hot humid forests of the Amazon basin. Chocolate is a mixture of roasted cocoa, cocoa butter, and a very fine sugar.

The word chocolate comes from the Mexican Indian "choco," foam, and "atl," water.

Queen Bona's Charlotte

A dessert fit for royalty, with an unexpected twist.
Queen Bona frosts her ladyfingers.

12 ladyfingers
1 envelope unflavored gelatin
½ cup sugar
⅛ teaspoon salt
4 large eggs, separated
1 (6-ounce) can frozen orange juice, thawed
3 tablespoons lemon juice
3 tablespoons water
½ teaspoon grated orange peel
½ teaspoon grated lemon peel
⅓ cup sugar
1 cup heavy cream, whipped (to add to egg whites)
1 cup heavy cream, whipped (to frost)
mandarin oranges

- Line the bottom and sides of a 9-inch springform pan with ladyfingers.

- Mix gelatin, ½ cup sugar, and salt in a heavy pan.

- Beat together egg yolks, orange juice, lemon juice, water, orange peel, and lemon peel. Stir into gelatin mixture.

- Heat over low heat (do not boil) until gelatin dissolves and mixture thickens slightly.

- Chill over ice water, stirring often until as thick as egg whites.

- In a separate bowl, beat egg whites until foamy. Add ⅓ cup sugar gradually and beat until they stand in soft peaks. Add whipped cream.

- Gently fold gelatin mixture into egg white mixture. Spoon into the lined springform pan.

- Chill until set. Remove band from springform pan and spread with whipped cream. Decorate with mandarin oranges.

- Yield: 12 servings

Festive Cranberry Torte

A sweet conclusion.

Crust

- 1½ cups graham cracker crumbs
- 2 ounces pecans, chopped (½ cup)
- ¼ cup sugar
- 6 tablespoons butter, melted

Filling

- 1½ cups fresh cranberries
- 1 cup sugar
- 2 large egg whites
- 1 tablespoon frozen orange juice concentrate, thawed
- 1 teaspoon vanilla
- ⅛ teaspoon salt
- 1 cup heavy cream, whipped

Glaze

- ½ cup sugar
- 1 tablespoon cornstarch
- ¾ cup cranberries
- ⅔ cup water

- To make crust: in a mixing bowl, combine graham cracker crumbs, pecans, sugar, and butter. Press into bottom and sides of an 8-inch springform pan. Chill.

- To make filling: in a large mixing bowl, combine cranberries and 1 cup sugar. Let stand for 5 minutes. Add unbeaten egg whites, orange juice, vanilla, and salt. Beat on low speed until frothy, then beat on high for 6 to 8 minutes, until they stand in stiff peaks.

- In small mixing bowl, whip cream to soft peaks. Fold in cranberry mixture and pour into crust. Freeze until firm.

- To make glaze: in a saucepan, heat sugar, cornstarch, ¾ cup cranberries, and water until bubbly. Cool to room temperature. Do not refrigerate.

(recipe continued on next page)

(Festive Cranberry Torte, continued)

- To serve: remove torte from pan and spoon glaze in the center.

- Yield: 10 servings

Cranberry Crunch

Make this in advance and place in the oven to warm just before serving. Try with other canned fruit instead of cranberries.

nonstick cooking spray
1¼ cups quick oats
1¼ cups flour
1 cup brown sugar
½ cup butter, softened
1 can whole berry cranberry sauce
½ cup nuts, chopped (optional)

- Preheat oven to 350°.

- Spray a 9 x 9-inch shallow pan with nonstick cooking spray.

- Mix together oats, flour, brown sugar, and butter.

- Pour half of oat mixture into pan. Cover with cranberry sauce. Top with remaining oat mixture and nuts.

- Bake 45 minutes to 1 hour, until top is golden brown.

- Yield: 9 servings

Fairy Sherbet

Heat lemons before extracting juice
for twice as much juice.

2 large eggs
⅓ cup sugar
¾ cup light corn syrup
2 cups buttermilk
⅔ cup lemon juice
1 tablespoon grated lemon peel

- With an electric mixer, beat eggs and sugar until the mixture forms a ribbon when the beater is lifted. Add corn syrup and beat the mixture for 1 minute. Stir in buttermilk, lemon juice, and grated lemon peel.

- Transfer the mixture to a shallow pan and freeze for 1 hour.

- Transfer the mixture to a chilled bowl, whisk until smooth and return to the pan.

- Cover and freeze the sherbet until it is firm.

- Yield: 1 quart

Real buttermilk — what's left after butter is churned — almost doesn't exist anymore. Today's buttermilk is cultured. A good substitute for buttermilk: add 1 tablespoon white vinegar or lemon juice to 1 cup milk and let stand for 5 minutes before using.

Kahlúa Chocolate Nut Squares

nonstick cooking spray
1½ cups sifted flour
¾ teaspoon baking powder
½ teaspoon salt
½ cup butter, softened
¾ cup brown sugar, firmly packed
1 large egg
¼ cup plus 1 tablespoon Kahlúa
1 cup semi-sweet chocolate chips
1 ounce walnuts or pecans, chopped
(¼ cup)
Brown Butter Icing
2 tablespoons butter
1 tablespoon Kahlúa
2 teaspoons milk or cream
1⅓ cups sifted confectioners' sugar

- Preheat oven to 350°.

- Spray a 7 x 11-inch baking pan with nonstick cooking spray.

- Resift flour with baking powder and salt.

- Cream butter and sugar. Beat in eggs. Stir in ¼ cup Kahlúa, then flour mixture. Beat well. Add chocolate chips and nuts. Pour into baking dish.

- Bake 30 minutes. Cool in pan 15 minutes, then brush with 1 tablespoon of Kahlúa.

- To make Brown Butter Icing: in a saucepan, heat butter until lightly browned. Remove from heat. Add 1 tablespoon Kahlúa, milk or cream, and confectioners' sugar. Beat until smooth. (May need to add more milk or cream to make spreadable.)

- Spread Brown Butter Icing on cake when fully cooled.

- Yield: 12 servings

Lemondown Fancies

½ **cup (1 stick) butter**
½ **cup confectioners' sugar**
1 **cup flour**
2 **large eggs**
1 **cup sugar**
½ **teaspoon baking powder**
¼ **teaspoon salt**
2 **tablespoons lemon juice**

- Preheat oven to 350°.

- Cream butter and confectioners' sugar. Add flour.

- Press evenly on the bottom of an ungreased 9 x 9-inch pan and bake for 20 minutes.

- With an electric mixer, beat eggs, sugar, baking powder, salt, and lemon juice until light and fluffy. Pour over hot crust and bake 25 minutes or until imprint remains when touched in the center.

- To serve: cool and cut into 2-inch squares.

- Yield: 16 squares

"How do they taste? They taste like more."
— *H. L. Mencken*

New Orleans Bread Pudding

Every good New Orleans cook has his or her own version, prepared from a jealously guarded secret recipe. Here is ours:

1 loaf French bread
4 cups milk
3 large eggs
2 cups sugar
2 tablespoons vanilla
3 tablespoons butter, melted
1 cup raisins
Whiskey Sauce
1 cup sugar
1 large egg
½ cup (1 stick) butter, melted
bourbon or whiskey

- Preheat oven to 300°.

- Pour butter in bottom of a 9 x 13-inch pan.

- Soak bread in milk. Crush with hands until well mixed. Add eggs, sugar, vanilla, and raisins. Stir well. Pour bread mixture into baking pan.

- Bake for 1½ hours, until firm. Cool to room temperature.

- To make whiskey sauce: in a saucepan, mix sugar and egg. Add melted butter and heat over low heat to dissolve sugar. Add whiskey to enhance taste, as well as make it smoother and creamier.

- Pour half of the whiskey sauce over the pudding and heat under broiler until bubbly. Slice heated bread pudding into cubes and put into individual dessert dishes. Serve remaining sauce on the side.

- Yield: 12 servings

Peaches Almondine

A very elegant presentation. Perfect for a party.

 ¼ **cup white wine**
 ½ **cup sugar**
 6 **ripe peaches, peeled, halved and pitted**
 12 **amaretti biscuits, crushed**
 1 **large egg yolk, beaten**
 3 **tablespoons heavy cream**

- Boil the wine and sugar for 5 minutes to form a syrup.

- Poach the peach halves in the syrup for 5 minutes, then lift out with a slotted spoon and let cool.

- In a separate bowl, whip the heavy cream. Fold in the amaretti crumbs and egg yolk. Spoon into peach halves.

- To serve: arrange the filled peaches on a serving plate and pour the remaining syrup around them.

- Yield: 6 servings

"After a good dinner, one can forgive anybody, even one's own relations."
 — *Oscar Wilde*

Strawberries Bourbonnaise

This deliciously simple recipe is too good to be true. Make it for no reason and it will be something nobody will forget. Make it for a special occasion and it will become a tradition.

1½ quarts strawberries, stemmed (the fresher the better)
2 cups sugar
¼ cup unsalted butter
½ cup heavy cream
½ cup bourbon
whipped cream

Bourbon adds a special touch to fruit desserts and other sweets. Why is this American corn whiskey called bourbon? It gets its name from its birthplace, Bourbon County, Kentucky.

- Use a heavy cast aluminum or black iron skillet and make sure bottom of pan fits burners.

- Place on medium heat until you feel heat penetrate through bottom of pan to hand held over pan. When pan is hot, immediately add sugar. Stir with long handled wooden spoon. As sugar starts to melt, stir gently until you have golden colored syrup.

- Remove from heat and add butter. When butter is melted, add heavy cream a little at a time...very carefully. Stir in bourbon.

- Let sauce cool down and pour into a glass container. Cover and refrigerate. When cool, this wonderful sauce will be caramelized.

- To serve: place strawberries in individual stemmed glasses. Pour caramel sauce over strawberries. Top with a dollop of whipped cream. Sauce can be kept in refrigerator for several weeks.

- Yield: 8 servings

Apple Walnut Cobbler

nonstick cooking spray
2 pounds Winesap apples, pared, cored and
  thinly sliced (makes about 5 cups)
  juice and grated peel of 1 lemon
¾ cup sugar
1 teaspoon cinnamon
3 ounces walnuts or pecans, chopped
  (¾ cup)

Topping
1 large egg
1 cup milk
⅓ cup butter
1 cup sugar
1 cup flour
1 teaspoon baking powder
  vanilla ice cream

- Preheat oven to 350°.

- Spray shallow baking dish with nonstick cooking spray

- Place sliced apples in the bottom of the dish. Sprinkle lemon juice and lemon peel over apples. Mix sugar and cinnamon together. Sprinkle over apples. Sprinkle nuts over apples.

- To make topping: beat egg and milk. With an electric mixer, cream together butter and sugar. Continue beating, adding the egg mixture. Slowly mix in flour and baking powder. Pour topping over apples.

- Bake for 50 minutes.

- Serve warm or cold, delicious topped with vanilla ice cream.

- Yield: 8 servings

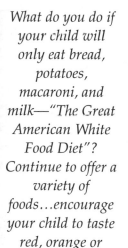

Cheery Cherry Tomato Salad

1 **pint cherry tomatoes**
6 **bacon slices**
¼ **cup mayonnaise**
1 **tablespoon tarragon vinegar**
2 **tablespoons olive oil**
1 **tablespoon chopped fresh basil**
6 **large romaine lettuce leaves, washed**
2 **tablespoons chopped chives**

- Wash and stem tomatoes. Dry completely.

- Cook bacon until very crisp; drain on paper towels. Crumble.

- Mix crumbled bacon, mayonnaise, vinegar, olive oil, and basil. Pour over tomatoes. Stir.

- Serve on lettuce leaves and sprinkle with chives.

- Yield: 6 servings

Cherry tomatoes are kid-sized and kid-friendly. They are available all year round and their flavor is consistently good, especially in winter when the "hot house" tomatoes are tasteless. Don't ever, ever refrigerate tomatoes!

Choo Choo Salad

*For engineers over 3, who are
experienced chew-chewers.*

**1 (10-ounce) package frozen green peas,
thawed**
2 large celery stalks, chopped
1 pint sour cream
**8 strips of bacon, cooked crisp, drained and
crumbled**
½ cup salted peanuts

• Mix peas, celery, sour cream, bacon, and
peanuts together in a plastic bowl and cover.
(If you can find a plastic bowl that has a cover,
that would be great).

• Refrigerate at least one hour before serving.

• Yield: 6 servings

Old King Cole Spinach

nonstick cooking spray
2 large eggs
**1 (10-ounce) package frozen chopped
spinach, drained**
1 pinch nutmeg

• Preheat oven to 350°.

• Spray a 1-quart casserole dish with nonstick
cooking spray.

• With an egg beater, beat eggs until foamy.

• Squeeze the spinach dry and mix with the eggs.
Sprinkle with nutmeg.

• Pour into the casserole dish and bake 30
minutes.

• Yield: 4 servings

Littlest Angel Biscuits

nonstick cooking spray
2 cups flour
3 teaspoons baking powder
1½ teaspoons salt
3 tablespoons butter, melted
⅔ cup buttermilk

- Preheat oven to 475°.

- Spray cookie sheet with nonstick cooking spray.

- Sift flour, baking powder, and salt into a bowl.

- Stir in the butter and buttermilk to make a soft dough.

- Lightly knead dough on a floured board until it can be rolled out.

- Roll out dough to ½-inch thickness (the same width as a plastic cassette box). Cut out biscuits with fun shaped cookie cutters.

- Place biscuits on the cookie sheet and bake 10 to 12 minutes. Serve warm.

- Yield: 24 biscuits

Let your child help with preparation.

These biscuits are fun to make, but a little messy. Mix the dough gently so they don't become tough and chewy. If you have a window in your oven door, you can watch them rise to two times higher than when they went in. Don't forget to clean up!

Ragamuffins

1 **large egg**
½ **cup milk**
¼ **cup butter, melted**
1 **cup apples, cored and coarsely chopped**
1½ **cups flour**
2 **teaspoons baking powder**
½ **teaspoon salt**
1½ **teaspoons cinnamon**
½ **cup sugar**
¾ **cup raisins (optional)**

- Preheat oven to 400°.

- Place muffin papers in a muffin tin.

- In a large bowl, beat egg. Stir in milk, butter, and apples.

- Combine flour, baking powder, salt, cinnamon, sugar, and raisins.

- Add dry ingredients all at once into the wet ingredients.

- Stir just to moisten. Spoon batter into muffin cups, filling two-thirds full.

- Sprinkle each muffin with additional sugar and cinnamon before baking.

- Bake for 20 minutes.

- Yield: 12 muffins

A great breakfast muffin. You get your fruit and fiber at the same time. Make a double batch; they freeze beautifully.

Brown Bag Chicken

12 chicken drumsticks
⅓ cup flour
1 teaspoon salt
¼ teaspoon pepper
1 teaspoon paprika
½ teaspoon curry powder
1 teaspoon sage
½ teaspoon thyme
½ teaspoon onion salt
⅓ cup butter or margarine

- Preheat oven to 450°.

- In a heavy brown paper bag combine flour with salt, pepper, paprika, curry powder, sage, thyme, and onion salt.

- Put butter in a baking pan and place in oven to melt

- Put two drumsticks in the bag at a time and shake to coat well.

- Place all the coated drumsticks in the baking pan and bake uncovered for 30 minutes. Turn drumsticks and bake 15 minutes longer. May be served hot or cold.

- Yield: 12 servings

" 'It's a comforting sort of thing to have', said Christopher Robin."
— "House at Pooh Corner", A. A. Milne

Chop Chop Suey

2 tablespoons cornstarch
3 tablespoons soy sauce
¼ teaspoon ginger
½ cup water
1 pound boneless lean pork
2 tablespoons oil
2 cups cabbage, thinly shredded
2 large celery stalks, thinly sliced (1 cup)
1 bunch green onions, thinly sliced
1 (16-ounce) can bean sprouts, drained
1 (8-ounce) can sliced water chestnuts, drained
3 cups hot cooked rice

- Combine cornstarch, soy sauce, ginger, and water in bowl; mix well.

- Cut pork into thin, bite-sized pieces.

- Heat oil in a large skillet. Brown pork in skillet over medium high heat, stirring frequently.

- Add cornstarch mixture. Mix well.

- Add cabbage, celery, green onions, bean sprouts, and water chestnuts.

- Cook for 5 minutes or until vegetables are tender crisp, stirring frequently.

- Serve over hot cooked rice.

- Yield: 6 servings

"If there is anything the Chinese are serious about, it is food. Eating is truly one of the great joys of life."
— *Lin Yutang*

Corny Cheesy Row Boats

6 patty shells, frozen
2 tablespoons butter
2 tablespoons flour
¼ cup milk
½ cup Cheddar cheese, shredded
1 (7-ounce) can corn kernels, drained
1 cup chopped cooked chicken
12 pretzel sticks

- Bake patty shells according to package directions.

- Heat butter in a medium pan. Stir in flour and cook over low heat for 1 minute.

- *Stir, stir, stir your boat gently over heat....* Add milk gradually, stirring until smooth. Stir constantly over medium heat for 5 minutes or until the mixture comes to a boil and thickens. Boil 1 minute more; remove from heat.

- Stir in the cheese, corn, and chicken.

- Divide mixtures into shells. Arrange pretzel sticks as oars and serve.

- Yield: 6 servings

Add eye appeal; like the oars of "Corny Cheesy Row Boats", or different shape cuts of vegetables, or decorate lunch bags with colorful stickers.

Filled French Rolls

2 French rolls
½ cup diced Cheddar cheese
1 teaspoon minced onion
2 small gherkin pickles, chopped
2 tablespoons tomato sauce
  dash pepper

- Preheat oven to 350°.

- Cut off the top ¼ of roll. Scoop out bread leaving a shell. Place bread in bowl and tear into small pieces.

- Mix bread with cheese, onion, pickles, tomato sauce, and pepper.

- Divide mixture between bread shells. Put top back on and wrap in aluminum foil.

- Bake for 30 minutes.

- Yield: 2 servings

Falling Leaves Fruit Cup

2 Red Delicious apples, cored
2 Bartlett pears, cored
2 bananas, sliced ½-inch thick
½ pound red grapes, halved
½ cup almond slivers, toasted
1 cup vanilla yogurt
1 teaspoon cinnamon
¼ teaspoon ground ginger
½ teaspoon nutmeg
1 tablespoon apple cider

- Chop apples and pears into 1-inch chunks.

- Combine apples, pears, bananas, grapes, and almonds in a glass serving bowl.

- In another bowl, mix yogurt with cinnamon, ginger, nutmeg, and apple cider.

- Pour over fruit and stir to coat evenly. Chill.

- Yield: 10 servings

Jolly Green Giant Shells

water
1½ teaspoons salt, divided
24 whole giant pasta shells
 1 tablespoon vegetable oil
 1 (10-ounce) package frozen chopped
   spinach
 2 tablespoons butter, melted
 1 small onion, minced
 2 cups cottage cheese
 1 large egg, beaten
 1 teaspoon black pepper
 1 (28-ounce) can tomato sauce
 4 ounces mozzarella cheese, shredded
   (1 cup)

- Fill a big pot with water and 1 teaspoon of the salt. Heat the water until boiling. Add pasta shells and boil for 9 minutes. Drain shells and put in a bowl. Gently toss shells in oil and set aside.

- Thaw frozen spinach and drain, squeezing out all water (like you would squeeze a wet washcloth).

- Heat butter in a skillet and sauté onion until soft. (The onions will be clear like cellophane tape.) Stir in spinach.

- Put spinach mixture in a bowl. Add cottage cheese, egg, ½ teaspoon of the salt, and pepper.

- Spoon mixture into each shell.

- Pour half of the sauce into the bottom of a 9 x 13-inch baking dish. Arrange stuffed shells in dish. Cover with remaining sauce.

- Bake at 350° for 30 minutes.

- Remove from oven. Sprinkle with mozzarella cheese. Return to oven until cheese is melted and bubbly, about 3 minutes.

- Yield: 6 servings

Miss Piggy Pies

nonstick cooking spray
1 cup ham, diced
½ cup diced pepperoni sausage
½ cup cubed Cheddar cheese
1 tablespoon grated Parmesan cheese
½ teaspoon salt
½ teaspoon pepper
1 large egg
1 cup flour
½ teaspoon baking powder
1 cup milk

- Preheat oven to 375°.

- Spray miniature muffin tins with nonstick cooking spray.

- In a large bowl; mix ham, pepperoni, Cheddar cheese, Parmesan cheese, salt, pepper, egg, flour, baking powder, and milk.

- Fill muffin tins three-fourths full. Bake for 20 to 25 minutes or until lightly browned.

- Yield: 3 dozen

What to do when your child will only eat one food... called a "food jag". Serve the "jag" food as long as the child wants it, but offer other foods with the meal. Food jags rarely last long enough to cause any harm.

This Little Pig Went to Market: A ham is a leg of pork that has been wet or dry cured and probably smoked. The word itself is derived from the Old English word for thigh, "hamm."

Cheesy Tuna Puffs

nonstick cooking spray
½ **cup water**
¼ **cup butter**
½ **cup flour**
dash salt
2 **large eggs**
1 **(7-ounce) can solid white tuna, drained**
1 **cup grated Parmesan cheese**
2 **tablespoons mayonnaise**

Did you know that rinsing canned tuna for about a minute washes away at least half the sodium without affecting the taste?

- Preheat oven to 425°.

- Spray cookie sheet with nonstick cooking spray.

- Place butter in water and bring to a boil.

- Sift flour with salt and add to butter mixture.

- Cook, stirring vigorously, until batter leaves sides of pan and forms a ball. Remove from heat.

- Beat in eggs, one at a time.

- Drop by rounded teaspoonful onto a cookie sheet. Bake at 425° for 10 minutes, then at 350° for 20 minutes. Cool.

- In a small bowl, flake tuna with a fork.

- Grate Parmesan cheese in a blender until powder fine. Mix cheese and mayonnaise into tuna. Mixture should be smooth.

- Cut off small piece of the cream puff for a lid and stuff tuna spread into cream puffs. Replace lids. Serve at your dolly's next tea party.

- Yield: 12 servings

Yams with Ham I Am!

4 large yams
½ pound cooked ham
2 tablespoons butter
½ cup brown sugar, packed, divided
¼ teaspoon cinnamon
⅛ teaspoon ground cloves
¼ cup orange juice
2 tablespoons butter, cut in bits

• Boil yams until they can just be pierced with a fork; cool slightly. When cool enough to handle, peel and slice lengthwise into ½-inch slices.

• Slice ham into ½-inch slices about as large as the yams.

• Melt butter and pour into a shallow 2-quart baking dish.

• Stir in ¼ cup brown sugar.

• Place the yams and ham slices in the baking dish in alternating rows, turning yams to coat with butter.

• Sprinkle top with remaining brown sugar, cinnamon, and cloves. Pour juice over all. Place bits of butter on top.

• Bake at 325° for 45 minutes or until top is brown.

• Yield: 4 servings

Rum Dum Diddley

1 small yellow onion, chopped
1 tablespoon butter
2 tablespoons water
1 (10-ounce) can tomato soup
8 ounces Cheddar cheese, shredded
1 tablespoon Worcestershire sauce
4 English muffins, split into eight halves

- Heat butter in saucepan. Sauté onion until tender.

- Add water and soup. Simmer for 3 to 4 minutes.

- Add cheese, stirring until melted. Add Worcestershire sauce.

- Serve over toasted English muffins or toasted bread.

- Yield: 4 servings

Have a non-traditional breakfast: leftover spaghetti, or pizza, peanut butter on apple slices, baked potato topped with cheese, steamed vegetables or chili.

Back Yard Banana Boats

1 banana, unpeeled
semi-sweet chocolate chips
miniature marshmallows
brown sugar

- Slit each banana lengthwise but not all the way through. Leave the skin on (do not peel).

- Put 1 to 2 teaspoons each of the chocolate chips and marshmallows in slit.

- Sprinkle lightly with brown sugar.

- Wrap tightly in foil, being sure to seal ends.

- Place on grill or over campfire, seam side up. Takes about 7 minutes to cook.

- Yield: 1 serving

Cowboy Cookies

If your child is under 3 or a picky eater
(picks nuts out of food),
make cowboy cookies without the nuts.

1 cup vegetable oil
1 cup sugar
1 cup brown sugar, firmly packed
2 large eggs
2 cups flour
½ teaspoon salt
1 teaspoon baking soda
½ teaspoon baking powder
2 cups quick oatmeal
1 cup shredded coconut
1 teaspoon vanilla
½ cup chopped nuts
6 ounces chocolate chips

- Preheat oven to 350°.

- Mix the sugars and oil together in a large bowl.

- Stir eggs into mixture.

- Add flour, salt, baking soda, baking powder, oatmeal, coconut, vanilla, nuts, and chocolate chips. Mix well.

- Drop dough by heaping teaspoonfuls onto a cookie sheet and bake until light brown about 8 to 10 minutes. Do not overbake.

- Yield: 2 dozen cookies

Place a piece of rye bread in a covered container with brown sugar to prevent lumping.

Potato Chip Cookies

1 cup butter, softened
½ cup sugar
1¾ cups flour
¾ cup plain potato chips, coarsely crushed
1 teaspoon vanilla
⅔ cup powdered sugar

- Preheat oven to 350°.

- With an electric mixer, cream butter and sugar. Beat until light and fluffy.

- Add flour, potato chips, and vanilla. Beat well.

- Drop dough by heaping teaspoonfuls onto ungreased cookie sheets.

- Bake for 10 to 12 minutes and edges are lightly browned.

- Cool on wire rack.

- Roll in powdered sugar.

- Yield: 4 dozen cookies

A wonderful shortbread kind of cookie. You will be so surprised to taste what the potato chips do in this cookie. Be careful, the bottoms brown very quickly. Bake them on the middle shelf of the oven.

Terrific Toffee Cookies

1 sleeve unsalted saltine-type crackers
2 sticks butter
¾ cup sugar
1 (12-ounce) package chocolate chips
1 cup pecans or walnuts, chopped

- Preheat oven to 400°.

- Line a cookie sheet with sides with aluminum foil and butter it completely.

- Melt butter and sugar in a saucepan.

- Layer saltine-type crackers on cookie sheet to cover foil. Pour melted butter mixture over crackers.

- Bake for 5 minutes.

- Immediately after baking, pour chocolate chips onto the crackers and spread chocolate until melted all over. Top with chopped nuts and chill 15 minutes.

- Peel off foil and cut into squares.

- Yield: 2 dozen or more, depending on how large you cut the squares

These cookies are so much fun to make and are so good to eat. At our house, these cookies are Santa's favorites. The plate is always clean.

Roasted Spring Garlic

12 medium cloves or 3 small heads of garlic
¼ cup olive oil (or more, as needed), divided
salt
pepper
several sprigs of thyme and rosemary

- Preheat oven to 300°.

- Cut the tops off each head of garlic, exposing just a bit of each clove.

- Place the heads in a baking dish, drizzle with 2 tablespoons of olive oil, sprinkle with salt, pepper, thyme, and rosemary.

- Cover with foil and bake for an hour.

- Uncover, baste with additional olive oil and continue baking for another half hour until completely tender.

- Let stand at room temperature until cool enough to handle, then squeeze the garlic from the peel.

- Serve with crusty bread, oven dried tomatoes and goat cheese mixed with heavy or sour cream. An alternate serving method is to leave the roasted head intact and serve with bread. A seafood fork is perfect for extracting the cloves.

- To make a Wonderful Roasted Garlic Soup: prepare the garlic as above and purée using a sieve or a food processor. Add 1-quart chicken stock, ½ cup cream and salt and pepper. To serve, top with croutons and Parmesan cheese.

Chef Christing Reynaud of the Silk Purse Restaurant

"There is no such thing as a little garlic."
— Arthur Baer

Garden Vegetable Terrine

1 **pound ground, skinless chicken breast**
2 **large egg whites**
8 **ounces heavy cream**
1 **teaspoon salt**
1 **tablespoon chopped dill**
1 **tablespoon chopped tarragon**
1 **tablespoon chopped basil**
¼ **teaspoon white pepper**
1 **pound carrots, medium dice**
8 **ounces artichoke bottoms, small pie cuts**
1 **pound spinach, deribbed leaves**
8 **ounces zucchini, seeded and diced**
8 **ounces shiitake mushrooms, coarsely chopped**
1 **pound red pepper, julienned**

- Prepare a day in advance of serving.

- Place the ground chicken and egg whites into a well-chilled bowl of a food processor. Process to a fine paste.

- Add the cream, salt, dill, tarragon, basil, and white pepper. Use quick on-off pulses until ingredients are just incorporated, do not over process.

- Put in a bowl and refrigerate. This is called a mousseline.

- Steam carrots, zucchini, artichokes, mushrooms, spinach, and peppers separately until tender. Drain and dry on several layers of paper towels.

- Coarsely chop the cooled, dried spinach.

- Gently fold all vegetables into the chicken mousseline.

- Preheat oven to 350°.

- Line two 12-inch enameled loaf pans or molds with plastic wrap. Divide terrine mixture

(recipe continued on next page)

(Garden Vegetable Terrine, continued)

evenly between the molds. Cover with plastic wrap and place in prepared bain-marie. (Put hot water in a baking pan large enough to hold the two molds. Water should cover at least three-fourth of the molds.) Place in preheated oven. Immediately reduce the heat to 275°.

• Check the water bath during cooking and maintain a fairly steady temperature of 170°.

• Terrines are done when an internal temperature of 140° is reached. Remove from water bath and take off plastic. Cool to room temperature, then refrigerate overnight before serving.

• To serve: slice terrines (½ to ¾-inch is good) and place on greens for presentation. Serve with fresh tomato salsa and sour cream on the side.

• Yield: 25 servings

Courtney Walker of Eagle Lodge Conference Center

The ancients believed that mushrooms sprang from bolts of lightning. While many Romans admired their taste, few among them were able to tell the edible from the lethal, and mushrooms eventually fell out of culinary fashion.

Trio of Exotic Mushrooms with Opal Basil Vinaigrette

5 ounces fresh shiitake mushrooms
6 ounces fresh oyster mushrooms
6 ounces fresh portabello mushrooms
½ cup olive oil, divided
1 leek (white part only), cleaned, julienned
4 medium garlic cloves, chopped (2 teaspoons)
4 teaspoons chopped shallots
¼ cup rice wine vinegar
salt and pepper
8 large leaves of fresh purple basil, julienned
2 heads Belgium endive (separated leaves)

- Remove stems from mushrooms. Clean and quarter mushrooms. Set aside.

- Heat ¼ cup of olive oil and fry leeks until brown. Remove from oil and drain on dish.

- Add mushrooms into same pan with oil and sauté for one minute. Add garlic and shallots; sauté for another minute.

- Deglaze with rice vinegar. Season with salt and pepper. Add remaining olive oil and basil.

- Divide onto four plates. Place five leaves of Belgium endive on plate to form a flower. Top with the crisp leek mixture.

- Yield: 4 servings

Kurt Wohlgemuth of The Atop the Bellevue

Mushrooms tend to absorb the water they are washed in, so rather than washing, wipe them clean with paper towels.

Quenelle of Red Pepper Mousse with Tomato Sauce

6 red peppers, blanched for 3 minutes in salted boiling water
1 cup chicken stock
1 teaspoon paprika
4 leaves of gelatin, soaked in cold water
1 cup heavy cream, whipped and kept cold

Sauce

4 ripe tomatoes, halved and seeds removed
juice from ½ of an orange
¼ cup sherry wine vinegar
salt

- Remove the skin of the blanched red pepper, the ribs, and seeds inside. Trim well and cut into pieces.

- Cook the red pepper pieces in the chicken stock for 30 minutes over low heat. Drain the liquid.

- In a blender, mix the red peppers with the paprika and the 4 soft gelatin leaves until smooth. Remove from blender and let cool in the refrigerator.

- Mix the whipped cream with the red pepper purée and season to taste. Place mixture in the refrigerator until set (3 hours minimum).

- To make tomato sauce: in a blender, mix the tomatoes with sherry wine vinegar, orange juice, and salt. Then pass the sauce through a fine strainer and refrigerate until cold.

- To serve: roll the red pepper mousse with a warm spoon (left in hot water). Place 2 or 3 quenelles on a cold plate and pour the tomato sauce around them. Garnish with chervil or parsley. Serve with a slice of toasted French bread.

- Yield: 4 servings

Chef Jean-Marie Lacroix of Four Seasons Hotel

Shrimp and Beans, Florentine Style

1 **pound small shrimp (40-50 sized), shelled and cooked**
1 **pound dried cannellini beans, rinsed**
1 **cup celery hearts, cut into small cubes**
1 **handful fresh basil, coarsely chopped**
4 **fresh plum tomatoes (peeled, if desired), cut into small cubes**
  virgin olive oil
  salt
  pepper

- Soak beans overnight.

- Rinse soaked beans and add water to cover. Cook on low fire until tender (about 45 minutes).

- Add celery, tomatoes, basil, and cooked shrimp. Add just enough olive oil to coat all the ingredients. Salt and pepper to taste.

- Serve at room temperature.

- Yield: 10 servings

Ristorante La Buca

Dried cannellini beans are usually found in the grocery store disguised as white kidney beans.

Basil, once so rare that only the "basileus," or sovereign, might cut it, became popular in Italy during the Middle Ages. Ther herb is a variety of mint and is indigenous to India, where it is considered an omen of happiness.

Gumbo Ya Ya

1 cup lard
2 cups flour
2 quarts chicken stock
½ cup clarified butter
1 pound chicken leg meat, cooked and diced
1 pound andouille sausage, cooked and diced
1 pound chicken tenders, cut in half
1 teaspoon minced garlic
1 teaspoon cayenne pepper
1 tablespoon salt
1 teaspoon black pepper
1 pound okra, sliced

• To make Cajun roux: sauté lard and flour, stirring constantly until copper-colored or arm breaks.

• To make gumbo base: combine chicken stock and Cajun roux in a pot and bring to a gentle boil.

• Heat clarified butter in a large skillet. Sauté chicken leg meat, andouille sausage, and chicken tenders.

• Add garlic, cayenne pepper, salt, black pepper, and okra. Cook thoroughly.

• Add chicken mixture to the gumbo base. Serve hot with rice.

• Yield: 8 servings

Thomas J. Downing of Café Nola

"If it ain't got okra, it ain't gumbo!"
— *Anonymous*

Soupe au Potiron (Pumpkin Soup)

1 **cup sliced leeks, white part only**
2 **tablespoons clarified butter**
2 **quarts raw, peeled, pumpkin pieces, cut into one-inch cubes (butternut squash makes an excellent substitution)**
⅓ **cup uncooked rice**
1 **tablespoon dark brown sugar**
2-3 **quarts chicken stock (enough to cover the pumpkin by two inches)**
2 **teaspoons of grated fresh ginger root**
2 **tablespoons tomato purée**
1 **cup heavy cream**
¼ **teaspoon (to taste) ground mace**
salt and pepper

- In a large stockpot, sweat the leeks in the clarified butter—until limp but not browned.

- Add the raw pumpkin, rice, brown sugar, the ginger, tomato paste, and chicken stock.

- Bring to a full boil over high heat; then adjust to a simmer, and cook for about 30 to 45 minutes, until the pumpkin is tender.

- Purée the soup using a food mill, or press through a fine sieve. Season with salt, pepper, and mace.

- Serve hot, garnished with fresh nasturtium blossoms and/or toasted pine nuts. The scooped out shells of very small pumpkins may be used as soup terrines.

- Yield: 10 servings

Chef Fritz Blank of Deux Cheminées

Oat Bran Muffins

¾ **cup oat bran**
¾ **cup oatmeal**
¾ **cup whole wheat flour**
2 **teaspoons baking powder**
½ **teaspoon salt**
¼ **cup brown sugar**
2 **egg whites**
¼ **cup maple syrup**
¼ **cup vegetable oil**
1 **cup low-fat milk**
fruits and/or nuts (optional)

- Preheat oven to 425°.

- Grease muffin cups.

- Combine oat bran, oatmeal, flour, baking powder, salt, and brown sugar. Set aside.

- Blend egg whites, maple syrup, vegetable oil, and low-fat milk.

- Fold the dry ingredients into the wet ingredients until only just blended. Add dried fruit or fresh fruit or nuts, if desired.

- Spoon into muffin cups and bake for 15 minutes.

- Yield: 12 muffins

Becky Roller of Roller's Restaurant

Dried fruits are good sources of potassium and iron, as well as fiber. But since they are also high in calories, be careful of the serving size.

Tomato Corn Clam Chowder

4 cups clam juice
1 cup white wine
1 garlic clove
2 sprigs fresh thyme
50 little neck clams
4 ears of corn (smoked over hickory chips)
  or 2 cups frozen corn with ¼ teaspoon
  liquid smoke
4 tablespoons butter
1 large onion, diced
1 leek, diced
1 carrot, diced
1 celery stalk, diced
2 cups heavy cream
6 plum tomatoes, cut each into 8 wedges,
  roast in oven for forty minutes at 400°
  degrees
  juice of ½ lemon
  salt and pepper

- Place in large pot: clam juice, wine, garlic, and thyme. Bring to a boil over high heat.

- Once it boils, add clams. Boil for 4 to 6 minutes or until clams open.

- Remove from heat, strain out clams and reserve broth.

- Strain broth through cheese cloth and set aside.

- Pick clams from shells and set aside.

- Cut corn off cobs and reserve both.

- Melt butter in large heavy bottom pot. Add onions, leek, carrots, and celery. Sweat until translucent.

- Add clam broth and corn cobs and simmer for 30 minutes.

(recipe continued on next page)

(Tomato Corn Clam Chowder, continued)

- Remove corn cobs and discard. Add lemon juice, tomato wedges, clams, and corn kernels. Salt and pepper to taste.

- Yield: 8 servings

Braddock's Tavern

Warm Spinach-Arugula-Basil Salad with Pinenuts and Roasted Pepper

1½ (10-ounce) packages spinach
1 bunch arugula
18 basil leaves
1 red pepper
½ cup extra virgin olive oil
¼ cup balsamic vinegar
1½ ounces pinenuts, toasted (about ⅓ cup)
¼ teaspoon salt
   freshly ground pepper
3 ounces chèvre, crumbled (optional)

- Wash and thoroughly dry the spinach, arugula, and basil leaves.

- Roast the pepper in a 450° oven until skin is blackened and blistered. Peel and julienne. Set aside.

- In sauté pan, heat the olive oil and vinegar to a boil. Add the pinenuts, salt, and pepper.

- Toss with the greens. Divide among six salad plates. Garnish with the roasted pepper and crumbled chèvre.

- Yield: 6 servings

Paul Roller Of Roller's Restaurant in Chestnut Hill

Cooper Hospital Award Winning Sticky Buns – "Best of Philly"

1 (1-pound 2-ounce) package hot roll mix
3 tablespoons butter, melted
3 tablespoons sugar
1 teaspoon cinnamon
⅓ cup raisins
¼ cup walnuts, chopped
1 egg white, whisked

Topping

½ cup butter, softened
½ cup dark brown sugar, packed
½ cup light brown sugar, packed
⅓ cup walnuts, chopped
⅓ cup raisins

- Follow box directions for sweet roll mix. Remove dough from bowl and put into a greased deep pan. Proof dough for 45 minutes at about 100°.

- Dust work area with flour and roll out dough into an 8 x 12-inch rectangle about ¼-inch thick. Brush off excess flour. Force air from dough. Brush with 3 tablespoons butter, leave one-inch space unbuttered at bottom of dough (for ease of sealing). Mix sugar and cinnamon together. Sprinkle cinnamon and sugar mixture, walnuts, and raisins on top of buttered dough. (If there is any butter remaining drizzle it over the sugar.) Roll up like jelly roll, starting from buttered end. Seal with egg wash. Slice into eight 1-inch wide rolls.

- To make topping: cream ½ cup butter with the brown sugars (if you don't have light brown sugar or if you only want to buy 1 package— we recommend the dark brown sugar) until light and fluffy. Spread into the bottom of a

(recipe continued on next page)

(Cooper Hospital Award Winning Sticky Buns - "Best of Philly", continued)

10-inch round pan. Sprinkle bottom of pan with walnuts and raisins.

- Place pieces of the rolled dough over topping in bottom of cake pan. Proof until double in size.
- Bake at 375° for 25 minutes. If topping has not caramelized, cover with aluminum foil and bake an additional 10 minutes.
- Yield: 8 buns

Chef Lewis Saunders

A Sunny Sunday Brunch

Bacon 'n Egg Sophisticate

Blueberry Pouffe Sunday Morning

Baked Crabmeat Remick

Irish Soda Bread

Cooper Hospital Award Winning Sticky Buns

Mimosas

Bloody Marys

Roasted Natural Amish Chicken With Roasted Vidalia Onions And Crayfish

10 **pounds whole live crayfish**
4 **whole Vidalia onions**
1 **teaspoon brown sugar**
  water
  salt
  pepper
1 **whole (5 pounds) Amish or free range chicken, fat trimmed**
8 **tablespoons (1 stick) unsalted butter at room temperature, divided**
1 **large sprig fresh rosemary, remove stem and chop leaves**
2½ **cups chicken stock**

- Boil the crayfish in water to cover for two minutes. Shell and set aside.

- Preheat oven to 450° degrees.

- Season Vidalia onions with salt and pepper. Place in roasting pan with 1-inch of water, brown sugar, and a tablespoon of butter. Cover with aluminum foil and bake for two hours. Baste occasionally. Remove foil at the end of the baking time until onions turn slightly golden brown. Remove onions and set aside.

- Cut the wings and tail off the chicken. Mix the rosemary with the remaining butter and stuff it under the skin of the chicken breast and thigh.

- Roast in oven for 45 minutes, taking care to baste at least four times. Remove from oven and let stand for 5 minutes.

(recipe continued on next page)

(Roasted Natural Amish Chicken With Roasted Vidalia Onions And Crayfish, continued)

- Remove the chicken from the pan; deglaze the pan with chicken stock and the juice from onion pan. Reduce to a nice consistency for sauce. Add crayfish and toss in sauce to cover.

- To serve: break onions open with fork. Cut chicken into four pieces and place on a plate. Surround the chicken pieces with onion pieces, and spoon crayfish and sauce over chicken and onions.

- Yield: 4 servings

Troy N. Thompson of the Ritz-Carlton

Yogurt and Herb Grilled Chicken Breast

½ **cup plain low-fat yogurt**
1 **ripe banana, sliced**
½ **teaspoon curry powder**
1 **tablespoon lemon grass, minced**
2 **garlic cloves, minced**
1 **teaspoon ground cumin, toasted**
1 **teaspoon crushed red pepper flakes**
4 **whole skinless chicken breasts, fat trimmed**

- Blend and pulse yogurt, banana, curry powder, lemon grass, garlic, cumin, and red pepper flakes for 15 seconds. Place chicken in marinade for 4 hours or overnight.

- Remove chicken from marinade, wiping off any excess marinade.

- Grill chicken approximately 5 minutes on each side.

- Serve with steamed carrots and wild rice.

- Yield: 4 servings

Vincent J. Alberia of Adams Mark Hotels

Yum Nurr

2 tablespoons fish sauce
2 tablespoons lemon juice
  pinch pepper
  pinch sugar
1 scallion, chopped (green part only)
1 tablespoon chopped onion
¼ pound flank steak
1 cup assorted greens
1 tomato, cut into wedges
¼ cucumber, sliced
  cilantro
  mint

- Combine fish sauce, lemon juice, pepper, sugar, scallions, and onions.

- Lightly grill beef. Thinly slice the beef and add to the spicy sauce.

- Serve over greens and decorate with tomato and cucumber.

- Garnish with cilantro or mint.

- Yield: 1 serving

Somsak Thai Cuisine

"Plant a little mint, Madame, then step out of the way so you don't get hurt."
— A British gardener

Mom's Chicken Chili

2 large onions, finely chopped
1 head garlic, crushed
2 sweet red peppers, finely chopped
¾ cup oil (corn or canola)
2-10 jalapeños (according to taste), chopped
1¼ pounds boneless, skinless chicken breasts, ground in food processor
2 (1-pound 12-ounce) cans crushed tomato
¼ cup chili powder
⅛ cup cumin
2 tablespoons Dijon mustard or hot and spicy mustard
2 cups water
2-3 (14-ounce) cans kidney beans

- Combine onions, garlic, red peppers, oil, and jalapeños in a deep sauté pan and cook over medium flame. Cook until onions are transparent and peppers are soft.

- Add chicken. Cook over medium heat for approximately 10 to 15 minutes or until chicken is cooked.

- Add crushed tomato, chili powder, cumin, mustard, and water. Cook over medium heat for approximately 30 minutes.

- Add kidney beans. Continue to cook until done, approximately 30 minutes.

- Yield: 10 servings

Michael Georgetti of Georgetti's Market

Alleged dying words of Kit Carson: "Wish I had time for just one more bowl of chili."

Sautéed Medallion of Pork Tenderloin

For ease of preparation, substitute fresh cherries with one 16-ounce can of drained, dark, sweet, pitted cherries.

½ **pound dark, sweet, pitted cherries**
1 **cup of beef broth**
¼ **cup of orange juice**
2 **tablespoons of brown sugar**
1 **tablespoon of granulated sugar**
1 **tablespoon of lemon juice**
2-3 **dashes of ginger**
4 **tablespoons butter, softened**
2 **ounces sun dried cherries**
2½ **pounds of pork tenderloin, cut and trimmed into 2-ounce medallions**
1 **cup of flour**
½ **cup of vegetable oil**
   cherry brandy
   salt
   pepper

- To make sauce: in a blender combine pitted cherries and beef broth. On medium speed, purée until smooth.

- Pour puréed cherries into a sauce pan. Add orange juice, brown sugar, sugar, lemon juice, and ginger. Bring to a boil, reduce heat and let simmer 5 to 6 minutes. Remove from heat, whisk in softened butter until smooth. Add dried cherries.

- Dust pork medallions with flour and sauté in a large pan with hot oil. Brown evenly on both sides.

- Discard oil and deglaze pan with a glug of cherry brandy. Reduce brandy by one-third.

- Add cherry sauce, salt, and pepper to taste. Continue to cook for about 3 to 4 minutes.

(recipe continued on next page)

(Sautéed Medallion of Pork Tenderloin, continued)

Remove from heat and serve.

• Yield: 6 servings

Luigi Baretto of Ram's Head Inn

Veal Riviera

8 (2-ounce) portions veal scaloppine from the loin, pounded
salt
pepper
flour for dredging
2 tablespoons olive oil
8 large shrimp, shelled
1 clove garlic, minced
½ teaspoon chopped basil
½ cup chopped fresh tomatoes
8 sun dried tomatoes, sliced in half
¼ cup white wine
¼ cup white veal stock (or chicken broth or vegetable broth)
1 teaspoon chopped fresh parsley

• Season veal with salt and pepper, dredge in flour, shake off excess flour.

• Sauté in hot olive oil approximately one minute on each side. Remove from pan, add shrimp and cook until shrimp turns pink.

• Drain excess oil from pan, then add garlic, basil, and both types of tomatoes, let cook for one or two minutes.

• Add white wine and reduce for one minute. Add veal stock and cook for three minutes. Add chopped parsley, season with salt and pepper.

• Plate the veal with a shrimp atop each medallion. Spoon over sauce and serve.

• Yield: 4 servings

Chef Benjamin C. Moñoz at La Collina Restaurant

Pan Seared Venison Filet with Asian Vegetables in Crispy Rice Paper

Marinade

- 1 **cup port wine**
- ½ **cup low sodium soy sauce**
- 2 **teaspoons minced garlic, divided**
- 2 **teaspoons chopped shallots, divided**
- 2 **teaspoons ground ginger, divided**
- ½ **teaspoon salt**
  pepper

Venison

- 4 **(6-ounce) venison filets**
- ½ **cup blended oil, divided**
- 2 **cups venison or veal stock or canned beef broth**
- ¼ **cup carrot, julienned**
- ¼ **cup daikon radish**
- ¼ **cup red pepper**
- ¼ **cup baby corn**
- ¼ **cup straw mushrooms, chopped**
- ¼ **cup bamboo shoots**
- ¼ **cup small broccoli florets**
- ½ **cup mirin (sweet rice wine)**
- ⅛ **cup chopped scallion**
- 1 **teaspoon finely chopped cilantro**
- 8 **rice paper wrappers**
- 1 **bowl water, room temperature**

- Combine port wine, soy sauce, 1 teaspoon of the garlic, 1 teaspoon of the shallots, 1 teaspoon of the ginger, salt, and pepper. Add venison and marinate for 2 hours in refrigerator.

- Preheat oven to 425°.

- Remove venison from marinade. To a heated sauté pan add 3 tablespoons oil. Sear both sides of venison for 2 minutes on each side or until browned. Remove and set aside.

(recipe continued on next page)

(Pan Seared Venison Filet with Asian Vegetables in Crispy Rice Paper, continued)

- Add marinade and stock to pan and bring to a boil. Reduce heat and simmer until sauce thickens.

- In another heated sauté pan, add ¼ cup oil. Sauté all vegetables for one minute. Add remaining garlic, shallot, and ginger. Add mirin. Sauté another two minutes. Remove from heat; add scallions and cilantro.

- Soften rice paper wrappers in bowl of water for one minute. Lay 2 wrappers on top of each other. Place one-third cup of the vegetables in the center of wrapper. Place venison on top of vegetables. Fold edges of wrapper around the top of venison. Flip wrapped venison over making sure edges are tucked underneath. Repeat for other three venison filets.

- Roast in oven for 10 to 12 minutes until it is medium rare and wrapper is crispy.

- To serve place venison in center of plate. Drizzle sauce around and garnish with remaining Asian vegetables.

- Yield: 4 servings

Jeffrey McKay, Rittenhouse Hotel

The Chinese believe that this life, in order to be properly lived, must be enjoyed in a civilized manner. Confucius, a lover of good food, taught that good taste in food was to be cultivated as a part of artistic living. The Chinese scholar became a gourmet as well. Many table customs and practices of etiquette date back thousands of years to Confucius. Cooking became appreciated as an art in which the chef, not unlike a great French chef, became free to create.

Sautéed Red Snapper With Toasted Pecan Pistachio Butter

½ **cup flour**
¼ **teaspoon cayenne pepper**
2 **teaspoons garlic powder**
¼ **teaspoon ground thyme**
4 **teaspoons paprika**
1½ **teaspoons salt**
4 **red snapper filets (1½ pounds)**
½ **cup milk**
¼ **cup peanut oil**
Toasted Pecan Pistachio Butter Sauce
⅓ **cup pecans**
⅓ **cup shelled pistachios**
⅛ **teaspoon ground white pepper**
⅛ **teaspoon cayenne**
4 **tablespoons butter**
juice from ½ medium lemon (1 tablespoon)
2 **tablespoons minced parsley**

- Mix flour, cayenne pepper, garlic powder, thyme, paprika, and salt in a medium bowl to make a seasoned flour.

- Dip each red snapper filet in milk, then dredge in the seasoned flour.

- Heat oil in a large skillet. Add snapper filets; sauté, turning once until golden brown, about 6 minutes.

- Remove snapper filets; cover and keep warm.

- To make sauce: sprinkle pecans and pistachios with white pepper and cayenne. Heat butter in the skillet. Add pecans and pistachios, sauté until browned lightly, about 3 minutes. Remove from heat and stir in lemon juice and parsley.

(recipe continued on next page)

(Sautéed Red Snapper With Toasted Pecan Pistachio Butter, continued)

- To serve: transfer a snapper filet to four warm plates. Spoon a portion of the sauce over each filet and serve immediately.

- Yield: 4 servings

Beau Rivage Restaurant and Wine Cellar

Golden Trout with Hazelnuts

4 golden trout filets, cleaned and boned
½ cup flour
  salt
  pepper
2 tablespoons olive oil
4 ounces hazelnuts, chopped (about ½ cup)
2 tablespoons butter
1 teaspoon diced red onion
1 tomato, diced
¼ cup white wine
3 tablespoons hazelnut liquor

- Season and flour trout. Sear in olive oil on both sides until lightly browned. Take out of pan. Reserve.

- Put hazelnuts, butter, red onion, tomato, wine, and hazelnut liquor in pan and cook until thickened.

- To serve: put trout on plate and spread the sauce across the top.

- Yield: 2 servings

John Schatz

Pan Seared Swordfish with Braised Greens and Roasted Tomato Aioli

Aioli
- 2 **cups vegetable oil, divided**
- ½ **cup garlic cloves, peeled (2-3 heads)**
- 2 **tomatoes, cored, halved and seeded**
- 2 **large egg yolks**
- 2 **tablespoons Dijon mustard**
- 1 **tablespoon tomato paste**
- ½ **cup red wine vinegar**
  juice from ½ lemon

Swordfish
- 2 **tablespoons vegetable oil**
- 1 **(8-ounce) swordfish steak, centercut**
  salt
  pepper
- 1 **teaspoon finely diced shallots**
- ⅛ **teaspoon finely diced garlic**
- 1 **pound collard or romaine washed, drained, torn into bite size pieces**
- 1 **tablespoon sherry vinegar**

- To make aioli: heat 1 cup of the oil on low heat. Roast garlic until light brown. Add tomatoes to heated oil. Cook for 3 minutes. Drain and reserve oil.

- Purée mixture in food processor with egg yolks, mustard, tomato paste, and vinegar until incorporated. Gradually add remaining oil and reserved oil and process again until incorporated. Check and add lemon juice. Set aside.

- To cook swordfish: heat medium pan in with 2 tablespoons of oil. When hot, gently add swordfish, salt and pepper to pan. Cook for approximately 3 minutes on each side until golden brown. Remove from pan.

(recipe continued on next page)

(Pan Seared Swordfish with Braised Greens and Roasted Tomato Aioli, continued)

- Quickly add shallots, ⅛ teaspoon garlic, and greens. Stir for minute.
- Deglaze pan with sherry vinegar and sweat greens for 1 minute.
- Place greens on the plate and then the swordfish on top. Coat with desired amount of aioli and garnish.
- Yield: 2 servings

> *Chef Barry Sexton of Jean Pierre's Restaurant*

Grilled Marinated Mahi-mahi

juice from 1 lemon (3 tablespoons)
4 tablespoons Japanese soy sauce
2 tablespoons tomato paste
4 tablespoons sesame oil
2 medium garlic cloves, finely chopped (1 teaspoon)
1 teaspoon oregano
½ teaspoon salt
freshly ground black pepper
2 pounds mahi-mahi

- Combine the lemon juice, soy sauce, tomato paste, sesame oil, garlic, oregano, salt, and black pepper to make marinade.
- Turn the fish in the marinade to coat evenly. Marinate the fish for at least 2 hours at room temperature, turning frequently.
- Preheat broiler.
- Place the fish on the broiler pan and broil for 5 minutes on each side, basting with the marinade two or three times until done.
- Yield: 4 servings

> *Sansom Street Oyster House*

Roasted Eggplant and Lobster Ravioli

Pasta Dough
- 1½ **cups flour**
- 2 **large eggs**
- 2 **tablespoons olive oil**
- 2 **tablespoons cold water**
- **salt**
- **pepper**

Filling
- 2 **tablespoons olive oil, divided**
- 1 **medium onion, diced**
- ¼ **cup roasted garlic**
- 5 **eggplants, spilt lengthwise**
- **salt**
- **pepper**
- 3 **tablespoon fresh thyme**
- 2 **cups sourdough bread crumbs**
- 2 **cups chicken stock**
- 1 **cup fresh lobster, cooked, shelled and diced**
- 2 **large eggs, beaten**

- To make pasta dough: combine flour and eggs and mix with dough hook of electric mixer at low speed; gradually add olive oil and water. Continue mixing until dough is smooth and has a silky texture. Season with salt and pepper.

- Let rest in refrigerator 4 to 6 hours. Then roll into thin sheets.

- To make filling: heat 1 tablespoon of oil in a skillet. Sauté onion and garlic until lightly brown. Set aside to cool.

- Brush eggplant with remaining olive oil and season with salt and pepper. Place on a sheet pan and roast in oven at 350° until brown. Let cool.

(recipe continued on next page)

(Roasted Eggplant and Lobster Ravioli, continued)

- Remove meat and discard skin.

- In a saucepot, combine eggplant, onion, garlic, thyme, bread crumbs, and chicken stock. Simmer on low heat until thickened, stirring constantly. Add diced lobster meat, season with salt and pepper. Let cool.

- Using a ravioli mold, lay one sheet of pasta on top ravioli mold. Brush lightly with beaten egg. Place one tablespoon of filling in each slotted spot of the mold. Place second sheet of pasta on top of filing and seal with a rolling pin. Unmold and separate raviolis.

- Cook in salted, boiling water for 3 to 4 minutes. Serve with desired sauce. Lobster-chive cream sauce recommended.

- Yield: 6 servings

Allan J. Vanesko of Passerelle

Entrecôte au Poivre

The following recipe is for two and is easiest done two at a time. For six people, have 2 friends following the same procedure using the other burners on your stove.

- 2 **sirloin steaks**
- 1 **tablespoon whole peppercorns, crushed**
- 2 **teaspoons butter, divided**
- ¼ **cup brandy**
- 1 **teaspoon mustard**
- ½ **cup heavy cream**
  salt
  pepper

- Rub both sides of steaks with crushed peppercorns.

- Heat a skillet until very hot. Add butter to skillet and sear steaks to the desired doneness. Remove from skillet.

- Put remaining butter and brandy in the same skillet and heat until almost brown. Add mustard and mix. Then add the heavy cream. Add salt and pepper to taste. Reduce. Pour over steaks.

- Yield: 2 servings

Omar Arbani

To crush peppercorns: place them on a board and crush them with the side of a wide chef's knife, pressing down hard with the palm of your hand. They will be just the right size.

Ultimate Chocolate Cake with Mocha Buttercream Frosting

Cake

- 3 scant cups flour
- 1½ teaspoons salt
- 2 cups sugar
- 1 cup unsweetened baking cocoa
- 2 teaspoons baking soda
- 1¼ cups butter, melted
- 2⅓ cups warm water
- 2 tablespoons vinegar
- 2 teaspoons vanilla

Frosting

- ½ cup (1 stick) butter, softened
- ½ cup unsweetened baking cocoa
- 1 pound confectioners' sugar
- 2 teaspoons instant coffee granules, dissolved in ¼ cup coffee

- To make cake: preheat oven to 350°.

- Butter a tube pan and dust with flour.

- In a mixing bowl; mix flour, salt, sugar, cocoa, and soda.

- In a separate bowl, combine butter, water, vinegar, and vanilla.

- Add liquid ingredients to dry ingredients. Beat until smooth.

- Bake in oven for 1 hour or until toothpick inserted in center is dry.

- To make frosting: combine confectioners' sugar and cocoa in a bowl. Stir well to combine. Add the softened butter and mix in gently. Add the coffee liquid, a small amount at a time, and beat with an electric mixer until smooth and spreadable. You may not need all the coffee liquid or you may need to add more.

Jim Lampman of Lake Champlain Chocolates

Chocolate Indulgence

Cake

> nonstick cooking spray
> 5 egg yolks
> ½ cup plus 2 teaspoons sugar
> 5⅓ ounces bittersweet chocolate, chopped fine (scant 1 cup)
> ½ cup plus 1½ tablespoons butter
> 2⅔ ounces almond flour (grind sliced almonds until fine in food processor with a steel blade) (heaping ½ cup)
> 2 tablespoons dark rum
> 5 egg whites
> ¼ cup plus 1 teaspoon sugar

Ganache

> 8 ounces semi-sweet chocolate
> 1 cup heavy cream

Crème Anglaise

> 2 cups whole milk
> ½ cup plus 2 teaspoons sugar
> 1 tablespoon plus 1 teaspoon cornstarch
> 8 egg yolks
> vanilla, rum, or Grand Marnier

- Preheat oven top 350°.

- Spray 9-inch torte pan with removable bottom with nonstick cooking spray. Dust with flour, shake off excess.

- To make cake: with an electric mixer, whip together egg yolks and ½ cup plus 2 teaspoons sugar until a thick ribbon stage.

- On the top of a double boiler, melt chocolate and butter. Add to egg yolk mixture while beating on the lowest speed. Add rum.

- Sift the almond flour. Fold into above mixture.

- In a separate bowl, whip the egg whites and ¼ cup plus 1 teaspoon sugar into stiff peaks but not dry. Fold meringue into chocolate mixture.

(recipe continued on next page)

(Chocolate Indulgence, continued)

- Bake about 20 minutes or until a knife inserted in the center produces a light crumb. Do not overbake. Let cool in pan and push bottom up to remove torte. Flip out onto a round cake plate.

- To make ganache: melt chocolate over double boiler. Remove from heat. Add cream all at once and stir until smooth. Let set until firm enough to pipe. Decorate cake with ganache.

- To make Crème Anglaise: heat milk to just at the boil. In a separate saucepan, combine sugar and cornstarch. Whisk in egg yolks until smooth. Slowly pour the hot milk into the yolk mixture. Return to heat and cook until it thickens, stirring constantly. Flavor with vanilla, rum, or Grand Marnier.

- Yield: 9-inch torte

  Chef Patrick D. Gauthron of Aux Petots Delices

The word cake comes to us from Middle English, and may have had earlier origins in Old Norse. From the earliest days of civilization, man has always considered cake a food for the gods as well as for himself. The Egyptians made cakes in animal, bird, and human forms for their various gods; Greeks offered honey cakes to their gods; and in the North honey cakes were offered to Thor at the winter solstice to ensure a fruitful year to come.

Black Bottom Butterscotch Pie

This crust is easy to make. It does not require rolling, just pressing into a 9-inch pie pan.

Crust
- 1 cup flour
- 3 tablespoons sugar
- 6 tablespoons unsalted butter
- 1 large egg yolk

Chocolate Bottom
- 2 ounces semi-sweet chocolate
- 2 tablespoons heavy cream

Butterscotch Custard
- 2½ cups whole milk, divided
- ¼ cup plus 1 tablespoon sugar
- ¼ cup plus 1 tablespoon unsulphured molasses
- 4 tablespoons unsalted butter
  pinch salt
- ¼ cup cornstarch
- 3 large egg yolks
- ½ teaspoon vanilla extract

Whipped Cream Garnish
- 1 cup chilled heavy cream
- 2-3 tablespoons sugar

- To make crust: preheat oven to 350°.

- Combine flour and sugar in a medium sized bowl.

- Cut the butter into small pieces. Drop the butter and egg yolk into flour mixture. With a pastry blender, or two knives, cut and work the butter and yolk into the flour until the mixture resembles coarse meal. Gather dough into a ball. Press evenly over the bottom and up the sides of a pie pan. Chill until very hard.

- Bake for approximately 20 minutes or until golden brown. Cool.

(recipe continued on next page)

(Black Bottom Butterscotch Pie, continued)

- To make chocolate bottom: melt semi-sweet chocolate and heavy cream together in the top of a double boiler until chocolate is just melted, whisking occasionally. Take off double boiler and cool until mixture is as thick as mayonnaise, remembering to keep whisking occasionally as mixture cools. Chill until firm.

- To make butterscotch custard: reserve ½ cup milk and pour into medium sized bowl.

- Put remaining 2 cups of milk in a heavy medium-sized saucepan with sugar, molasses, butter, and salt.

- Add cornstarch to reserved ½ cup of milk, and whisk until smooth and free of lumps. Whisk in egg yolks. Heat milk mixture in saucepan over moderate temperature until steaming and just ready to boil.

- Pour milk and cornstarch mixture into milk and sugar mixture in a steady stream, whisking constantly. Bring to a full boil. Lower flame and boil about two or more minutes, whisking occasionally. Shut off flame and whisk in vanilla. Let cool one minute and cover surface of custard with a piece of plastic wrap. Cool to room temperature.

- Spread over chocolate-lined pie shell. Chill.

- To make whipped cream garnish: whip cream and sugar (to taste) in a medium sized mixing bowl until thick and stiff peaks can be formed. Cover surface of pie with cream or pipe with a pastry bag for a more decorative effect.

Fran & Ava Hirsch of Heart's Content Bakery

Poached Stuffed Pears with Sauce Anglaise

Sauce Anglaise
- 1 cup milk
- 1 cup heavy cream
- 4 large egg yolks
- ½ cup sugar
- ¼ cup Grand Marnier or Cognac

Pears
- 6 firm pears
- 2 ounces walnuts, finely chopped (makes ½ cup)
- ½ cup raisins, chopped
- ⅓ cup honey
- 2 cups sugar
- 1 cup water
- 1 inch vanilla bean
- a few chopped pistachio nuts

- To make the Sauce Anglaise: heat the milk and cream to the boiling point. Keep hot.

- Beat the egg yolks and sugar together lightly over hot water in the top of a double boiler. Gradually add the hot milk mixture, stirring vigorously. Stir constantly until the custard coats a wooden spoon. Do not allow the water to boil and do not overcook or the egg yolks will curdle.

- Meantime, heat the Grand Marnier or Cognac to boiling point in a small pan to volatilize the alcohol. When the custard mixture just coats the spoon, stir in the alcohol and cook gently a minute or two, then poor sauce into a bowl and cool.

- To prepare the pears: peel the pears and core them from the bottom, leaving the stem in.

- In a food processor, make a paste of the walnuts, raisins, and honey. Stuff the pears with this paste.

(recipe continued on next page)

(Poached Stuffed Pears with Sauce Anglaise, continued)

- Make a syrup with the sugar, water, and about an inch of vanilla bean and poach the pears in it until just tender. Cool and serve with Sauce Anglaise. Decorate with the chopped pistachio nuts.

- Yield: 6 servings

Frank H. Jelinek of Gourmet Corner

New England Pudding

2 (8-ounce) cans chunk pineapple, drained
4 apples, cored and cubed
1 tablespoon lemon juice
7 ounces walnuts, chopped
(makes 1½ cups)
1 cup brown sugar, firmly packed
4 large eggs
2 cups sugar
2 cups flour
1½ cups (3 sticks) butter, melted

- Preheat oven to 350°

- Place pineapples and apples in bottom of a 9 x 13-inch pan. Sprinkle with lemon juice. Top with walnuts and brown sugar.

- To make topping: with an electric mixer, whip eggs and mix in sugar. Add flour and melted butter, mix completely .

- Spread topping over center of pan. Do not touch ends or sides.

- Bake in oven until golden brown, about 40 minutes. Serve warm with ice cream.

- Yield: 12 servings

Pace One Restaurant and Country Inn

Maple Walnut Crème Brûlée

2⅓ cups heavy cream
⅔ cup milk
¼ cup superfine sugar
3 whole large eggs
3 large egg yolks
2 teaspoons vanilla extract
1 teaspoon maple extract
½ cup light brown sugar
½ ounce walnuts, powdered (⅛ cup)

- Preheat oven to 300°.

- Heat cream, milk, and sugar in heavy saucepan.

- In a separate bowl, beat whole eggs and egg yolks. Beat together well.

- Gradually whisk the heated mixture into the eggs, then return mixture to pan. Cook over moderate heat, stirring with a wooden spoon until the custard coats the back of the spoon (approximately 3 to 4 minutes).

- Remove from heat. Stir in vanilla and maple extract.

- Pour custard into six individual dishes or a shallow baking dish about 9-inches across. Set dish or dishes in a large pan on the middle rack of the oven. Pour hot water in the outer pan up to the level of the custard. Bake 35 to 45 minutes until the center of the custard is set.

- Remove custard from water bath. Cover and chill.

- Well before serving, preheat broiler.

- Sift brown sugar and walnuts over the custard. Spread evenly to the edge. Set custard under the boiler as closer to heat as possible. Broil until browned but not burned. Serve.

- Yield: 6 servings

Dilworthtown Inn

Contributors

Joan Abele
Andrea Abiuso
Ellie Aumock
Laura G. Barclay
Nancy Barclay
Teri Barlow
Maureen Barnes
Grace Barr
Jeanne Bartley
Regina Baumgartner
Jeanne C. Beck
Stella Gentile Berg
Linda E. Berry
Joe Biggs
Marie Birks
Elvana Bodine
Kathy Bohan
Judy Boswell
Charlotte Bowers
Emma Brandon
Carolyn Brann
Nancy Brennan
Emmy Lou Brick
Lynn Brill
Debby Brown
Peter Brust
Anita P. Bulei, M.D.
Nancy Calabretta
Doris Armstrong Carr
Carol Carroll
Mary Jane Cheeseman
Linda Chiachetti
Marjorie J. Chodikoff
Ruth Clark
Sandra H. Coles
Dolores H. Corson
Elaine S. Coward
Doris Cox
Gretchen Coyle
Loveann Cranshaw
Marilyn H. Crocker
Marguerite Culver
Mary Cuthbertson
George Davidson
Ella R. Davis
Annette DeFeo
Lynne Demmerly
Susan Demmerly
Frank Demmerly, Jr.
Frank Demmerly, IV
Rita Dib
Jinny Dickenson

Kathy Dickey
Lynn Dietz
Lauretta Dimenna
Michael L. Dolfman, Ph.D
Carmel Dorsey
Michele Dougherty
Joan Douglas
Ruth W. Douglas
Mary Ann Driscoll
Ruth G. Duffy
Linda Eckenhoff
Jane Edwards
Kathy Ellis
Patty Familiar
Elaine Fanjul
Sarah Fanjul
Laurie Fantacone
Louise Farr
Lynne Marie Flynn
Elayne Foegelson
Shelly Foell
Bernadette Formoso
Sandra Frame
Micahel W. Franks
Eleanor Gaines
Thomas Gaither
Mary Gamon
Kathy Gandolfo
Gloria Gardner
Mary M. Garippa
Rosalind Chadwick-
  Garrigle
Jean Gertz
Alison Gibson
Betsy Gildhaus
Dottie Gore
Marie Goulburn
Loretta Grande
Edith Graulich
Peter Graulich
Walter Graulich
Phyllis Green
Karen Halpern
Karen S. Harbeson
Page Harbeson
Susan Harris
Lew Hegyi
Edith Henderson
Olga Henderson
Judy Heuisler
Cathy Hice

Carol Hirsch
Rosemary Hughes
Jane Hunter
Kathryn Hutton
Betty Ibbeken
Isabel Ingram
Meg Irish
Emily Johnson
Patsy Johnson
Sharon Johnson
Linda Joseph
Sharon Johnson
Linda Joseph
Marilyn Kalellis
Crys Kavalunus
Jo Anne F. Kay
Karen Keegan
Judith Keenan
Marion Keller
Helen Kelley
Joan Kelly
Linda Kelly
Jim Knipp
Anne Bridget Koch
Cheryl Kronenberger
Patricia Kronenberger
Anne M. Krout
Eleanor Kruger
Helen C. Kulp
Carol Lake
Nancy Lampman
Shirley Landgraf
Penny Laufer
Francis Lax
Ruth Leaman
Jane Leek
Peggy Leone
Maryann Levengood
Rhea Cottler Levine
Peg Lippincott
Eleanor C. Long
Bob Lumpe
Diane Lydic
Virginia MacNeal
Gail Ann Marley
Barbara Marsella
Sabina Marshall
Rosemary Mason
Bobbi McCloskey
Patrice McCrindle
Susan McCrindle
Bette McElwee

INDEX

A

B

Patrons

Mrs. Joan Abele
Carolyn Adamson
Advance Auto Supplies, Inc.
Anita Alic
Marlene Ances
Baby Beeper, Inc.
Debby & Brian Baratz
Mr. & Mrs. David Barclay
Mr. & Mrs. William J. Barr
Jeanne V. Bartley
Mrs. Richard C. Bean
Grace Beck
Carolyn Bekes
Dr. & Mrs. Gordon D. Benson
Carol C. Berardelli
Marty Lou Berglund
Dr. & Mrs. C. Miller Biddle
Carolyn & Ned Brann
Dr. & Mrs. James E. Brennan
Lorraine Briglia
Mrs. Frederick Brink
Karen Brubaker
M. Linda Burke, M.D.
MaryAnn Campling
Mr. & Mrs. Allen G. Carr, Sr.
Fran Cassidy
Dr. & Mrs. John Catalano
Mrs. Jerome Check
Maryetta Cook
Cooper Court Restaurant
Coriell Institute for Medical Research
Mrs. Charles W. Coward, Jr.
Doris C. Cox
Tina L. Cressman
Monica S. Deacon
Annette DeFeo
Lynne L. Demmerly
Jamey H. DeRenzo
Dorothy Warren Derham
Virginia P. Dickenson
Irene C. Dickey
Lynn Dietz
Dietz Roofing Co. Inc.
Dr. & Mrs. Michael L. Dolfman
Joan Douglass
Mary Ann Driscoll
Peter E. Driscoll, Esq.
Mr. & Mrs. John T. Dutton
Sally Price Eynon
Eleanor Vail of Haddonfield
Elaine Fanjul

Louise Z. Farr
Penny Ferrara
Dr. & Mrs. Stuart C. Finch
Joan Fiorella
Mrs. Richard D. Fitch
Mrs. John L. Gaines
Mary P. Gamon
Mrs. George B. German
Jean Gibson
Cheryl Glick
Evelyn Goodwin
Dorothy Giordano
Mrs. Walter Graulich
Catherine Gerew
Margaret Groh
Karen & Kevin Halpern
Page Harbeson
Mr. & Mrs. Robert G. Harbeson
R. Admiral & Mrs. Brooks Harral
Susan Harris
Paul Hayaux
Judith H. Heuisler
Kathy Higgins
Mrs. Richard Hineline
Carol & Les Hirsch
Hazel Shaffer Horner
Mrs. Frank J. Hughes
Mrs. James Hunter, III
Mrs. Gunther H. Ibbeken
Emily & Howard Johnson
Marilyn W. Kalellis
Dr. & Mrs. Lewis A. Kay
Dorothea Z. Kelchner
Marion Keller
Kathy Kellmer
Joan & Bill Kelly
Jack & Cheryl Kronenberger
Rob & Sandy Kugler
Mrs. Howard G. Kulp, Jr.
Peg Kurtz
Frances R. Lax
Rosemary O. Leach
Sylvia Lehrer
Kathy Lilly
Dr. & Mrs. Charles P. Lisa
Art & Peggy Littleton
Mrs. Robert L. J. Long
Marie Maxwell
Mrs. Robert McElwee
Stan Meltzer
Mrs. Robert D. Mervine

Mrs. Howard B. Miller
Linda M. Mottlin, Consultant
Mrs. Stanley Mroz
Ralph & Tonya Olson
Dr. & Mrs. John S. Owens
Ruth G. Kain-Palmer
Nanci Pastorius
Patricia D. Patterson
Mrs. Edmond J. Pearson
Mr. & Mrs. Philip A. Piro, Sr.
Charles & Gail Poliero
Mrs. George D. Prestwich
Mrs. George F. Prestwich
Mr. & Mrs. Ernest L. Previte
Letitia Orlando Principato
Mrs. Ann Ramage
Diane Reid
Joanne B. Riebel
Virginia C. Ritchie
Mrs. John Rittenhouse
Nancy & Tom Rocereto
Mrs. Hugh R. Rogers
Mrs. George W. Roney
Sheila L. Rosenfield
Dr. & Mrs. Harold W. Rushton
George & Pat Scerba
Patricia T. Schipper
Claire C. Scott

Hon. & Mrs. A. Morton Shapiro
Bill & Cathy Sharrar
Mrs. J. William Siebenson
Mrs. Vincent P. Small, Jr.
Barbara Smith
Mrs. Herbert J. Stayton, Jr.
Mrs. George McClellan Snyder
Mrs. Estelle Soppe
Mr. & Mrs. Robert P. Stebbins
Mrs. Gilbert Stein
Maureen Sullivan
Betty Jones Tatem
Patricia L. Taylor
Mrs. Oren R. Thomas
Town & Country Auxiliary
Dr. & Mrs. Edward Viner
Barbara & Marvin Waxman
Mrs. John W. Weatherby
Dr. & Mrs. William A. West
Sandra & Ron Weiss
Rosalind White Williams
Mrs. Paul E. Wright
Write On! ...fine stationary
Dr. and Mrs. Michael E. Zank
The Zavaglia Family in Memory
 of Joseph Zavaglia, Sr.
Barbara Zimmerman
Ada Zimmerman

FOOD FABULOUS FOOD

Volunteer Office - Cookbook Committee
Cooper Hospital/University Medical Center
One Cooper Plaza
Camden, NJ 08103-1489

Please send me _____ copies of *Food Fabulous Food* @ $19.95 each $ _____

Plus postage & handling @ $ 3.50 each $ _____

Tax for New Jersey residents @ $ 1.20 each $ _____

TOTAL $ _____

Name _____

Address _____

City _____ State _____ Zip _____

Make checks payable to *Women's Board, Cooper Hospital/UMC*
Please allow 3 to 4 weeks for delivery.

FOOD FABULOUS FOOD

Volunteer Office - Cookbook Committee
Cooper Hospital/University Medical Center
One Cooper Plaza
Camden, NJ 08103-1489

Please send me _____ copies of *Food Fabulous Food* @ $19.95 each $ _____

Plus postage & handling @ $ 3.50 each $ _____

Tax for New Jersey residents @ $ 1.20 each $ _____

TOTAL $ _____

Name _____

Address _____

City _____ State _____ Zip _____

Make checks payable to *Women's Board, Cooper Hospital/UMC*
Please allow 3 to 4 weeks for delivery.

FOOD FABULOUS FOOD

Volunteer Office - Cookbook Committee
Cooper Hospital/University Medical Center
One Cooper Plaza
Camden, NJ 08103-1489

Please send me _____ copies of *Food Fabulous Food* @ $19.95 each $ _____

Plus postage & handling @ $ 3.50 each $ _____

Tax for New Jersey residents @ $ 1.20 each $ _____

TOTAL $ _____

Name _____

Address _____

City _____ State _____ Zip _____

Make checks payable to *Women's Board, Cooper Hospital/UMC*
Please allow 3 to 4 weeks for delivery.